Hope and Its Hieroglyph

ÆR

American Academy of Religion
Studies in Religion

Editor
Lawrence S. Cunningham

Number 57
HOPE AND ITS HIEROGLYPH

by
Richard H. Roberts

HOPE AND ITS HIEROGLYPH
A Critical Decipherment of Ernst Bloch's
Principle of Hope

Richard H. Roberts

Scholars Press
Atlanta, Georgia

HOPE AND ITS HIEROGLYPH

by
Richard H. Roberts

© 1990
The American Academy of Religion

Library of Congress Cataloging in Publication Data

Roberts, Richard H., 1946-
    Hope and its hieroglyph : a critical decipherment of Ernst Bloch's
    Principle of hope / Richard H. Roberts.
    p.   am. -- (Studies in religion ; no. 57)
    Bibliography: p.
    ISBN 1-55540-369-7
    1. Bloch, Ernst, 1885-1977. Prinzip Hoffnung. 2. Hope.
3. Imagination. 4. Utopias. 5. Creation (Literary, artistic, etc.)
I. Title. II. Series: AAR studies in religion ; no. 57.
B3209.B753P7537   1989
193--dc20   89-35948
                                                          CIP

Printed in the United States of America
on acid-free paper
∞

CONTENTS

ACKNOWLEDGEMENTS

I am deeply grateful to my friends and colleagues Mr. Robert Morgan of the University of Oxford, and Dr. Ann Loades and Dr. David Jasper of the University of Durham for encouragement and stimulating interchange over a text that represents a writer subjected to repeated denigration, even abuse, in the Anglo-Saxon world. Without the practical intervention of Professor Robert Detweiler of Emory University this book might well have never been finished, here again I owe a debt, as I do to Professor Lawrence Cunningham of the University of Notre Dame for acute appraisal of the text. I should also acknowledge the steadfast support of Professor Daniel W. Hardy, my close colleague who has done his utmost to support intellectual endeavour in the University of Durham during a period of unprecedented stress and difficulty.

I am indebted to Mrs. Joan Trowbridge who has word-processed with skill and patience a developing manuscript fraught with German and extensive notes.

Quotation of the translation of *Das Prinzip Hoffunung* is by permission of the MIT press and Basil Blackwell of Oxford, England. The extract from *Speech Genres and Other Late Essays* by M.M. Bakhtin, translated by Vern W. McGee (Copyright-(C) 1986) is reprinted by permission of the University of Texas Press.

INTRODUCTION : RESISTANCE AND RECEPTION

The following book arose out of the commissioning of a lengthy review-article of the English translation of Ernst Bloch's *Das Prinzip Hoffnung*[1] which served to crystallise my longstanding research interest in the relation between Christianity and Marxism, and in the formation, inversion and transformation of the German idealist and dialectical traditions in the nineteenth and twentieth centuries. The contrast between the initial German (notably the West German) reception of *The Principle of Hope* and the recent critical response to the English translation in North America and Britain could scarcely be starker: the heroic intellectual "Magus of Tübingen" had now become a "Stalinist mountebank" peddling Marxist-mystical fantasy. I believe that that recent critical reaction to the translation has been both misguided and to a considerable degree unjust; and this book is intended to provide an introductory guide to the masterpiece of an important, even indispensable, but admittedly problematic writer.

Bloch's writings are extensive and although early abortive attempts were made to arrange a translation of *Das Prinzip Hoffnung*[2] was not until 1986 that a complete text appeared in English.[3] Many of Bloch's other works remain untranslated not least because of their resistant style. The transient enthusiasm for Bloch's work in the 1960's is understandable, as a Marxist thinker (albeit highly unorthodox) his role in the student movement of West Germany was analogous to that of Herbert Marcuse in North America.[4] It is possible to attribute some of

[1] R.H. Roberts, "Review article : An Introductory Reading of Ernst Bloch's *The Principle of Hope*" in the *Journal of Literature and Theology*, March 1987, Vol.1 No.1, pp.89-112.

[2] As Bloch's biographers and, in particular Karola Bloch recall, Oxford University Press considered the possibility of a translation under the title *Dreams of a Better Life*, see Karola Bloch et al (eds.) *Ernst Bloch Briefe 1903-1975* (Frankfurt am Main: Suhrkamp Verlag, 1985), p.11.

[3] Neville Plaice, Stephen Plaice and Paul Knight (trs.),*The Principle of Hope*, (Oxford, Basil Blackwell, 1986), 3 vols.

[4] The negative side of this influence is alluded to by J.P.Stern, who, in reviewing *The Principle of Hope*, regarded Bloch's failure to do justice to the evil of the Third Reich and to dissociate himself sufficiently from anti-Semitism as providing the "system of beliefs from which the Baader-Meinhof group draw its picture of the world", "Marxism On Stilts", *The New Republic*, 9.3.1987, p.38. This article is reprinted in substantially the

the venom recently directed against Bloch to a significant change in social and political circumstance: economic crisis, *perestroika* and *glas-
nost* in the Soviet Union; a rightward movement in the United States
and the Thatcherite "elimination of socialism" in Britain are all relevant factors. Those who enthused over Bloch earlier now find their intellectual arteries hardening, they appear to have lost patience or
have conformed. For them, Bloch's own question, the title of his inaugu-
ral lecture in Tübingen: "*Kann Hoffnung enttäuscht werden?*" ("Can
Hope be frustrated?") has been answered in the affirmative. For those
of either liberal or socialist political outlook the last decade has been
one of practical and ideological retrenchment in an era of violence and
of increasing contempt for consensus and for human life itself. Bloch
has, for many, truly become the "Prophet of the unbecome",[5] a bitter
reminder of illusions.

Why, then, produce a reading of Bloch's *magnum opus* in such a cli-
mate? There are, I believe, three good preliminary reasons to do so:
first, *The Principle of Hope* is a synthetic work conceived on a huge
scale that confronts and challenges the pervasive fragmentation and
dilution characteristic of much contemporary culture; it thus provides
an image for Western European humanity which, however questionable, is both comprehensive in scale and yet conceived with democratic
intention. Second, *The Principle of Hope* contains a consistently
worked-out, but imperfectly understood resolution of the German
Hegelian tradition, comparable with, but different to those of other
nineteenth and twentieth-century philosophers and theologians; this
needs to be understood in the English language context. Third, as regards the interaction of the Christian and Marxist traditions, Bloch's
work was significant not only in the period of so-called "dialogue" but
continues to be of importance. All these three points are related in terms
of the basic postulate of Bloch's thought: that he articulated an all-
embracing conception of reality putatively determined by the *future*
rather than by the past. However implausible in principle this may
seem (and Bloch's venture is open to the objections directed against the
structure of a transcendence conceived more traditionally in relation to
the past or the present) he was nevertheless prepared to develop a consistent, cumulative argument grounded in the conviction that things are
not as they should be and that goal-oriented change in the human condition is both necessary and possible. The "front" of the future is the

same form in *Encounter*, July-August, 1988, vol. LXXI/2 pp.27-33 under the title "Ernst
Bloch, Philosopher of 'Hope'". Given contemporary British political circumstances, in
particular those affecting university education, Stern's account is an astounding fusion of
literary acuteness with political naivety.

[5]Michael Tanner, *The Times Literary Supplement*, 22.8.86, p.923.

categorical imperative of change, an imperative conveyed through the subversive utopian tradition (both religious and secularised); it is this latency that all the forces of reaction seek either to suppress or perversely to exploit.

Bloch stood apart as a relatively isolated figure estranged from orthodox Marxism, but also as an atheist, distanced from his ancestral Judaism. Fundamental to this isolation is Bloch's articulation of the dimension of a futurity purged both from the "narrow-gauge" and "cold" form of Marxist-Leninist orthodoxy and from the de-eschatologised religion of the West. *The Principle of Hope* therefore proposes a transformation of the culture that culminated in the great narratives of Hegel's *Phenomenology of Mind* (1807) and Goethe's *Faust*, but which also includes within its ambit the whole tradition extending back to St. Augustine's *City of God* and beyond to Plato, Aristotle and the pre-Socratic philosophers. Bloch's conception may appear to the casual observer merely to be constructed out of the tedious repetition of an obsessively-held insight, the notion of *Noch-Nicht Sein*, that is "Not-Yet Being". This would be a manifest injustice given Bloch's first-hand assimilation of an astounding range of primary materials. In reality he provides a total alternative "reading" of the tradition that challenges its established, de-eschatologised postulates.

The Principle of Hope is the summation of this interpretation in which can be found the many-layered location, "deduction" and extended development of the category and the categorical imperative of anticipation and futurity. In this book we attempt to penetrate beneath the dense style of Bloch's text in order to expose and recapitulate its inner structure. This exercise is difficult enough given the author's powers of synthesis, and so in order to contextualise and justify *The Principle of Hope* we refer extensively to Bloch's other works, primarily in the footnotes. Above all, it is our intention to introduce and to decipher a resistant text thus allowing the reader to penetrate through its dense surface into the inner structure.

Ernst Bloch was, unlike his near contemporary and fellow secularised Jewish Marxist intellectual, T.W. Adorno, a militant optimist and a relentless visionary. Bloch makes acute demands upon the patience of the reader which originate not only in the styles he exploited but also, more problematically for the English reader, in the intrinsic capacities of the German language. The latter lends itself to the creation of ontological narrative that is the occasion of the manifestation of being. This is a "speech genre" well-developed in German thought: thus Bloch's *Principle of Hope* and Karl Barth's *Church Dogmatics* (and in particular the fourth volume) both stand in the extended shadow of Hegel's *Phenomenology of Mind* as monuments to the capacity of the German language to embody and as it were realise reality. The German philosopher does not retreat from this task through self-deprecating irony and sometimes facile humour like the English, nor like the French does he seek the transparency of Cartesian clearness and distinctness (and the dubious delights of *différance*). By contrast, the German embraces the linguistic virtuality of Goethe's phrase, *"wie schönes, wie seiendes"*, in order to promote ontological fructification on a grand scale. This capacity of the German language is one of the factors which enables and emboldens his "refunctioning" (*Umfunktionierung*) of the whole tradition in terms as comprehensive in its own way as Nietzsche's "transvaluation of all values" (*Umwertung aller Werte*).

Silvia Markun points out in her brief biographical survey[6] that Bloch's life and thought are inseparable and that a wholly adequate study of Bloch would fully comprehend both; this, however, lies beyond the scope of the present book. We take *The Principle of Hope* as the centerpiece of Bloch's work and in the light of this proceed as follows. First, in chapter 1, we provide an outline of Bloch's life and thought which distinguishes well-marked stages corresponding with his voluntary and enforced movements and later emigration and the corresponding intellectual encounters that took place. Second, in chapters 2-6, we expound and analyse the major divisions of *The Principle of Hope* in relation to the collected works. Sustained attention is given to the first volume which contains the foundations of the theoretical critique and the conceptual innovations. We briefly review the second volume in chapter 7 and present the third in chapters 8 and 9, where the originality and persisting imperative of Bloch's *atheistic* appropriation of *religious* insight becomes apparent. In conclusion, on this basis in chapter 10 we evaluate the issues that arise out of the past and the possible future reception of Bloch's masterpiece.

Bloch's epic work *The Principle of Hope* is the *magnum opus* of an oeuvre largely conceived free from the constraints of academic teaching. The result is often a repetitive prolixity and pointed failure of systematisation which can only be partially explained or rationalised in terms of the stylistic and structural demands of writing from, as it were, the standpoint of the future. Thus, whilst Fredric Jameson's representation of Bloch is far superior to most other contributions by British or North American critics (Wayne Hudson and George Steiner being the notable exceptions), his sophisticated theoretical apologetic is nevertheless too generous in the allowances it makes for Bloch's sheer self-indulgence and quantitative excess. Thus Jameson applies his own view

---

[6]S. Markun, *Ernst Bloch in Selbstzeugnissen und Bilddokumenten* (Reinbek bei Hamburg: Rowohlt Verlag, 1977), p.7.

that art is a "displaced prophetic vocation" to the work of Bloch himself and argues that;

"Mainly, however, the neglect of Bloch is due to the fact that his system, a doctrine of hope and ontological anticipation, is itself an anticipation, and stands as a solution to the problems of a universal culture and a universal hermeneutic which have not yet come into being. It thus lies before us, enigmatic and enormous, like an aerolite fallen from space, covered with mysterious hieroglyphs that radiate a peculiar inner warmth and power, spells and the key to spells, themselves patiently waiting for their own ultimate moment of decipherment."[7]

Jameson's contrast between philosophy and hermeneutics is likewise somewhat strained in face of the peculiarity of a project so dependent upon the past that at the same time purports to transvalue the present from the standpoint of a future that is not yet. Hence we suggest that the notion of a "speech-genre" which resists reduction but escapes the dangers of unbridled linguistic autonomy is perhaps a happier way of characterising the distinctiveness of Bloch's text: Thus M.M. Bakhtin presents the "speech genre" as follows:

"Language is realised in the form of individual concrete utterances (oral and written) by participants in the various areas of human activity. These utterances reflect the specific conditions and goals of each such area not only through their content (thematic) and linguistic style, that is, the selection of the lexical, phraseological, and grammatical resources of the language, but above all through their compositional structure. All three of these aspects - thematic content, style and composition of structure - are inseparably linked to the whole of the utterance and are equally determined by the specific nature of the particular sphere of communication. Each separate utterance is individual, of course, but each sphere in which language is used develops its own relatively stable types of these utterances. These we may call speech genres."[8]

The provisional licencing of Bloch's approach by these means, that is as "speech genre", shifts our critical discussion away from reduction-

[7]F. Jameson, *Marxism and Form Twentieth-century Dialectical Theories of Literature* (New Jersey : Princeton University Press, 1971), pp.158-9.

[8]M.M. Bakhtin, "The Problem of Speech Genres, V.W. McGee (tr.) *Speech Genres and Late Essays* (Austin : University of Texas Press, 1986,) p.60.

ist attack into what we might term the morality of post-modernism, that is towards the legitimacy of rehabilitating modes of discourse seemingly distanced, even extinguished, by transformations of the tradition as a whole, including its religious and mythological aspects. We thus maintain that serious grappling with the past in the interests of the present and the future entails the simultaneous intellectual management of pre-critical tradition, critical modernity and postmodern re-appropriation. Bloch's work contains all three dimensions and although it is ostensibly dependent upon the future, and thus the *eschatalogical* (and not merely the utopian) dimension, it inevitably raises many questions about the interpretation of the tradition *as a whole*. Processes of de-eschatologisation and secularisation and a series of complex displacements underlie Bloch's project; decipherment of the latter depends upon the reader's willingness and ability to juxtapose these three critical dimensions.

Within *The Principle of Hope* there are the remnants of the ancestral structures of German idealist thought and we first seek to understand Bloch from the standpoint of this relatively familiar perspective. Bloch's extraordinarily wide range of reference and allusion has to be contained in order to preserve clarity and this is achieved by the extensive use of footnotes which are intended to indicate: first, where further investigation would prove fruitful; second, the points at which Bloch's own primary texts in the *Gesamtausgabe* are an obvious and significant commentary upon and expansion of *The Principle of Hope* and, third, to refer (again without endangering the mainly introductory and expository character of this book) to the extensive, and predominantly German, secondary literature.

Bloch's *The Principle of Hope* can be experienced as the textual embodiment of Goethe's exhortation to *"Sterbe, und werde"* which is a demand that makes peculiarly heavy demands upon the reader. Whoever resists this call to "Die, and Become" will be less than equal to the task of interpretation. Yet the Anglo-Saxon reader can take heart, Bloch's owl of Minerva flies not at dusk but at dawn. Hope beckons and even if we might not care for the colour of Bloch's dawn (*Morgenröte*) it is our contention that *The Principle of Hope* deserves a far fuller measure of critical recognition than it has up to now, generally speaking, received.

What follows is an interpretation: we neither imply nor demand any acceptance of Bloch's views. We believe that it is important to understand the nature of his argument and to appropriate critically that space for reflection, that urge to think and act from the future and to grasp reality proleptically that Bloch presents with unique vigour. This writer clears space, he opens possibilities and refunctions the past in the name of the future. As such Bloch articulates indispensable middle ground between nostalgic regression into the past and capitulation to the coming nemesis of technological domination that overshadows the future. In his ambitious thought-experiment Bloch re-awakens a lost past through the category of the hidden future and exploits the idea of the possible so as to threaten all ideological rigidities. At his best Bloch crosses the boundaries that enforce subliminal limitation and confine us within the borders of the apparent, rather than the real. His is a call to freedom that must be heard.

CHAPTER I

ERNST BLOCH'S LIFE AND WORK: AN OUTLINE

Ernst Bloch is an intrinsically difficult writer whose style, thought and actions are not readily assimilable into any single or simple framework. Because of this, he is liable to remain the victim of either something approaching dogmatic partisanship on the part of a small minority of devotees or, alternatively, be subject to arbitrary dismissal by those lacking the energy or will to engage seriously with a thinker who provides a comprehensive and sustained (even if finally questionable) synthesis of, and commentary upon large areas of the whole Western tradition. The sheer range of Bloch's knowledge and the absence, until his first academic post taken up near retirement age, of any obligation to explain his views with regularity to a student audience compound the situation. Bloch regarded his works as a synthetic unity and resisted the ordering of the *Gesamtausgabe* in strict chronological sequence, and the absence of a critical apparatus and organisation in the standard edition puts near insuperable obstacles in the path of the uninformed reader. Also problematic was Bloch's practice of revising early texts for re-publication, thus sometimes making the precise determination of the original content uncertain.[1] In practical terms we have nevertheless to rely primarily upon the collected edition of Bloch's works whilst not wholly ignoring, for example, the excision of laudatory comments upon Stalin from the East German first edition of *Das Prinzip Hoffnung* prior to its re-publication in the West. We respect the intentions of the author in the first instance but refer to original editions where they are available. The scale, complexity and the alien character of Bloch's work has discouraged most Anglo-Saxon writers. Indeed, despite the pioneering study by Wayne Hudson,[2] in

---

[1]This practice has earned Bloch some harsh criticism. The major revision of texts like the early *Geist der Utopie* presents no particular problem whereas the scale of alteration in other works is difficult to assess without detailed critical comparison of texts, some of which are now extremely difficult to obtain. Most commentators take the *Gesamtausgabe* as the basis of their assessment and this precedent is followed here. All references to the Gesamtausgabe (GA) are to the second edition of 1977.

[2]Wayne Hudson, *The Marxist Philosophy of Ernst Bloch* (London: Macmillan, 1982). Both Hudson and S. Unseld (ed), *Ernst Bloch zu ehren* (Frankfurt am Main: Suhrkamp,

which he focuses upon Bloch's innovations within Marxism, there is as
yet no comprehensive presentation in English of an oeuvre that matured
over many decades according to laws of development conceived and applied in relative isolation, and worked out in occasional but intense interaction with a group of writers and thinkers drawn from the elite of
the twentieth-century left-wing German-speaking intelligentsia.

Whilst the published form of Bloch's work tends to obscure the
steps in his intellectual development, it is nevertheless important to
understand how the major works relate to the main stages of a life
largely devoted to the accumulation of learning and its organisation
around a single, fundamental principle, what Hudson calls a "central
operator", the category of "Noch-Nicht Sein" (Not-Yet Being), the
precise meaning of which will be explained later. Bloch's life fell into
five basic phases: first, the period from his birth in 1885, his youth and
education at school and university up to the publication of his first major work Geist der Utopie (Spirit of Utopia) in 1918; this text established Bloch as a significant, if eccentric figure in the context of what
was to become the culture of the Weimar Republic. Second, the period
from the end of the First World War until his exile in 1933, during
which Bloch travelled and interacted with Georg Lukács and later
with Walter Benjamin and wrote a series of works including a notable
historical study of the radical Reformer Thomas Münzer als Theologe
der Revolution (Thomas Münzer as Theologian of Revolution) published in 1921, and a second, heavily revised version of Geist der
Utopie that appeared in 1923. Third, in 1933 Bloch went into exile in a
number of European countries with his third wife Karola Piotrkowska
(who outlives him) and eventually passed the Second World War in
the United States, during which time he wrote (but did not publish) a
series of major works, including Das Prinzip Hoffnung. Fourth, in 1949
Bloch responded to a call to the Chair of Philosophy at the reconstituted University of Leipzig in the Eastern, Russian zone of Germany.
Apart from brief travel abroad Bloch remained in the DDR until 1961,
but it was only until his enforced retirement in 1956 that he enjoyed official status. During a visit to West Germany in 1961, on hearing of the
construction of the Berlin Wall Bloch stayed in the West and was invited to take up a guest professorship at the University of Tübingen.
Here, in the fifth and final stage of his life Bloch exerted enormous influence upon the student generation of the 'sixties and early 'seventies
and devoted himself assiduously to the revision and preparation of all
his works for the full Gesamtausgabe completed in 1977. Bloch died in
the same year at the age of 92; so ended a life of exceptional vitality

1965), pp.397-403 provide detailed information on the chronology of Bloch's publications.
See also Biographical Outline below, pp. 229

which bequeathed to posterity a collection of texts that illuminate an intellectual career fraught with diverse ambiguities whilst caught up in the conflict of twentieth century totalitarianisms.

The main body of this chapter consists in an outline of these stages in Bloch's life which draws upon the standard biographical accounts[3] but concentrates attention upon the texts that frame, as it were, Bloch's masterpiece, *The Principle of Hope*. The latter work has about it a breathless virtuosity, it contains an amalgam of styles and is the product of a relentless belief in the intrinsic power of language. It is essential to be aware of the immense energy invested in the supportive texts which offer a highly original commentary on the history of philosophy, theology, and in a less systematic way, literature, besides the many shorter occasional writings which themselves vary in style and genre from Kafka-esque episodic short stories to political and cultural journalism pursued at a high level.

I. EDUCATION AND EARLY DEVELOPMENT (1885-1919)

Ernst Bloch was born on the 8th July 1885 in Ludwigshafen, the son of Max Bloch, a Bavarian railway official, into a liberal Jewish family. Although Bloch underwent the ritual initiation of *Bar Mitzvah* he was from an early age a convinced atheist. Despite an unimpressive school record Bloch's precocious early development was evident in extra-curricular correspondence with Ernst Mach, Theodor Lipps, Eduard von Hartmann and Wilhelm Windelband. All commentators record the decisive influence of the contrasting social and cultural realities of Mannheim and Ludwigshafen, one of the great monuments to the German economic and industrial expansion of the *Gründerzeit*.[4] The *Residenz* and the Court Library of Mannheim contrasted with the proletarian slums of Ludwigshafen, and this provided for the young Bloch a living exemplification of the class struggle: the contrasting poles of the nineteenth century social order confronted each other directly. Silvia Markun makes much of this form of direct education and its effect upon Bloch; significant were the extraordinary diversity of ideas drawn from the social realities of the growing chemical industry, the

---

[3]Erhard Bahr, *Ernst Bloch* (Berlin, 1974); W. Hudson, op.cit; Sylvia Markun, *Ernst Bloch in Selbstzeugnissen und Bilddokumenten* (Hamburg: Rowohlt, 1977) and Peter Zudeieck, *Der Hintern des Teufels Ernst Bloch Leben und Werk* (Moos: Elster Verlag, 1987). David Drew provides an excellent introduction to Bloch's musical interests in the collection translated by P. Palmer, *Essays on the Philosophy of Music* (Cambridge: Cambridge University Press, 1985) pp.xi-xlviii

[4]Capitalist industrialization on a comprehensive scale came relatively late to Germany, during the *Gründerzeit* entrepreneurial expansion took place with unprecedented rapidity and attendant distressing social consequences.

ancestral *Jahrmarkt* and its colportage, and, above all, the Court Library. The latter contained the works of the great German thinkers of Romanticism and the Enlightenment, but its contents precisely failed satisfactorily to explain the genesis of the stark juxtaposition of the rampant capitalist development and the architectural and social relics of absolutism. Thus whilst Bloch absorbed Karl May,[5] Hegel, Kant, Fichte and, above all, Schelling,[6] he also supplemented his prodigious reading with socialist writers such as Marx, Engels, August Bebel and Rosa Luxemburg. Bloch's lifework actually consists in an extraordinary attempt to combine the fruits of classical culture with consistent materialism and socialist revolutionary theory, however implausible a project this may appear to be. From an early stage Bloch's interests extended into philosophy, psychology, music and physics, besides European literature in general. At 13 Bloch wrote an essay, *"Das Weltall im Lichte des Atheismus, Renaissance der Sinnlichkeit"* ("The World-All in the Light of Atheism, Renaissance of Material Nature") which even then indicated the fundamental orientation of his life-long preoccupation with the reworking of materialism into a philosophy adequate to the totality of cosmic reality and human experience.[7] The particular form this project would take becomes apparent in his later school text *"Über Kraft und ihr Wesen"* ("On Power and its Essence") of 1902 in which the seventeen year old Bloch fought his way out of the enclosure of the Hegelian and idealist system with the assertion that: *"das Ding an sich ist die objective Phantasie"*, the "thing in itself is objective fantasy", that is "objective imagination".[8] As early as 1901 his school exercise books reveal the emergence of an extraordinary style later to be identified as "Expressionist", that is an acceptance of invasive fragmentation and the exploitation of indirect means of communication, directed in Bloch's case towards a single, obsessively-held goal, the as yet undiscovered land of the future.

---

[5]With characteristic humorous exaggeration Bloch recalled his youthful reading in conversation seventy years later: *"Es gibt nur Karl May und Hegel, alles dazwischen ist eine unreine Mischung"*, cited by Michael Landmann *"Ernst Bloch im Gespräch"*, in S. Unseld, op.cit., pp.345ff.

[6]Bloch's affinity with the late Schelling, most notably in his celebrated lectures *Philosophie der Offenbarung*, is often commented upon. Jürgen Habermas' intellectual sketch (1960) *"Ein Marxistischer Schelling"* in *Philosophisch-politische Profile* (Frankfurt am Main: Suhrkamp Verlag, 1981), pp.141-159 develops this parallel.

[7]The autobiographical fragment *"Der Lebensgott"* in *Spuren,GA* I, pp.65-72 affords insight into the mind of the young Bloch: school was abominable, all other kinds of attractions, (especially the *"Kaiser-Panorama"*, were preferable. But as Bloch later recalled in his school essay of 1896, *"Das Weltall im Lichte des Atheismus"*, his earliest conviction was: *"Ich bin ein Atheist"*, loc.cit., p.67.

[8]*Philosophische Aufsätze zur objektiven Phantasie*, GA10, p.133.

After passing his *Abitur* without distinction in 1905, Bloch matriculated at the University of Munich in order to study philosophy, music and physics with his former correspondent, the philosopher and psychologist Theodor Lipps. At this time Bloch became acquainted with the Neo-Romantic phenomenology and psychology of Max Scheler and Edmund Husserl, both of which left their mark upon his later work. Lipps' "act psychology" did not satisfy Bloch and in 1907 he transferred to Würzburg into the ambit of Oswald Külpe, a notable representative of the Neo-Kantian school of philosophy. Here Bloch encountered another pupil of Külpe, the young Martin Heidegger who was at that time in his Neo-scholastic phase and regarded by his then teacher as embodying a link between Kant and St. Thomas Aquinas. During a stay in Würzburg Bloch wrote the text which was to prove the key to his life's work: *"Über die Kategorie Noch-Nicht"* ("On the Category of the Not-Yet"). Upon this Hudson comments:

> Henceforward, Bloch had one fundamental idea important enough to set him apart from other thinkers, which he developed for the rest of his life: the idea that man possessed an anticipatory consciousness which gave him not-yet conscious knowledge of future postulates.[9]

Characteristically, this paper was not published at the time nor did it later appear in full in the *Gesamtausgabe*; nevertheless in this early text of the twenty-two year old Bloch we find the moment of birth of the system which was to be developed over the following seventy years. In Würzburg Bloch became acquainted through a Jewish friend with the Cabbala and Jewish mysticism and this familiarity is an additional factor to be taken into account in understanding the stylistic genres exploited with great freedom by the mature Bloch. After six semesters of study in Würzburg Bloch was *promoviert* in 1909 with a doctoral thesis published under the title: *"Kritische Erörterungen über Rickert und das Problem der modernen Erkenntnistheorie"* ("Critical Questioning concerning Rickert and the Problem of modern Epistemology")[10]. Bloch's thesis has to be understood against the background of one of the most important, yet least well understood epochs in German intellectual life, that of Neo-Kantianism, during which the once seemingly all-powerful inheritance of German idealism surviving in *Lebensphilosophie* collapsed when it was obliged to face the necessity of re-defining the role of philosophy

9Hudson, op.cit., p.6.

10Parts of the Würzberg dissertation are reproduced in the *Ergänzungsband zur Gesamtausgabe Tendenz - Latenz - Utopie*(Frankfurt am Main: Suhrkamp, 1978), pp.55-107.

in relation to the development of experimental psychology. Bloch's dissertation on the neo-Kantian Heinrich Rickert, contained, Hudson informs us, an attack upon Rickert's "dualistic oscillation between positivism and apriorism" and it "tried to show how a critique of neo-Kantianism could lead to a new utopian philosophy".[11] As will become apparent in the ensuing chapters Bloch's own presentation of the category of the Not-Yet and the utopian principle is not constructed in terms of an overt dialogue with neo-Kantianism as such, but as a re-engagement with the original thinkers of classical German philosophy, Kant, Schelling, Feuerbach, and supremely, Hegel.

It was not the intellectual renown of Lipps or Külpe alone which drew Bloch to Munich and then later to the relatively obscure University of Würzburg. A seventeen year old actress also had some influence and it is of some significance to note that she was one of a series of beautiful, intelligent (and preferably wealthy) women with whom Bloch had serious relationships throughout his life. Unlike many leading twentieth century male intellectuals Bloch's attitude[12] was one of consistent if not unambiguous appreciation, an attitude emphasised by his thoroughgoing absorption of the Romantic spirit. There is with Bloch no whiff of the canker of misogyny evident in some thinkers with progressive reputations.

Bloch took a decisive intellectual step and entered into the mainstream of German culture when he moved to Berlin in 1908. Here at the centre of the pre-War Wilhelmine Reich Bloch commented ascerbically upon the aesthetic inwardness (*Innerlichkeit*) of the German bourgeoisie and its aggressive imperialism, which at that time co-existed in close proximity with the sharpest political and cultural opposition to it. In this tense and electric environment Bloch gained access to the brilliant circle associated with Georg Simmel's[13] private colloquium. This had only twelve places and on the basis of a half hour exposition of his ontology of the Not-Yet Bloch was admitted, and a brief friendship began which was further encouraged when he and Simmel went away together on a three week tour to Italy to mark the latter's

[11]Hudson, op.cit., p.6. The passage cited in the *Ergänzungsband* (See note 10 above) is an extended philosophical praeparation for the introduction of Bloch's new category into the seeming wasteland of neo-Kantian logicism.

[12]Bloch's fragment, "*Der lange Blick*" is indicative, in writing about the sexual act he observes: "*Selten haben Untreue und höchliste Treue eine schrecklichere Verbindung im gleichen Akt: die mannliche Liebe erlischt leicht im Nichts-als-Liebe, das der Frau das Alles ist*", *Spuren* GAI, p.85.

[13]Georg Simmel (1858-1918) is a figure of great importance heavily overshadowed in the Anglo-Saxon mind by Max Weber. Simmel's pessimism strongly influenced Lukács and Weber besides Bloch, and his conceptions of alienation, the individual and of reification were of general long term significance.

fiftieth birthday. Simmel was a polymath who united the philosophy of history, sociology, the philosophy of culture and metaphysics in a richly diverse *Weltanschauung*. From a philosophical point of view Bloch initially saw some significance in Simmel's doctrine of perspective, his emphasis upon the "lived moment" and concept of a universal hermeneutics of the soul and the doctrine of "perhaps".[14] It was, however, the development of Bloch's relationship with Georg Lukács, whom he had met during a visit to Budapest, that had a greater long term impact. Whilst Lukács was then under the influence of the poet Stephan George and the *Wandervogel* movement[15] their interaction was to be intense: friendship, sympathy, enthusiasm, and love combined in a late-flowering explosion of Romantic sensitivity. This was despite Bloch's devastating later judgement passed upon the "mediocrities" in the *Georgekreis* in his essay *"Die Okkulten von 1913"* published in the collection *"Durch die Wüste"* ("Through the Desert") after the War in 1923.[16] Relations with Simmel soon deteriorated as Bloch came to think of him as a "wholly empty, purposeless man", a disillusionment which deepened when the latter enthusiastically endorsed the war policy of imperial Germany in 1914.[17]

In 1911 Bloch established a Swiss home in Garmisch where in 1913 he married his first wife Else von Stritsky, a sculptor from Riga, whose religious and mystical Christian outlook had a lifelong influence upon Bloch, despite his longstanding engagement with Marxism. Of all the major twentieth-century Marxist revisionists (with the exception, perhaps of Walter Benjamin), Bloch was to be by far the most sympathetic to the religious dimension, in that he understood it to be an indispensable aspect of human development.[18] In 1912 Bloch's life was divided

---

[14]See Bloch's short comment: *"Weisen des 'vielleicht' bei Simmel (Zum 100. Geburtstag, 1958)"* GA10, pp.57-60.

[15]Bloch's relationship with the dominant forces in contemporary cultural innovation was characteristically ambiguous: he often drew inspiration from what he reacted against and later might denounce. Stephan George and the *"Georgekreis"* and the *"Wandervogel"* youth movement were active in the widespread revulsion against the mechanisation of life through *"Technik"* and advocated a return to the virtues of mystical and rural life.

[16]*Durch die Wüste* (Berlin, 1923), new edition (Frankfurt am Main: Suhrkamp, 1964). This collection is reproduced piecemeal in the *Gesamtausgabe*.

[17]Here Bloch's reaction to Simmel and those academics who gave their support to the parliamentary resolutions and declarations on the outbreak of war in 1914 is similar in some respects to that of Karl Barth. It is, furthermore, interesting that both these great quasi-metaphysical thinkers passed the time of the War on neutral Swiss territory. Bloch was excused service on account of his defective sight; Barth was of course himself a neutral of Swiss nationality. Bloch's judgment upon Simmel is to be found in *"Schulphilosophie heute"* again published in *Durch die Wüste*, pp.91ff.

[18]For an account of the place of religion in human development see relevant literature cited in chs. 8 & 9 below.

between Garmisch and Heidelberg, where he gained access to the brilliant intellectual circle associated with Max Weber. In the Webers' home the German mandarin academic tradition confronted a bohemian, educated youth overflowing with an exuberant mixture of ideas drawn from psychoanalysis, socialism, incipient feminism and renascent mythologies of redemption, a situation acutely observed by Marianne Weber in the biography of her husband. Whereas Georg von Lukács (who then still bore a title of nobility) was appreciated in the Weber's salon for his proposals in aesthetics, Bloch was viewed with less warmth by Frau Weber,[19] who recorded that: "a new Jewish philosopher had just come - a young man with an enormous crest of black hair and a self-confidence equally excessive, who obviously took himself to be the forerunner of a new Messiah and insisted that everyone would recognise him as such".[20] With the outbreak of war Bloch and Else left Germany and settled in Grünwald in Switzerland where they congregated with other disaffected, messianically-conscious intellectuals. At this time Bloch's interest was aroused in Franz von Baader, Thomas Münzer and the humane religious socialism of Wilhelm Weitling[21], and he began work upon Geist der Utopie, first published in Munich in 1918. This work, a densely-written text combining Expressionist style and cultural critique with utopian ideas and revolutionary Messianism, is the public departure point of Bloch's intellectual odyssey. It is a document which (along with Lukács' early works and, in the theological sphere, Karl Barth's Römerbriefe of 1919 and 1922), was projected into the febrile social and political chaos and cultural vacuum, that followed upon the Armistice. Bloch, like Karl Barth, was capable of exceptionally intense application and both men substantially revised their earliest contributions to the post-War "crisis". Their contrasting but analogous intellectual strategies are mutually illuminating when seen together in context.[22]

---

[19]Bloch did, however, eventually contribute an essay on "Politische Programmes und Utopien" in Switzerland to Max Weber's Archiv fur Sozialwissenschaft und Sozialpolitik 1919,vol.46, pp.140-162.

[20]Marianne Weber, Max Weber - ein Lebensbild (Tübingen, 1926) p.476. Frau Weber's sketch is confirmed by Bloch's strident exclamation in a letter to Lukács in 1911: "Ich bin der Paraklet und die Menschen, denen ich gesandt bin, werden in sich den heimkehrenden Gott erleben und verstehen", Ernst Bloch Briefe, p.67.

[21]Bloch's predeliction for heretical and marginalised figures in theology and socialism is a complementary adjunct of his refreshing and highly distinctive hermeneutic of the tradition which is largely dedicated to a reversal of approaches usually accorded "orthodox" status..

[22]The affinities and dissimilarities between the immediate post-war contributions of Lukács, Bloch and Barth, all seminal texts in their own spheres of interest merit the closest contextual examination. See David Drew, op.cit., for an account of their relationships with each other and with Adorno.

Geist der Utopie is an extraordinary book which deserves fuller description, as it is upon this foundation that Bloch's understanding of cultural transmission, his overall hermeneutic of the tradition, is built.[23] This technique, described by Hudson as "recursive modernism", contrasts in important ways with the work of his distinguished older contemporaries Simmel and Emil Lask, and even with that of Lukács, to whose early publications Bloch's text clearly relates. Bloch's relationship with Lukács was fundamental to the first edition of this demanding work and nowhere is this more clearly seen than in the passage "*Zur Theorie des Dramas*" ("On the Theory of Drama")[24] where insights drawn from Lukács' essays on the "methodology of literary history" and the sociology of modern drama are combined and reinterpreted as a prefigurement of Bloch's own conception of the heroic destiny of mankind. Apart from the direct personal communication and correspondence between Bloch and Lukács before the War the only works published by the latter in German prior to the appearance of *Geist der Utopie* (and thus directly accessible to Bloch) would appear to be *Die Seele und die Formen* (The Soul and the Forms)[25] besides *Von der Armut am Geist. Ein Gesprach und ein Brief* (On Poverty of the Spirit. A Conversation and Letter)[26] and *Zur Soziologie des modernen Dramas* (On the Sociology of Modern Drama).[27] From Lukács, Bloch took the conception of the hero whose right it is to experience tragic death, a fate which he demands: for "*der Held erlangt sein Schicksal*".[28] The preMarxist Lukács, like Bloch, explicated *Mythos* not as a spiritual refuge but as a "truth", true only because the world is itself false. Bloch proceeds to transform this insight into the goal of the self-realising hero; thus in the decipherment of tragic myth there is exposed:

a becoming of God, a disclosure of the God who is now living and sleeping in man alone, an internal monologue within the crea-

[23]Earlier comment on Bloch's style and method is particularly relevant here, see Gert Ueding, *Glanzvolles Elend. Versuch über Kitsch und Kolportage* (Frankfurt am Main: Suhrkamp, 1977).
[24]*Geist der Utopie Erste Fassung, GA,16*, pp.67-77.
[25](Berlin: Egon Fleischel, 1911).
[26]*Neue Blätter 2*, 1912, pp.67-92.
[27]*Archiv für Sozialwissenschaft und Sozialpolitik*, 1914, pp.303-45, 662-706. For an account of this period from Lukács' standpoint (and bibliography in English translation) see A. Arato and P. Braines, *The Young Lukács and the Origin of Western Marxism* (London: Pluto Press, 1979), ch.3. See also A. Münster, M. Lowy, N. Tertulian (eds.) *Verdinglichung und Utopie Ernst Bloch und Georg Lukács zum 100, Geburtstag* (Frankfurt am Main: Sendler Verlag, 1987) for a comprehensive overview of the relation between Bloch and Lukács.
[28]*Geist der Utopie, GA 16*, p.68.

ture, a self-disclosure of God before himself, in which, however, the transcendent God is brought to life.[29]

The paradoxical Jesus, the "comic" hero Don Quixote, and Moses (as
presented in cabbalistic saga) are presented as exemplary participants
in a Promethean realisation of the divine-human tragedy of human becoming, which is experienced in an unresolved tension between sustained existence and its ever-threatening end.

Despite the appropriation and development in apocalyptic terms
of Lukács' own response to the Weberian "iron cage" of the human condition, there is no clear, formal structure apparent in *Geist der Utopie*,
but a series of passages gathered under the heading of "*Die
Selbstbegegnung*" ("The Meeting with the Self", or, more simply "Self-
meeting"). Bloch's characterisation of the then contemporary bourgeois
cultural situation was brutal and extreme: the "triumph of stupidity,
guarded by the gendarme, celebrated by intellectuals".[30] Through this
he had to hack a way forward on the basis of the motivation afforded
by active "fantasy" (that is the active imagination); that which is not
has to be called into being; we must, Bloch exclaims:

> build out into the blue, build ourselves into the blue and there
> seek out that which is the true, the real, where that which is
> simply factual disappears – incipit vita nova.[31]

The new life begins, but it is realised through the revolutionary
transcendence of the old. Bloch begins *Geist der Utopie* with a cryptic
meditation on an ancient mug, a drinking vessel that bears within itself
the impress of past generations and yet is latent with future possibility. In three lengthy passages on the production of the ornament, the
comic hero (Don Quixote), and the philosophy of music[32] Bloch exam-
ines by means of prolix analysis the mediation of the self, the *Ich*,
through architecture, literature and music. It is, above all, the Gothic

---

[29]"*Sie ist ein Gottwerden, eine Enthüllung des nur noch im Menschen lebendigen,
schlafenden Gottes, ein Monologisieren in der Kreatur, eine Enthüllung Gottes vor sich
selbst, aber der immanente Gott erweckt darin den transzendenten zum Leben*", *Geist der
Utopie, GA* 16, p.69.

[30]*Geist der Utopie, GA* 16, p.9.

[31]*Geist der Utopie, GA* 16 ibid. Bloch's projection of "blue" as the colour of openness
and emancipated future-orientedness is pervasive throughout his work. Dante's words
from the *Inferno* in the Divine Comedy are repeatedly exploited: Incipit Vita Nova is a
key leitmotif in *The Principle of Hope.*

[32]Extracts from this have recently been translated, see P. Palmer (tr.) op.cit. Bloch's
"philosophy" of music has always attracted lively criticism as Margarete Susman noted
in her reply to the musicologist, Paul Bekker's attack on the details in Bloch's approach.
See the "*Erwiderung*" of 17.4.1919 in S. Unseld, op.cit., pp.393-4.

imposition of life upon the supremely resistant medium of stone and the achievements of the heroic genius of Beethoven as he burst through the material and ideal conceptions of inwardness characteristic of Mozart and Bach, that enjoy paradigmatic status. Bloch attempts to formulate the as yet unconstructed question of the end or goal, latent glimmers of which are already carried within us. Pervasive throughout is a response in terms of the analysis of *Sehnsucht*, a striving towards that which is now lost in the past and the object of nostalgia, or, more paradoxically from the writer's standpoint, of anticipation of the future. This juxtaposition of negative critique and positive re-appropriation is everywhere characteristic of Bloch's method of "refunctioning" the intellectual and cultural inheritance of the West in the light of its forward-orientated possibilities. The final section with the striking title *"Karl Marx, der Tod und die Apokalypse"* ("Karl Marx, Death and the Apocalypse") contains a heightening of the tension between materialist immanence expressed thus: "I must die. But before this I want to eat and drink. For tomorrow morning I am dead",[33] and the future *parousia* of the narrow, the tragi-heroic "hope" that resists ruin. Throughout *Geist der Utopie* religious conceptions are used to break through the limitations of a wholly immanent inwardness, but this is attempted without at any point relapsing back into a simplistic (and impermissible) revival of past theistic answers. Bloch excludes traditional theism but retains the sense of God understood as resistance to foreclosure. It would be a mistake, however, to oversystematize this strange and eccentric text which is written in a style that almost obscures its essential intentions.

The strange qualities of *Geist der Utopie* were grasped by Margarete Susman in a justly famous review[34] in which she discerned both the contemporary importance and the future direction of Bloch's thought. For Susman in the dark, stormy night of war a light glimmered, that of a new German metaphysics. In an age of material welfare, external growth and endless commerce, humanity had drawn back from our "first birthright as children of God".[35] In an age in which doubt about God is the norm this new philosophy presented a single hope: *"In uns allein brennt noch Licht"* (Bloch). It is therefore the recognition of the absolute responsibility of humanity for its own condition which necessarily presents an ultimate encounter with the self as the final dream of the world.[36] With characteristic Germanic dy-

---

[33]*Geist der Utopie, GA* 16, p.393.

[34]"Geist der Utopie", originally in the *Frankfurter Zeitung* on 11.1.1919, reproduced in S. Unseld, *Ernst Bloch zu Ehren*, pp.383-93.

[35]Susman, op.cit., p.384.

[36]*"Selbstbegegnung ist der letzte Traum der Welt"*, Susman, op.cit., p.385.37.

namism this *Selbstbegegnung* is understood an encounter which will only come about through the explosive breaking through of the limitations imposed upon existence, so as to attain the final homecoming of humanity. The creative drive towards apocalypse engaging the whole person is thus seen as no arid, narrowly-defined, theoretical knowledge but an ultimate, emancipatory realisation. Not only is cultural fragmentation thereby overcome but historical relativism likewise falls away into irrelevance. The goal of all knowledge is anchored in a yearning to construct the final identity of mankind itself. The rooting of humanity in *Sehnsucht* and its Messianic representation through the Expressionist mode of discourse, must be understood as a rejection of both classicism and naturalism.[37] In this, Bloch's Nietzschian "joyful night of death" (*bunten Sterbenacht*), music is the last veil over the mystery that attains transparency in the metaphysics of the secret of life itself.[38] Unlike later critics, Susman correctly understood Bloch's critical juxtaposition of ancestral *anamnesis* and the utopian drive; the mutual indispensability of both as realised in their highest form in music is the key to comprehension of the text. Bloch's "system of theoretical Messianism" prefigured in *Geist der Utopie* was built upon what seemed a fundamental paradox, that is the *positive* outworking of the "left-wing" Hegelian critique of theology in terms that would entail "the completion of the designation of God on the basis of our own capacities".[39] This programme, the positive recovery of the divine in the human, rather than the negative (and orthodox Marxist) exclusion of God as illusory projection, is central to Bloch's thought. Margarete Susman crystallised the structure of Bloch's first major work and her analysis supports our contention that the religious assimilation of atheism is a central, and possibly the dominant theme of the oeuvre that culminates in his masterpiece, *The Principle of Hope*.

II. BLOCH AND WEIMAR: THE EXPRESSIONIST ERA AND ITS CRITIQUE (1919-1933)

During his residence in Switzerland Bloch came to know Walter Benjamin and they remained friends until the latter's suicide on the Franco-Spanish border in 1940. Both shared recondite interests in the

[37]Susman defines Expressionism as follows: "*immer form fremder, immer klassischer und unnaturalistischer zugleich, immer mehr nie selbst: unser eigenes fragendes, unruhiges Selbst. Dahin geht der Expressionismus*", op.cit., p.388.

[38]"*Musik ist der letzte, schon durchsichtig werdend Schleier über dem Mysterium*", Susman, op.cit., p.388.

[39]"*Wie alles allein durch uns geschehen muss, wie wir auch das Letzte und Äusserste noch: die Ernennung Gottes aus eigener Kraft vollbringen mussen*", Susman, op.cit., p.391.

mystical and apocalyptic dimensions of the Judaeo-Christian tradition. From an orthodox Marxist standpoint Bloch was then and later seen as a syncretist, the proponent of a "political mysticism". In 1919 he returned to Berlin and participated in the Expressionist movement and began a career as a major political and cultural essayist. Bloch's first substantial publication in the post-War period was the appearance in 1921 of *Thomas Münzer als Theologe der Revolution*.[40] This book was conceived by Bloch as a "coda" to *Geist der Utopie*.[41] In 1923 Bloch published a second, heavily revised edition of the latter in which by the introduction of sub-headings and demystification of the more obscure passages he tried to communicate more directly. In *Thomas Münzer* Bloch relinquished the more uncompromising features of the Expressionist style of the original *Geist der Utopie* and introduced a structured historical narrative as the basis of theoretical development. In this book Bloch propounded a "revolutionary romanticism" that reinforced his view of the need for a *subjective* dialectic within Marxism. Thus the relatively inchoate theoretical insights of 1919 were clarified and tested in 1921 in relation to an historical individual. This proof of initial hypotheses further prepared the ground for the imposing synthesis in the *Principle of Hope* itself.[42]

Thomas Münzer is a remarkable book, more immediately accessible in both style and purpose than *Geist der Utopie*. After a compact account of Münzer's life its substance consists in a striking analysis of the underlying tendencies of Münzer's preaching and theology. The context is established through an adaptation and development of the Weberian analysis of the socio-economic correlates of the various theologies of the Reformers: Bloch attacks Luther's role in the Peasants' War and his "secret Manicheeism" (which later helped to legitimate a political absolutism uncontained by natural law) and then looks more sympathetically at Catholic theology, drawing an interesting and important parallel between St. Thomas and Hegel.[43] Against all *Tyrannophilie*, be it that of Luther, Schleiermacher or indeed that of Karl Barth, Bloch set the proto-Hegelian dialectic of Münzer, that is the way of the "absolute man" and thus of "break-through". The very kernel of Münzer's thought is seen in a "phenomenology of God-preparation" (*Phanomenologie der Gottbereitung*), in which the German speculative mystical tradition is combined with the Reformation redis-

---

[40](Munich: Kurt Wolff, 1921) Referred to as *Thomas Münzer*

[41] See "*Nachbemerkung*" (1969), *TM, GA2*, p.230.

[42]See again "*Nachbemerkung*", ibid, "*Seine revolutionäre Romantik findet Mass und Bestimmung in dem Buch 'Das Prinzip Hoffnung'*".

[43]*TM, GA 2*, p.161. Some commentators have cast Bloch in the role of an atheistic St. Thomas.

covery of the Word and culminates in an ascesis and the experience of absolute abandonment. The latter state Bloch describes in strikingly existential terms as a:

> suspensionem gratiae, where the soul's abyss is finally made perfectly empty, and man, in the quietest and most profound abandonment and detachment, becomes at last aware of God's word.[44]

Münzer is for Bloch the prototypical religious man, who, having repudiated the security of Luther's understanding of faith, prefigures Kierkegaard through the reinstatement of a real "spiritual yearning" (*geistlicher Sehnsucht*).[45] The notion of *Sehnsucht* links the structure of human self-understanding isolated in the examination of Romanticism and its forerunners examined in *Geist der Utopie* with its theological analogate, even, given the hypothesis of progressive secularisation, its antecedent. Bloch's interpretations of Münzer and his "Expressionism of experience" (*Expressionismus des Erlebnisses*)[46] and pneumatological hermeneutics[47] are of first rank importance on their own terms. Bloch expands and illuminates this with reference to the Jewish Cabbalah, Anabaptism, the later Fichte, and, above all, Schelling. A latent "theology of revolution" is understood to arise out of the transformation of faith in God, that is a faith not drawn down onto something represented mythologically in the present but an experience extending towards a future "Kingdom of the freedom of the children of God".[48] Truth is *apocalyptic*, and so at the heart of Münzer's teaching Bloch finds a universal principle constitutive of all revolutions (including, significantly, that of Karl Marx):

> To this world of faith rises the smoke of the pure dawn of the Apocaplypse and precisely in the Apocalypse it gains its final criterion, the metapolitical, indeed metareligious Principle of

---

[44]*TM, GA* 2, p.189.

[45]More fully Bloch puts it thus: *"Hochst paradoxal also exaltiert Münzer, über jeglicher Verwesung in Christo, seine Anspannung geistlicher Sehnsucht, gott-rufender Subjektivität, seine aller-hochste Apologie der Unwissenheit und der Tränen; bis Gott die völlig zerbrockene Kreatur mit der Menschwerdung seines Sohnes auch ganz und gar vergotte."* *TM, GA* 2, p.193.

[46]*TM, GA* 2, p.197. See pp. above and S. Markun, op.cit., p.26.

[47]*TM, GA* 2, pp.198-9.

[48]*TM, GA* 2, p.209. The original German is as follows: *"Der Glaube an Gott ist damit nicht auf einen mythologisch Vorhanden bezogen, sondern auf ein künftiges 'Reich der Freiheit der Kinder Gottes'"*.

all revolution: the beginning of the freedom of the children of God.[49]

The miracle (that is the *Wunder*) of entry into this new world is no individualistic, mystical sinking into subjective identity but the universal realisation within the collectivities of the Old and the New Adam of the mutual "Not-Yet" of the humanity that reverses relations of *Herrschaft* or lordship.[50] The miracle of faith entails stepping across the limits of everyday existence in the notion of *Überschreiten*, a transgression of limits.[51] This quasi-revolutionary sensibility recurs, so Bloch argues, in Lessing's *Erziehung des Menschengeschlechts* (*Education of the Human Race*), which after the manner of Joachim of Fiore, posits a time of fulfilment, an age of brotherly equality.[52] In *The Principle of Hope*, Bloch draws together these fundamental impulses in a text that is to be an "education of the human race" for our own time. Münzer himself recreated an impulse that originates not merely with Joachim of Fiore but which is traceable right back to the Christ of the Fourth Gospel. As a dimension frequently repressed (as in the late Schelling's *Philosophie der Offenbarung*)[53] this nevertheless glints through in the "subterranean history of revolution",[54] which invites the seeker to join the "stormy pilgrimage" and to recognise a universal human homesickness. It is the benign subversion of all history and culture by this suppressed consciousness that permits Bloch to make the following assertions which express the fundamental unity of purpose that unifies and sustains the whole adventure of *The Principle of Hope* and its attempt at a fusion of Marxism and universal culture:

> High above the ruins and fractured spheres of the culture of this world the spirit of unobstructed Utopia shines in, certain of its centre only in the innermost Ophir, Atlantis, Orpid, in the house of the absolute appearance of ourselves. In this way at last Marxism and the dream of the undetermined join forces in

[49]*TM, GA 2*, p.210.
[50]*TM, GA 2*, ibid.
[51]*TM, GA 2*, p.216.
[52]*TM, GA 2*, p.218.
[53]*TM, GA 2*, pp.222 ff. Schelling's lectures given in 1841/42, *Philosophie der Offenbarung* (Frankfurt am Main, 1977) is one of the most important, yet possibly neglected *religious* texts of the nineteenth century. The subsequent reception of these lectures in the intellectual histories of the members of the extraordinary audience who witnessed them and those who later read them deserves fuller investigation. Bakunin, Kierkegaard, Engels, Burckhardt, Savigny, Trendelenburg, Ranke and A. von Humboldt were, for example, present.
[54]*TM, GA 2*, p.228.

an identical campaign; that is as the driving force of the end
which brings to an end the voyage of the whole world around
us, in which man is an oppressed, a despised and lost being; as
reconstruction of the planet earth and call of creation, the
forced entry of the kingdom: Münzer with all the Chiliasts remains the one who summons us to this stormy pilgrimage.[55]

It is this mutual indebtedness and concomitant identity of purpose
that Bloch was later to see as suppressed in the "cold" stream of orthodox Marxism; but this "spirit", latent in the utopian, anticipatory
aspect of the Western (and indeed the wider human) inheritance, informs the unity of his oeuvre. *Geist der Utopie* and its "coda" *Thomas
Münzer als Theologe der Revolution* taken together on the one hand,
and their realization in *Das Prinzip Hoffnung*, on the other, constitutes
an ellipse in relation to which the justifications, explorations, and indeed, the ornamentation characteristic of the whole of Bloch's "open
system" may justifiably be understood. Bloch's continuing use of the Expressionist style should not, however, mislead us; this is not simply the
case of an ever more ambitious repetition of a single unifying theme
that permits the recovery of a tradition through mere eclectic salvage.
Any interpreter of Bloch's Marxism is obliged constantly to ward off
the accusation that Bloch's work is merely dilettantisme writ large; as
Hudson comments: it is possible to "mistake his quotations from Gnostic,
biblical, Romantic and other sources for pastiche".[56] Hudson has difficulty in defending Bloch as a transmitter of culture through
"refunctioning" of the tradition, precisely because in regarding Bloch as
an innovator *within Marxism* as such, he emphasises the weakest and
most problematic aspect of his work. We attempt to demonstrate the
presence of cohesive, purposive thought within *The Principle of Hope*
in which Marxism is rhetorically present but in substantial terms predominantly supportive, even marginal. This in consequence indicates
the dangers of interpreting Bloch as *primarily* a Marxist thinker. It is,
we shall argue, the universality of the anticipatory category that relativises both the impulse towards universal cultural recovery and that
which implies a Marxist realisation. The quest for totality and the
demand for openness are lines of intellectual perspective that thus extend even beyond Bloch's own resolution of them in his "open system".
Thomas Münzer with its combination of communism with chiliasm put

[55]*TM, GA* 2, p.229.
[56]Hudson, op.cit., p.7.

Bloch beyond the pale of the orthodoxy of the Third International and established his distinctive approach in the public domain.[57]

After his return to Berlin in 1919 Bloch associated closely with Lukács and Benjamin, and more distantly, with Adorno. It was with Lukács that there later took place the famous public disagreement on the political nature of art in the "*Expressionismusdebatte*".[58] Bloch's "revolutionary romanticism" and his eventual public defence of the legitimacy of Expressionism over against Lukács' attack upon of it was to put him in a characteristically difficult and ambiguous position. It was in the context of this debate between the defenders of cultural modernism and the ideologues of social realism that Bloch formulated his contrast between "cold", "narrow gauge" Marxism and a "warm", catholic and inclusive counterpart. Bloch's enduring friendship with Walter Benjamin began in 1917 and one of the main themes to emerge from this intellectual partnership was the conception of the "*objektive Hieroglyphe der Sache*",[59] a cultural hermeneutic in which things in the world are understood as both the encipherment of reality and the focus of appearance, objects thus conceal and disclose their secret essence as symbolic figures or "hieroglyphs".

Sylvia Markun suggests that Bloch's preparation of *Thomas Münzer* may have been a "Purgatorium" after the premature death of his first wife, Else, in January 1921. Bloch was deeply affected and retired from the sight of his friends for a year. His remarriage in July 1922 to Linda Oppenheimer, an artist from Frankfurt, was a failure and ended in divorce in 1928. In 1923, *Geist der Utopie* was reissued in the new, heavily revised edition that was better fitted to its role as an introduction to his philosophy. Again in 1923 Bloch published a lengthy review of one of Lukács' most important works, *History and Class Consciousness*,[60] in which he promulgated a fusion of utopian philosophy

---

[57]The main later texts are presented in *Erbschaft dieser Zeit GA* 4.

[58]Translations of the main contributions appear in Ronald Taylor (ed.) *Aesthetics and Politics* (London: NLB, 1977).

[59]See S. Markun, op.cit., p.33 and *Über Ernst Bloch* (Frankfurtam Main: Suhrkamp, 1971), pp.17ff. Contrasting theoretical interpretations of this way of seeing the world as distanced from itself, as a "hieroglyph" alienated from its counterpart, is a major early twentieth century theme owing much to Jewish influence (as mentioned earlier with regard to Lukács) and is likewise present in the work of the more pessimistic T.W. Adorno. See Gillian Rose, *The Melancholy Science An Introduction to the Thought of T.W. Adorno* (London, 1978).

[60]"*Aktualität und Utopie zu Lukács' Geschichte undKlassenbewusstsein*" (1923), in *Philosophische Aufsätze zur objektiven Phantasie, GA* 10, pp.598-620. Bloch recognised in Lukács' work the reinterpretation of Marx's relation to Hegel and with this the reappearance of the subject-object problem central to classical German philosophy within the context of Marxism itself. The problem of the lost object, the *Ding an sich*, and its solution in terms of a reworking of the philosophical tradition from the standpoint of dialectical materialism was in danger of premature resolution by Lukács who lacked a full enough

with Marxism, and also the collection of essays *Durch die Wüste*, which embodied his response to contemporary events. The essayist style pioneered by Lukács equally suited Bloch and the post-War generation which included Benjamin, Siegfried Kracauer, Adorno and others provided a commentary upon and analysis of the deepening crisis of Weimar culture and society which has only recently become more fully accessible to an English readership.

The Marxist-revisionist "lament over reification" with which Bloch was associated was expressed in a mutual style and method in which politics, philosophy and aesthetics were combined in a cultural critique directed against the fragmentation and individual abstraction of human life experienced under late capitalism. Bloch's shared esoteric interests with Walter Benjamin in Messianism, eschatology and the Cabbala tended to set him apart, especially after Lukács' conversion to orthodox Marxism (he joined the Hungarian Communist Party in 1918). The evolving critique embodied in a "hermeneutic of everyday life", a genre in which, following Freud's lead in *The Psychopathology of Everyday Life*, Adorno wrote *Minima Moralia*,[61] Benjamin *One Way Street*,[62] and Bloch *Spuren* (Traces), first published in Berlin in 1930.[63] Each sought to cast light upon a mode of existence that seemed at root perverted. The question of literary strategy became a fundamental political issue. Marxist orthodoxy, increasingly drawn into its own web of "socialist realism", conceived of modernism and above all Expressionism as desperate products of decaying capitalism. Bloch, by contrast, saw in modernism a protest against a humanity constructed out of reified relationships. Adorno's conception of the *Brüche*, the "breaks" in such a reality and Bloch's *Spuren* or "traces" likewise pointed to a distinction between the facade of existence, a seamless presentation of reality constructed through the commodity dialectic, and a "beyond" accessible only through episodic, indirect means. Expressionism afforded such means of emancipation in that its strategy of literary disruption inhibited dogmatism and resisted any premature imposition of spurious rationality upon what was in reality an irrational life-condition.

Bloch does not appear to have been tormented by the Marxist intellectual's sense of an ever threatening dissociation of theory and practice. A dominant factor in his personal survival was his unfailing awareness of an individual destiny or vocation dedicated to the rediscovery, exposition and application of a single, fundamental idea: the

---

appreciation of *"Das metaphysische Gesamtthema der Geschichte"*, discerned, not surprisingly, in *Geist der Utopie*, and identified with Bloch's own utopian principle.

[61] *Minima Moralia – A Marxist View of Everyday Life* (London: NLB, 1974).

[62] (London: NLB, 1979)

[63] *Spuren*, (Berlin: Paul Cassirer, 1930) *GA* I, 1977.

lost utopian dimension. Bloch never decisively committed himself either in politics (he did not join the Communist Party) or in his writings. Despite the insights present in his controversial essays published throughout the period 1921-1932, Bloch carefully refrained from the fuller development of the conceptions which had first been stated in *Geist der Utopie* and *Thomas Münzer*: his was a reserved truth.[64]

IIIA. EXILE AND THE SYSTEMATISATION OF THOUGHT (1933-1949)

Exile brought Bloch the opportunity to complete a series of works, the centrepiece of which is *The Principle of Hope*. In exile in Vienna (1934), Paris (1935) and Prague (1936-8) Bloch continued to apostrophise the "cold" and "Roman" communism of Moscow and the tragic separation of bread and violin, but his paradoxical loyalty to Stalin throughout the Moscow trials rightly brought obloquy upon him.[65] The pursuit of the "objective imagination" (*objektive Phantasie*) remained central to Bloch's life even after Hitler's *Machtergreifung* in 1933.[66] Exile in the United States (1938-49) confirmed Bloch's ideological detestation of capitalism, despite his acceptance of American hospitality. Bloch remained relatively isolated and depended upon his wife, Karola, for financial support.[67] The German exiles, and Bloch was in contact with Berthold Brecht, Hans Eisler, Georg Grosz, Thomas Mann, Paul Tillich and Hermann Broch, had to take up an attitude towards a future Germany and respond to the fate of the German language itself.[68] Bloch, Brecht and Lukács were to return to the communist East after the end of the War. Bloch completed the preparatory work on *Das*

[64]See *Erbschaft dieser Zeit, GA 4*, pp.255-278, which contains short papers in which Bloch had to defend Expressionism against both communist and fascist adversaries.

[65]Markun argues that Bloch's apology for the Moscow trials is a stumbling block. The question of Bloch's conduct stays open and remains problematic.

[66]There are many interesting similarities and significant differences between the intellectual careers of Bloch and Karl Barth. The latter's *Theologische Existenz heute!* (Munich, 1933) indicated a decisive turn to abstract reflection in theology as marked in its own way as Bloch's consistent dedication to "metaphysical Messianism".

[67]The one amusing incident recalled in Markun's somewhat over-respectful short biography is Adorno's humiliation of the destitute Bloch. Horkheimer had not extended to him the support of the exiled Frankfurt School's wisely invested funds, consequently Adorno appealed for support, but *"dabei falschlich behauptete, Bloch habe seinen Lebensunterhalt als Tellerwascher verdienenmussen und sei wegen zu langsamen Arbeitstempo entlassen worden"*, op.cit., p.43. Bloch brought this upon himself: *"Als Tellerwäscher bin ich entlassen, weil ich mit dem Tempo nicht mitkam"*, letter to Adorno of 18.10.42, *Ernst Bloch Briefe 1903-1975*, p.443

[68]George Steiner has relentlessly pursued this theme in the context of contemporary literature. Thomas Mann was the key figure in this debate largely conducted in the United States.

Materialismusproblem seine Geschichte und Substanz (1936-7) *(The Problem of Materialism: its History and Substance)*[69] and then in the United States worked on *Das Prinzip Hoffnung,*[70] *Naturrecht und menschliche Würde (Natural Law and Human Dignity),*[71] and *Subjekt-Objekt-Erläuterungen zu Hegel (Subject Object: Clarification of Hegel).*[72] Apart from parts of *Das Prinzip Hoffnung* these other works were not published in their final form until the 1960's. Bloch's self-imposed delay and a tactical hesitance enabled him to write his greatest works, whether heeded or ignored, for posterity rather than for his contemporaries. Bloch's masterpiece is supported by this cluster of related texts which function as the outlying defences of a work that taken entirely on its own might be misunderstood merely as an exercise in strident mythopoesis.

Bloch's *Materialismusproblem,* written in 1936-7, is an immense survey expounding and defending the conviction of his early youth that reality is to be understood in consistent materialist terms and it includes in the revised and expanded text eventually published in 1977 a fascinating study of "Left-wing Aristotelianism" and the philosopher Avicenna. Bloch's dialectical materialism can be understood as an attempt to widen and enhance Engels' "dialectics of nature", thus bringing this conception into a fuller historical perspective.[73] The most imaginative flowering of Bloch's renewal of the "dialectics of nature" is to be found in *Das Prinzip Hoffnung* where the dynamic latency of *Noch-Nicht Sein* is expanded into an alternative social and cultural hermeneutic applied to the full history of social and cultural development.

In *Naturrecht und Menschliche Würde,* Bloch again reviewed the totality of the tradition in an attempt to overcome the Marxian[74] and Marxist repudiation of "human rights" as a class-interested, bourgeois concoction to be swept away with the extinction of that class. Here Bloch located an intellectual task of great and continuing importance within both socialism and capitalism. In *Subjekt-Objekt* Bloch attempted to come to a comprehensive reckoning with Hegel through the recognition that the latter's recapitulative synthesis of the whole tra-

---

[69]*GA,* 7.
[70]*GA.* 5.
[71]*GA,* 6.
[72]*GA,* 8.

[73]The real origin of this discussion is to be found in Marx's doctoral thesis of 1838-41 *Differenz der demokratischen und epikureischen Naturphilosophie, MEGA* I/2, which is directed at the question as to how consciousness can arise out of matter understood exclusively in terms of atomism.

[74]"Marxian" refers to the views of Marx himself, "Marxist" to those of Marxism.

dition provided, both in its strength and weaknesses (and above all in its conception of *anamnesis*), the dominant temporal dialectic that had to be "refunctioned". Bloch is the sole twentieth-century Marxist thinker to have worked on such an all-comprehensive and integrated scale. His project involved a re-conception and expansion of Marxist categories through the Aristotelian notion of the latent energy of matter and its *subjective* dialectical expression in the interpretation and transformation of the total temporal and historical process. This synthesis has yet fully to be understood and assimilated in the Anglo-Saxon world.

IV. PROFESSOR OF PHILOSOPHY AND
STATE IDEOLOGUE (1948-1961)

In 1948 Bloch returned to the Russian Zone and to what was to become the German Democratic Republic (DDR) fully prepared to participate in the realisation in terms of concrete social praxis of the utopian vision that only Marxism had, so he claimed, the power to enact. Unlike Russia, in which philistinism had triumphed, Bloch hoped that the divorce of "bread" and "violin" in the implementation of communist socialism would be avoided in the exemplary society of the new Germany and its re-appropriated ancestral culture. Here again the parallel has to be drawn between Bloch and Lukács (who also chose to return to his homeland, Hungary, from Moscow, rather than from the United States). Both attempted to reforge elements of the Marxist inheritance within the context of a social system that, under the guise of the Party's interpretation and realisation of the dictatorship of the proletariat extended the control of the state over all aspects of life. Bloch's attempt to generate a German philosophical renaissance and his veiled critical attitudes towards Stalinist orthodoxy ensured both his prominence in the DDR and his eventual downfall. Bloch's role as an intellectual apologist for the regime was never unambiguous and although his wife joined the Party, he did not. In 1949 there appeared in East Berlin the first edition of *Subjekt-Objekt, Erläuterungen zu Hegel*, in 1952 *Avicenna und die Aristotelische Linke (Avicenna and Left-wing Aristotelianism)*, and in 1953 *Christian Thomasius, Ein deutscher Gelehrte ohne Misere (Christian Thomasius, a Merciless Learned German)*. All are, in effect, not only historical studies but also coded, indirect criticisms of a dogmatic Marxism distorted by the ruthless imposition of the official Stalinist interpretation of Lenin's lamentable *Materialism and Empiro-criticism*. Thus in *Subjekt-Objekt* Bloch challenged the Stalinist dismissal of Hegel as a "reactionary idealist"; in *Avicenna* he proposed a new, extended Marxist concept of matter; and in *Christian Thomasius* he confronted the Marxist tradition with the issue of natural law. The creative dimension of these efforts is parallel in some ways to Lukács' *Ontology of Social Being*; both purport to convey what ought to be the form of a truly socialist social order. Bloch with his (later imprisoned) associate Wolfgang Harich edited the *Deutsche Zeitschrift für Philosophie* which was the sole organ of philosophical independence operating within the constraints of Stalinist cultural hegemony.

This period of Bloch's life, in which he did his utmost to project a positive public image of communist socialism, was crowned by the publication in 1954-5 of the first two volumes of *Das Prinzip Hoffnung*. In 1955 Bloch received the National Prize of the German Democratic Republic and became a member of the Academy of Sciences. This was the apogee of his academic career in the communist East, but the forces of opposition were gathering, posed for an onslaught which was to culminate in renewed exile. Whilst the first two volumes of *Das Prinzip Hoffnung* had earned their author heavy criticism, it was Bloch's provocative lecture, *"Differenzierung im Begriff Fortschritt"* ("Differiations in the Concept of Progress") published in 1955,[75] which touched upon sensitive philosophical issues such as relation of freedom and determinism, that presaged a more direct conflict with the authorities. Attacks upon *Deutsche Zeitschift für Philosophie* were challenged by Bloch and his courageous allies. At this time Bloch called for and on occasion participated in Christian-Marxist dialogue where he argued for the admission of a fuller intellectual input into the process out of which the theory and practice of a genuine Marxism might emerge. The crisis finally broke in the events surrounding the 20th Congress of the Communist Party of the Soviet Union in 1956.

On the academic level it was Rugard Otto Gropp, a problematic colleague and later Bloch's enemy and the erstwhile protector of dialectical materialist "pure doctrine", who in 1954 launched a general attack on the separation of theory and practice implied by the revisionist re-Hegelianisation of Marxist philosophy.[76] Ironically, in 1955 Gropp had edited Bloch's 70th birthday Festschrift, a collection remarkable for the almost total absence of substantial comment on the latter's work, apart from an isolated Swiss contribution.[77] It is evident that the inner discipline involved in living under any totalitarian regime was at work: no-one dared to be committed on paper to an indi-

[75](East Berlin, 1957).

[76]"*Die marxistische dialektische Methode und ihr Gegensatz zur idealistischen Dialektik Hegels*", *Deutsche Zeitschrift fur Philosophie*, 1954, vol. 2/1, pp.69-112.

[77]Otto Morf's "*Ernst Bloch und die Utopie*" stands out in the collection, R.O. Gropp (ed), *Ernst Bloch* (East Berlin, 1955).

vidual or to a position that might and indeed did lose favour. In March 1956 Bloch addressed the philosophy section of the Academy of Sciences upon the extremely sensitive subject of *"Das Problem der Freiheit im Lichte des wissenschaftlichen Sozialismus"* ("The Problem of Freedom in the Light of Scientific Socialism")[78] in which he advanced the view that freedom was not only a social category (*eine gesellschaftliche Kategorie*) but also, at a more profound and fundamental level, an anthropological reality pertaining to the very essence of human nature. It is perhaps Bloch's courageous willingness to move beyond the limitations of "narrow gauge" Marxism within the actual setting of a totalitarian regime that affords grounds for the defence of his character against those who condemn him out of hand for his support of the Moscow trials before the war. Bloch's fall from official approval (or rather a state of studied toleration) was sudden. On the 14th November 1956, the occasion of the 125th anniversary of Hegel's death, Bloch delivered a provocative oration, published much later under the title *"Hegel und die Gewalt des Systems"* ("Hegel and the Power of the System"),[79]. In this address he drew an unambiguous contrast between the immense, all-comprehensive achievement of Hegel and the centralised and compartmentalised control of official German communist "philosophy": unless dialectical materialism re-admitted Hegel's system in modified form then it in effect forfeited its claim to be philosophy in the true sense.

Shortly afterwards Bloch's assistant Wolfgang Harich was sentenced to ten years imprisonment and Bloch himself was retired in the beginning of 1957 and summarily relieved of his editorship of *Deutsche Zeitschift für Philosophie*. The unfortunate Harich was the object of Walter Ulbricht's public denunciation and this was followed by a process of repressive philosophical "normalisation". R.O. Gropp masterminded as unnamed editor a collective attack upon Bloch's *"Revision des Marximus"*[80] which was described as an "anti-Marxist doctrine of world-salvation".[81] Meanwhile, Bloch's arrest was ordered but then rescinded on political grounds; he was then banned from publication and philosophical association. This did not prevent Bloch's rapprochement

[78]Full title: *"Das Problem der Freiheit im Lichte des wissenschaftlichen Sozialismus. Protokoll der Konferenz der Sektion Philosophie der Deutschen Akademie der Wissenschaften zu Berlin 8.-10 Marz 1956"*. This was subject to limited circulation and suppressed following Bloch's disgrace. Parts are cited in *Philosophische Aufsätze* under the title *"Freiheit, ihre Schichtung und ihr Verhältnis zur Wahrheit"* GA 10, pp.573-595.

[79]Reproduced in *Philosophische Aufsätze*, GA 10, pp.481-500.

[80]*Ernst Blochs Revision des Marxismus Kritische Auseinandersetzungen marxistischen Wissenschaften mit der Blochschen Philosophie* (East Berlin, 1957).

[81]See *"Ernst Blochs Hoffnungsphilosophie - eine anti-marxistische Welterlösungslehre"*, op.cit., pp. 9-49.

with Adorno at a Hegel conference in Frankfurt am Main in 1958, but such incidents were rare during a period of enforced isolation. Finally in 1961 whilst on a visit to Bayreuth, Bloch decided to apply for political asylum after hearing of the construction of the Berlin Wall. In response to a call to become a guest-professor in Tübingen, an invitation issued after considerable pressure exerted by friends on his behalf, Bloch's opening lecture, *"Kann Hoffnung enttauscht werden?"* ("Can hope be disappointed?"), could not have been more pertinant, both then and now.

V. MAGUS OF TÜBINGEN (1961-1977)

The final period of Bloch's life is the most remarkable testimony to the prodigious energy of an elderly man who nevertheless produced a series of powerful new books and re-issued in revised form many of his earlier works. Thus it was in rapid succession that *Naturrecht und menschliche Würde* (1961), *Philosophische Grundfragen. Zur Ontologie des Noch-Nicht-Sein* (*Basic Questions of Philosophy. On the Ontology of Not-Yet-Being*) (1961); *Verfremdungen I* (*Estrangements*) (1962); *Tübingen Einleitung in die Philosophie* (*Tübingen Introduction to Philosophy*) (I, 1963; II, 1964); *Verfremdungen II* (1964); *Literarische Aufsatze* (*Literary Essays*) (1965); *Atheismus in Christentum* (*Atheism in Christianity*) (1968); *Philosophische Aufsatze zur objektiven Phantasie* (*Philosophical Essays on Objective Fantasy*) (1969), *Politische Messungen, Pestzeit, Vormärz* (*Political Evaluation, Plague Time, Eve of Revolution*) (1970); *Das Materialismusproblem* (1972); *Experimentum Mundi* (1975); and *Leipziger Vorlesungen zur Geschichte der Philosophie* (*Leipzig Lectures on the History of Philosophy*) (1977)[82] brought to a conclusion an astonishingly rich and prolific literary production which is, as yet, scarcely absorbed within Germany, never mind more widely in the English-speaking world. Bloch's participation in Christian-Marxist dialogue and the exploitation of his thought by theologians both Protestant and Catholic, his support of the "Prague Spring" and his condemnation of the American involvement in Vietnam, together with exceptional literary productivity kept Bloch near the centre of West German cultural consciousness until his death on 4th August 1977.

Bloch's work would appear to represent a serious, long-standing commitment to the formulation of an improved form of Marxism, a "revision", even a "reform", intended to make it capable of responding positively to the cultural tradition out of which it had originally

[82]For details of publication see *Select Bibliography* pp.233ff below.

grown, and which, in the name of "dialectical" and "historical materialism" and "socialist realism", it constantly, but misguidedly, condemned as the perverse product of a degenerate bourgeois order. It is, however, the neglected but in our view fundamental religious dimension of Bloch's attempt to effect a rebirth of the totality of a tradition in transmogrified form that informs our brief study of *The Principle of Hope*. Bloch's success or failure as a Marxist theoretician, and the particularities of his status within Marxism as a consistent and hardline *Ketzer* (heretic) have been extensively handled elsewhere. Indeed Hudson in his study of Bloch's revisionism tends to minimise what we conceive to be one of the greatest tensions in an oeuvre which on the one hand recapitulates in heroic terms a Promethean cultural inheritance and, on the other, demands its democratic and socialist, realisation. It is Bloch's drive towards human universality and the humanistic ingestion of the religious impulse which dominates *The Principle of Hope*. Nevertheless we agree with Hudson that Bloch was indeed:

> a world figure, whose passing included not only the end of a great world of German Jewish hope, but a break with a range and intensity of knowledge which may not be achieved again in our century.[83]

It is this sense of ending, of historical and cultural hiatus identified with Bloch's life and work that compels our attention. His philosophy belongs to that genre of literature that ventures a dialectical and systematic recovery of a past totality. Its contemporary analogates are Proust's *'A la recherche du temps perdu* and the great *Church Dogmatics* of the Swiss German theologian Karl Barth. All three such narratives are directed towards the past in terms of recovery and reiteration. All three conjure with time, the category that persists in the aftermath of ontological metaphysics. All three operate in the era of the dark "afterlife" of religion (George Steiner) and renovate visions intrinsic to our culture. At the heart of Bloch's work there is a wholehearted commitment to the fullest recovery of the human *without* a flight from reality; the core of this recapitulation lies in *The Principle of Hope* to which we now turn our attention.

[83]Hudson, op.cit., p.19.

CHAPTER II

THE PROLEGOMENA TO HOPE: THINKING MEANS VENTURING BEYOND

The writings of Ernst Bloch provoke contrasting and equally extreme reactions of hostility and enthusiasm amongst both those who
precipitately pronounce upon their quality as well as on the part of the
small minority who take the trouble to read his texts with care.
Bloch's exaggerated rhetoric and his strident, oratorical style tend to
alienate those who value above all a restrained appreciation of evidence and linear argument. In *The Principle of Hope* Bloch exploits a
literary mode that threatens to overwhelm and seduce the unwary
reader through the repetitive accumulation of words organised around
a single, even if internally complex motif: the so-called "discovery" of
Not-Yet-Being (*Noch Nicht Sein*). *The Principle of Hope* is not a work
of philosophy in the "contemplative" mode but:

> a particularly extensive attempt is made in *this book* to bring
> philosophy to hope, as to a place in the world which is as in-
> habited as the best civilised land (*Kulturland*) and as unex-
> plored as the Antarctic. (*P.H.I,6*)

We are, as it were, already in unconscious possession of a territory
that awaits discovery. "Hope" is posited in the context of confusion and
anxiety: the questions "Who are we? Where do we come from? Where
are we going? What are we waiting for? What awaits us? (*PHI,3*) go
largely unanswered. This state of anxiety may give way to fear; the
fear that has been learned through the events of the century. By contrast, the learning of hope is an act that challenges renunciation and
passivity. What Bloch calls the "emotion of hope" (*Affekt des
Hoffens*)[1] precipitates activity that opens, broadens and frees; we are
to throw ourselves into what is becoming (*ins Werdende*) and not merely
be passively thrown in "What Is" (*ins Seiende*).[2] Bloch's insistence

---

[1]"Emotion" is a weak rendering of the word "*Affekt*" which here implies a causal role
in response to disturbance rather than a mere state of mind, that is a solipsistic
modulation of inwardness.

[2]Readers of Bloch have to brace themselves for a style which, like that of Heidegger
and many other German writers who express themselves with a supreme confidence in the

upon an active rather than a passive existence, an existence characterised by the verb "thrown" (*Werfen* and its cognates) can be understood as a pointed repudiation of the great German alternative to
Bloch's philosophy of human existence in the early Heidegger of *Sein
und Zeit*. The caged-in "dog's life" (*Hundeleben*) of passivity, anxiety
(*Angst*) and fear (*Furcht*) is not, Bloch hints, a natural state; it has its
creators (*Urheber*) and these are challenged through hope.[3] Hope as an
active protest against nameless anxiety and its formulation in fear is a
feasible enterprise: "this work ... looks in the world itself for what can
help the world; this can be found" (*PHI*,3). Bloch's starting-point is
therefore immanent, and intrinsic to human nature; hope is located in
the pervasive and persistent occurrence of "daydreams" (*Tagtraümen*).
The anthropological starting-point, the conjunction of "hope" as
"feeling" (*Affekt*) with the "daydream" might well seem weak to a casual reader. Clearly Bloch will in the course of his exposition have to
drive towards the progressive universalisation of a category that is as
yet inchoate and confined within his account of human subjectivity.[4]
Whatever the apparent vulnerability of a starting-point grounded in
the manifestation of "hope" through the "daydream", Bloch immediately recognises the ambiguity of the latter. The dreams may in part be
"enervating escapism" (*entnervende Flucht*) open to manipulative exploitation or they may more interestingly be provocative and resistant
to the attitude of "renunciation" (*Entsagung*).[5] It is the latter
"daydream" that Bloch wants to locate, clarify, train and develop;
thus, he argues, a "ripening" may take place as these dreams experience into mediation[6] through the course of the events themselves. So we
can already see that Bloch's version of the "dialectic" of human life is

power of language to act as the epiphany and bearer of "Being" and its future-orientated
counterpoise, "Becoming". German philosophers and theologians in the idealist and Romantic tradition from Hamann, Herder and Hegel through to the interwar period in this
century exemplify this tendency.

[3]As will become increasingly apparent it is Bloch's heroic optimism that gains him
many enemies amongst those who sanction pessimism or nihilism as the only possible alternatives.

[4]Bloch's reconstruction of a wide-ranging ontology on the basis of the extrapolation of a
single transcendental principle somehow escaping the strictures of the Kantian critique or
its later counterparts is not, of course, unique. Thus in this setting Friedrich Schleiermacher's theological anthropology grounded in the *schlechthinniges Abhängigkeitsge-
fuhl* is likewise to be understood as the recreation of a lost completeness upon new, but
limited ground.

[5]Here Bloch takes up Nietzsche's protest against the repristination of secularised
sacrificial motifs in, for example, the later Wagner and his aesthetic representation of
cultic renunciation and ecstatic despair.

[6]The notion of "mediation" (*Vermittlung*) again indicates how Bloch is to appropriate
and re-use with rehabilitated meaning concepts drawn from the ancestral German tradition, in particular as embodied in Hegelian thought.

not confined to given static categories but organised around the juxta-posed realities of the "participating" reason which encounters "the New" (*das Neue*) as opposed to the merely "contemplating" reason of the impotent subject.[7]

I. DENKEN HEISST ÜBERSCHREITEN: VENTURING BEYOND

This phrase, which we render "Thinking means venturing beyond" (*PHI*, p.4)[8], is a key interpretative term, almost a slogan, that demands precise characterisation if it is not to mislead. A number of possible alternatives have to be excluded if Bloch's text is not to be taken as mere expressivist posturing in the face of nihilism. Unless a reasonably secure starting-point is secured in the prolegomena contained in the brief, but highly compressed and complex *Introduction* to *The Principle of Hope* then the whole structure that is to follow comes into question. Bloch is striving to unify, albeit dialectically, a series of factors which might on first sight appear incompatible. In order to expose and clarify the submerged dimensions of this intellectual iceberg we shall cite an extended passage at length and then comment. The following analysis is intended to be exemplary and will not be repeated, but it does indicate the kind of reception required by a writer who employs a variety of literary techniques that render his argument largely opaque to a reader unacquainted with both the visible, as well as the less ob-vious premises. Such an exposition will help us lay hold of the hermeneutic necessary to an adequate comprehension of Bloch's work as a whole.

> Thinking means venturing beyond. But in such a way that what already exists is not kept under or skated over. Not in its depri-vation, let alone in moving out of it. Not in the causes of depri-vation, let alone in the first signs of the change which is ripen-ing within it. That is why real venturing beyond never goes into the mere vacuum of an In-Front-of-Us, merely fanatically,

---

[7]Here is a first indication of how the "dialectic" undergoes re-orientation as the subject engaged in an active mode with regard to the future is thereby freed from the merely contemplative epistemological stance against which Marx polemicised in the *Theses on Feuerbach* of 1845, a text quite central to Bloch's highly qualified appropriation of Marx. See Ch. 6 below. Bloch contrasts the *bloss betrachtenden* with the *beteiligten Verstands*, that is "purely contemplative" as opposed to "participatory (i.e. engaged) reason". This interpretation of Marx's *Theses* has also been immensely influential in liberation theol-ogy.

[8]"Uberschreiten" is once more a powerful and theory-laden word in Bloch's intellec-tual world, it combines the senses of an active stepping across boundaries and transgres-sions of the expected, the mundane; it is part of Bloch's consistent protest against the un-questioning acceptance of mundane mediocrity as the norm.

merely visualizing abstractions. Instead, it grasps the New as something that is mediated in what exists and is in motion, although to be revealed the New demands the most extreme effort of will. Real venturing beyond knows and activates the tendency which is inherent in history and which proceeds dialectically. Primarily everybody lives in the future, because they strive, past things only come later, and as yet genuine present is almost never there at all. The future dimension contains what is feared or what is hoped for; as regards human intention, that is, when it is not thwarted, it contains only what is hoped for. Function and content of hope are experienced continuously, and in times of rising societies they have been continuously activated and extended. Only in times of a declining old society, like modern Western society, does a certain partial and transitory intention run exclusively downwards. Then those who cannot find their way out of the decline are confronted with fear of hope and against it. Then fear presents itself as the subjectivist, nihilism as the objectivist mask of the crisis phenomenon: which is tolerated but not seen through, which is lamented but not changed. On bourgeois ground, especially in the abyss which has opened and into which the bourgeoisie has moved, change is impossible anyway even it if were desired, which is by no means the case. In fact, bourgeois interest would like to draw every other interest opposed to it into its own failure; so, in order to drain the new life, it makes its own agony apparently fundamental, apparently ontological. The futility of bourgeois existence is extended to be that of the human situation in general, or existence per se. Without success in the long run, of course: the bourgeois emptiness that has developed is as ephemeral as the class which alone still expresses itself within it, and as spineless as the illusory existence of its own bad immediacy with which it is in league. Hopelessness is itself, in a temporal and factual sense, the most insupportable thing, downright intolerable to human needs. (*PHI*, 4-5)

What is the meaning and the real implication of this passage? We have seen how Bloch defines thinking not merely in instrumental or contemplative terms but as an active confrontation in hope with the pregnant future; thus: "*Denken heisst Überschreiten*", thinking is a venturing beyond. Recourse to venturesome thought must not imply a suppression or elision of consideration of what actually exists (*Vorhandenes*) in so far as this is characterised by need and distress or seen in terms of the signs of change within it. The "real venturing" (*wirklichen Überschreiten*) is no leap into empty space energised by a fanatical (*schwärmend*) resolve arbitrarily informed by abstract visualisations. In other words, the "real venturing" does not involve an alienation of the self into an abstract (i.e. transcendent) realm divorced from how things are; it is, furthermore, no leap into utopian fantasy conceived as an alternative to the exigencies of the given. On the contrary, and here Bloch exposes the nerve-ending of his motivation, the grasping of the New (*das Neue*) is not a step into nothing, that which has not yet happened and an empty "In-Front-of-Us" (*Vor-uns*), but engagement with a reality that is "mediated" in "what exists and is in motion" (*das Neue als eines, das im bewegt Vorhandenen vermittelt ist*). Bloch's juxtaposition of the German terms for that which exists (*Vorhandenen*) and that which is in motion (*bewegt*) puts his argument directly into that strand of the metaphysical tradition that has, since Aristotle, construed existence in terms of movement.[9] Thus in grasping the New as mediated in what exists and in motion Bloch is emphasising that active hope engages with a reality-to-be that actualises itself within immanence, that is within all-comprehending contingency. In the face of this form of manifestation *within*, rather than *apart* from contingency (as would be the case for the normal, untransformed, non-*umfunktionierte* appearance of the utopian dream) a massive effort of discernment is called for: the laying-open, the enactment of exposure (*um freigelegt zu werden*) "demands the most extreme effort of will".[10] So it is that Bloch appears to unfold the possibility of venturesome thought without recourse to "grace", albeit in any residual secularised form.[11]

As in Heidegger's *Being and Time*, here Bloch's subject is on its own within contingency and there thus is no softening of the rigorous demand for a form of "authentic existence", to use a term implied, but not actually employed. Unlike Heidegger, however, Bloch then steps from his first relatively informal outline of the phenomenology[12] that is to un-

---

[9]Bloch's treatment of being in terms of "movement" has (in terms of its post-Hegelian systematisation) affinities with Kierkegaard's critique of Hegel and locates the unreality of Hegel's "system" in the detemporalisation of movement.

[10]It is this restless assertiveness that gives the work of Bloch its capacity to outrage readers who remain in the postures of contemplative, unengaged thought against which the future-orientated demand is directed.

[11]Despite the explicit denial of grace there is a powerful sense of intellectual ascesis as extraneous diversions are pared away in order to establish the authority of the future over minds enslaved by the past or overwhelmed by the present.

[12]Bloch's work is "phenomenological" in two related senses: first, it owes an obvious debt to Hegel's *Phenomenology of Mind* (and what is seen as its counterpart in Goethe's *Faust*), see Chs. 8 and 9 below; second, in terms of the history of the early twentieth century German philosophy emerging from Neo-Kantianism, Bloch's account of forward-ori-

dergo reiteration and development throughout *The Principle of Hope* to a consideration of its context, that is to a view of history conceived as dialectical process. The "real venturing" is not conducted over against an ontological void but activates the latent dialectic. Reflecting critically upon an understanding of time current in Western thought since St. Augustine,[13] Bloch argues against the tradition that has focussed upon the *past* in recollection (that is in *anamnesis* understood as the bedrock for the construction of human identity) by stressing the *future* as the locus of human intentionality. Bloch admittedly grants, with Augustine and the tradition, the fleeting ungraspability of the present but his focus upon the future is radical and original: he disturbs the standard, accepted, even, it might be said, the enforced view of reality as bounded by the past in tradition and subverted by the transient moment that is never present but past. The orientation towards the future that is truly constitutive of the human is the directedness towards a dimension that is double-edged: the future contains what we both fear and hope for. But, and this is a crucial qualification, for human intention (*Intention*) when unfrustrated (*ohne Vereitlung*) the future contains only what is hoped for.

Bloch's argument has, so far, run within the confines of a phenomenological analysis of subjectivity and it is directed against and in certain ways outside the temporal analyses of Augustine and Heidegger. Bloch as a Marxist steps beyond the limits of the latter tradition in recognising a causal connection between the social and historical context and the perception of the future and its possibilities. As a society rises so the interplay between the intensionality of hope as "function" and its meditation through historical events, its "content" are a continuous and expanding experience. When an old society declines so the dark side of intention manifests itself: those trapped in the decline experience fear in the face of, and against, hope. The resultant frame of mind, and here Bloch directs his observations against modern Western society, is one of subjective fear and objective nihilism.[14] These conditions are tolerated even though bewailed but are ultimately unaltered in a crisis that has, as it were, its own form of interlocking social logic. This re-presentation of the catastrophic self-enclosedness of Western society and its culture is not merely a formal denunciation congruent with the

entated inwardness is a mythologised variant of the self-consciously "scientific" phenomenology of Husserl.

[13] Bloch's engagement with the theological tradition is remarkable feature of his work, see ch. 9 below.

[14] It is well to bear in mind that Bloch's direct experience of nihilism in the period of post First World War Weimar culture was of radical extremity, as becomes apparent when the early works of Bloch, Lukács, Adorno and the theologian Karl Barth are seen together in their contemporary context.

ideology of the regime Bloch tried to serve when he published the first volume of *The Principle of Hope*. In fact, his position owes as much to Oswald Spengler[15] as it does to Marx and it was rooted in a continuing awareness of the crisis of Weimar culture seen most clearly in the struggle with nihilism, which we believe remained a life-long factor in Bloch's thought.

Where, however, Bloch clearly does show his Marxist colours is in the subsequent step in the argument: the quintessential representation of this condition of "no-hope" is to be found in a single class, the bourgeoisie. The latter, functioning in classic Marxian terms, universalise and project their own failure into a reified ontology; their agony (*Agonie*) is but "apparently fundamental" (*scheinbar grundsätzlich*) and "apparently ontological" (*scheinbar ontologisch*).[16] Not only do the bourgeoisie assume here a role of historic criminality but they assert themselves through an ideological hegemony that carries with it the implication of an unreal, falsely objective truth.[17] It is not, however, without a complex irony that Bloch's own project might well be conceived as precisely such an attempt to generate and project a comprehensive interpretation of the nature of reality. The imprisoned existence of the bourgeoisie is, despite its pretensions to universality, ephemeral inasmuch as it will, as a class, pass away into history and as without real substance as it colludes with its own "bad immediacy" (*schlechten Unmittelbarkeit*),[18] that is with its own ideological construct that falsely purports to represent the human condition as such.

---

[15]The image of Bloch as the crude reversal of Spengler is a misleading denigration. One of Bloch's strengths is his capacity to grapple with different genres as tokens that through their content and style manifest the social reality of the context of their production and cultural consumption. In this he is similar to the other Marxist revisionists of the Frankfurt School from whom Bloch was later in personal terms at some distance. Oswald Spengler's *Der Untergang des Abendlandes Umrisse einer Morphologie der Weltgeschichte* (Munich: C.H. Beck, 1918/23) and subsequent reinforcing texts crystallised the socio-cultural ethos of an era, and this is a fact to be recognised, as Bloch does, regardless of the intrinsic merits of this much criticised representation of cyclic *Weltanschauungen*. The close relation of Bloch to Spengler is implied in the light of Armin Baltzer's presentation of the latter in *"Weltangst und Weltsehnsucht"* in *Philosoph oder Prophet? Oswald Spengler Vermächtnis und Voraussagen* (Neheim-Husten, 1962), pp.100-113.

[16]Bloch's repeated attacks upon the "agony" of bourgeois existence is one of the less attractive features of the Marxist revisionist tradition whose practitioners were almost invariably eduated in the classic bourgeois mould and whose skill as critics of culture would be inconceivable without their incomparable intellectual formation or *Bildung*.Bloch was an aristocrat of the intellect with a loathing for intellectual mediocrity but he also had an uninhibited readiness to identify with certain aspects of "low life" and its attendant genres.

[17]For an analogous critique by Antonio Gramsci, see Q. Hoare, G.N. Smith (trs.) *Selections from the Prison Notebooks* (London: Lawrence and Wishart, 1971) esp. pp. 323-377.

[18]This is a humorous play upon Hegel's concept of a "bad infinity", that is of infinity as boundless and uncontainable within an interpretative structure, see C. Taylor, *Hegel*. (Cambridge, 1975), pp. 114ff. and pp.240-244.

There is in the final assertion of this passage something of a sublime inferential pragmatism: hopelessness is incompatible with human needs; therefore it must needs be banished.[19]

II. The Discovery of the Front

We attempted in an extended commentary on a section of the opening argument of *The Principle of Hope* to show how it contains a wide-ranging synthesis of ideas not traceable to any single source. Less formal in stylistic and philosophical terms is Bloch's subsequent expansion of the theme that, given that bourgeois existence expressed in philosophised terms represents a systematically self-enclosed hopelessness, then what of *its* attempts at hope? Here Bloch lets all restraints fall away as he polemicises against the preachers from the pulpit who work with "flatteringly and corruptly aroused hope" directed at "mere inwardness" (*blosse Inwendigkeit*)[20] or the "empty promises of the other world" (*Vertröstung aufs Jenseits*), (*PHI,5*). In mocking Brechtian tones Bloch describes the sign outside the "No Future night club" that lures humanity into a wholly nihilistic destiny: there must against this somehow be found a middle way between illusion and nihilism. Drawing upon the cruder aspects of the polemical style of Marx (and more pointedly, Lenin), the latest Western philosophies trade upon a continued exploitation of the idea of transcendence (*Übersteigens*); they live, as it were, upon borrowed capital. Clearly Bloch is going to have to justify his appeal to the "daydream" with some care if his own claims are to survive in contradistinction to the "fraudulent hope" of the purveyors of transcendence. Out of the texture of suggestive polemic the following aphoristic conclusion emerges:

> Thus, knowing-concrete hope subjectively breaks most powerfully into fear, objectively leads most efficiently towards the radical termination of the contents of fear. Together with informed discontent which belongs to fear, because they both arise out of the No to deprivation (*Mangel*). (*PHI,5*)

[19]Jurgen Moltmann's passionate denunciation of bourgeois immanence in the opening passages of *The Theology of Hope* (London: SCM, 1967) reflects Bloch's polemic: "That we do not reconcile ourselves, that there is no pleasant harmony between us and reality, is due to our unquenchable hope", p.22. See also chs. 8 and 9 below.

[20]Bloch's use of the word *Inwendigkeit* is significant, it implies a specifically biblical resonance. See, for example "Jakob Böhme"in *Zwischenwelten in der Philosophiegeschichte, GA* 12, pp.227-241.

This summary statement points to three dominant themes: first, the Hegelian notion of dialectic as the attainment of truth through "trial by death" (*Bewahrung durch den Tod*) is present in a form reminiscent of the *Phenomenology of Mind*; and, second, there is a profound recognition of the role and conquest of fear in human self-development which owes much to Freud. But, third, Bloch relates "fear" to need, that is to a Marxist conception of scarcity rather than to the genetic explanation in Freudian sexual terms. It is, above all to Marx that Bloch attributes the "turning-point in the process of concrete venturing becoming conscious" (*PHI*,5). The reasons for the repression of the discovery of hope as venturesome thought are cryptic: "Lazy substitution, current copying representation, the pig's bladder of a reactionary, but also schematizing Zeitgeist" (*PHI*,5). Bloch does not attribute the suppression of hope to a class-based conspiracy but more to a pervasive sloth; indeed, if he did not, he would not be in a position to confront the problem in the terms of the universal pattern of enlightenment he has chosen to assert and develop. Bloch's references to class determination and the centrality of the proletariat as opposed to the evils of the bourgeoisie are pointed, even strident, but in reality they are peripheral to the main argument which is concerned with the universals of human existence itself. In this, Hegel certainly triumphs over Marx in Bloch's appropriation of the tradition. Despite the bald assertion of Marx's indispensable discovery (something which Bloch does not spell out in unambiguous textual terms) "deeply ingrained habits of thinking cling to a world without Front" (*PHI*,5). In a not wholly convincing way Bloch attributes to Marx a categorial discovery which has otherwise remained atrophied and stultified:

> Not only man is in a bad way here, but so is the insight into his hope. Intending is not heard in its characteristic anticipating tone, objective tendency is not recognised in its characteristic anticipatory powerfulness. The desiderium, the only honest attribute of all men, is unexplored. (*PHI*,5)

It is vital to any well-founded interpretation of Bloch that we understand fully his conception of the latency of the realm to be explored. Beyond all else it is the Marxian discovery which allegedly renders concrete the mostly-hidden latencies encoded in the history of the utopian dream that becomes conscious in the "No to deprivation"; that is, as a *negation of*, rather than *acquiescence in* the face of given reality, which in this instance is conceived under the conditions of late capitalism. "Informed protest" rather than resignation (however sophisticated in its form of philosophical expression) is the correct posture,

first finalised by Marx in the *Theses on Feuerbach* of 1845, that has to
be nurtured. The *Theses* are the determinative point of contact between
Bloch and Marx, a *locus classicus* which for Bloch functions as a kind of
canon within the canon influencing all aspects of his interpretation of
the Marxian corpus. The structure and strategy of such protest cannot but
be different from its predecessors, for, as Marx well understood, the
whole pattern of previous thought (that is apart from the half-con-
cealed, underground history of protest) involved a merely contemplative posture, a reflective adjustment to, rather than critical-practical
reaction within history and contemporary reality, be it social or individual. Our extended gloss upon Bloch's text indicates how his standpoint arises; it is a "hermeneutic" that emerges out of the combative
posture. Not surprisingly this hermeneutic entails the opening up of a
"Front" (*Front*) and the consequential discernment of allies and enemies
across the whole range of human knowledge and experience. Above all,
the latent war on behalf of, and the incipient victory of the New
(which later becomes more distinctly hypostatised into the *Novum*)
must be provoked into a declared and formal conflict. Bloch, the radical (yet bourgeois) intellectual, conceives and formulates a strategy of
recovery of the past and probing of the present in the name of the future,

> The Not-Yet-Conscious (*Das Noch-Nicht-Bewusste*), *Not-Yet-
> Become* (Noch-Nicht-Gewordene), although it fulfils the
> meaning of all men and the horizon of all being, has not even
> broken through as a word, let alone as a concept. This blossom-
> ing field of questions lies almost speechless in previous philos-
> ophy. Formal dreaming, as Lenin says, was not reflected on, was
> only touched on sporadically, did not attain the concept
> (*Begriff*) appropriate to it. Until Marx, expectation and what
> is expected, the former in the subject, the latter in the object,
> the oncoming as a whole did not take on a global dimension, in
> which it could find a place, let alone a central core. The huge
> occurrence of utopia in the world is almost unilluminated ex-
> plicitly. Of all the strange features of ignorance, this is one of
> the most conspicuous. (*PHI*,5-6)

This passage provides us with further clues to Bloch's ambitious
project, hence his "particularly extensive attempt" to "bring philosophy to hope, as to a place in the world which is as uninhabited as the
best civilized land and as unexplored as the Antarctic" (*PHI*,6). Such
an ambitious project might seem on a superficial level clear and
straightforward, but on the contrary it involves a concomitant new

mode of thought. The apparent forgetting of the future tense by a whole cultural tradition (except, as we shall see by its dissident minority, an intellectual "underworld") brings about a kind of exclusion:"an overwhelmingly static thinking did not name or even understand this condition, and it repeatedly closes off as something finished what has become its lot".(*PHI,6*) In other words, we might say that humanity is here conceived as having built its own prison, declared the world beyond the walls non-existent and then felt free to throw away the key fitting the exit door. This is what Leibniz called "a palace of fateful events" from which there is no escape. In a particularly literal translation of Bloch's words we read that, "As contemplative knowledge is by definition solely knowledge of what can be contemplated, namely of the past, so it bends an arch of closed form-contents out of Becomeness over the Unbecome" (*PHI,6*).[21] Thus contemplative knowledge is by its very nature confined to past events; but, from this material it constructs a kind of vault of closed knowledge (that is of things that *have happened*, i.e. "Becomeness") which precludes the possibility of the knowledge that strives through and into the future composed of the things that cannot now happen, (i.e. the "Unbecome"). Consequently we live within a "world of repetition" (*Welt der Wiederholung*), a "great Time-and-Again (*des grossen Immer-Wieder*, literally "always-again").[22] Knowledge therefore becomes an obsessive celebration of the past rather than an active grasp upon the latent future. Not only Kant and Hegel, but Bloch argues, all earlier philosophers went about their work with what amounts to closed-off categories; and consequently, form, idea and substance are understood as subsisting, finished and complete. Hope and its positive correlate, the as yet uncompleted determination of that which exists, is absent from the conceptual vocabularies of the sciences taken in the widest sense, and indeed from the reality they seek to interpret.

Bloch conceives of his masterpiece as the culmination of the earlier works when he here refers in particular to *Spuren, Geist der Utopie, Thomas Münzer, Erbschaft dieser Zeit* and *Subjekt-Objekt* in which, we

[21]The German is remarkable: "*Ist als betrachtendes Wissen per definitionem einzig eines Betrachtbarem, nämlich der Vergangenheit, und uber dem Ungewordenen wolbt es abgeschlossene Forminhalte aus der Gewordenheit*", p.4. The grammatical and syntactical structure of this passage give some indication of the difficulties in translating Bloch's exalted, as opposed to his commentary and expository style,

[22]Bloch's use of the motif of the "world of repetition" is highly suggestive. It is, in the conceptuality of Bloch's hermeneutic a "refunctioning of Nietzsche's " myth of the eternal return" and the reversal of its later negative, pessimistic application by Spengler. For further comment on the genesis of this conception see K. Löwith, "*Nietzsches Wiederholung der Lehre von der ewigen Wiederkehr*" in *Weltgeschichte und Heilsgeschehen Die theologischen Voraussetzungen der Geschichtsphilosophie, Sämtliche Schriften* (Stuttgart: J.B. Metzler, 1983) vol.2, pp.228-239; and *Nietzche*, op.cit., vol.6.

recall, there resides the pervasive latent principle that is now to find fullest expression in *Daz Prinzip Hoffnung*. It is of course of fundamental importance that the latency everywhere characteristic in Bloch's view of reality as determined by the category of "Not-Yet-Being" implies in turn a literary unfinishedness in its textual representation. In so far as the contemplative knowledge of the past reflects its own presupposition of an essential completeness, it has happened; so with regard to the hope and the future it is incomplete, even as yet, not fully uttered. By its very nature, however, it *cannot be* so uttered; the consequence of this is a stylistic and conceptual stumbling block, an inherent *skandalon* built into the mode of utterance itself.[23] Over-specificity would actually reduce and negate the representation of the very dimension of openness and unfinishedness to which Bloch refers. Thus in order for the horse to make the journey successfully it must be hobbled.

The hermeneutic of the future bears within itself limitations comprised in the style and structure of Bloch's utopian genre which encode rather than crudely expose the reflected reality that is not yet. Such knowledge, surfacing in the hermeneutic of "longing" (*Sehnsucht*),[24] "expectation" (*Erwartung*), and "hope" (*Hoffnung*) cannot be divorced from the occasion of its occurence. *Docta spes*, that is "comprehended hope" arises in a specific context and this is at the point at which the "In-Front-of-Us" (*das Vor-Uns*) dawns. Now we see why Bloch's owl of Minerva flies at dawn, not dusk. The "Novum demands its concept of the Front" (*PHI*,6); the occurrence of the engagement with hope and the venturesome thinking which we have outlined is in the midst of the turbulence created when present encounters future. We ride (risking the imposition of another image) precariously upon the foaming crest of a wave of time in constant danger of tumbling back into the mere past or falling forwards into irrational speculation or ungrounded fantasy. Bloch is thus to attempt the extraordinary, and in every way taxing feat of balancing in this zone of marginality. That there are inevitable stylistic consequences and perplexities entailed by this new form of indirect communication is to be expected, however unwelcome and distasteful this might prove to be for an unimaginative reader. That said

[23]In terms of a literary-theoretical approach to Bloch's *Principle* its textuality can be understood as an attempt to implant a powerful reader-response that on the one hand involves the destruction of an abject, passive dependence upon the past and, on the other, a positive invitation to walk out boldly along a plank lacking visible support at the outward extremity; it is, in Nietzschian terms, a provocation to "live dangerously".

[24]The pursuit of the post-Kantian parallel of Schleiermacher and Bloch as aestheticians of feeling would indicate that whereas the former provides a phenomenology (and implied ontology) "of absolute dependence" the latter constructs their counterparts in terms of the Romantic yearning, the temporal reversal of the *Sehnsucht* quintessentially encapsulated for example in Heine's poem "*Kennst du das Land*". Bloch naturally insists upon a forward orientation of such intentionality.

(and stylistic obscurity cannot lightly be tolerated as a necessary condition of successful expression) Bloch's goal is nevertheless clear, his intellectual task implies the gargantuan rehabilitation of a lost, repressed category:

> Expectation, hope, intention towards possibility that has still not become; this is not only a basic feature of human consciousness, but, correctly corrected and grasped, a basic determination within objective reality as a whole. (PHI, 7)

Here is posited a universal determining category which in Bloch's estimation is a constitutive as any of the traditional categories[25] previously employed in the history of philosophical reflection. In *The Principle of Hope* there is a consistent hypostatisation of the key concepts employed and indeed without this the intentional dimension could not reach adequate expression. In this technique Bloch is very much a product of the German tradition. As a self-declared (although always, from the standpoint of "orthodoxy") a never unproblematic Marxist, Bloch attributes an analogous, if perhaps not wholly identical philosophy to Marx himself. This cautious attribution is significant, as the precise role of *Marxism* in Bloch's thought has yet to be established:[26]

> Since Marx, no research into truth and no realistic judgement is possible at all which will be able to avoid the subjective and objective hope contents of the world without paying the penalty of triviality or reaching a dead-end. *Philosophy will have conscience of tomorrow, commitment to the future, knowledge of hope, or it will have no more knowledge* (Bloch's emphasis). And the new philosophy, as it was initiated by Marx, is the same thing as the philosophy of the New, this entity which expects, destroys or fulfils us all. (PHI, 7)

---

[25]Bloch's interest in Aristotle and in the renewed Averrhoeist attack upon scholasticism is here explained.In fact Bloch's claim to be a philosopher in restricted Anglo-Saxon technical sense would rest upon the quality and consistency of his historical mastery of the tradition of reflection upon the categories stemming from Aristotle's *Categories* and *De Interpretatione* and continued through the work of St. Thomas Aquinas and his critics which was consummated in immanence in the "transcendental deduction" of the pure concepts of understanding in Kant's *Critique of Pure Reason*, see N. Kemp Smith (tr.) (London: Macmillan, 1933), pp.120-175.

[26]It is precisely the manifest categorial *reductions* within Marxism that Bloch seeks to correct. This leads to difficulties when Bloch has to distinguish Marx from the tradition that takes his name; hence his heavy concentration upon the transformatory epistemology of the *Theses on Feuerbach*.

The attributability of this vision to Marx is not without its difficulties; there is doubtless a certain apologetic motif in Bloch's writing
here, for on the assumption that heresy springs from innovation, he is
bound to defend the status of the philosophy of hope as pre-existent in
the Marxist tradition.[27] Ironically, it is precisely the static *foreclosure*
of social development enacted in the history of socialist societies as
structured by the ideology of Marxism-Leninism in its Stalinist form
that has provided the contemporary setting of Bloch's intellectual
warfare against "narrow-gauge" Marxism. It will be increasingly apparent that Bloch has almost as selective and transformative a relationship with the thought of Marx as with the other past figures
whose contemporary resonance is recognised and developed.

III. TRACES, TRUTH AND THE DIALECTIC

Bloch has now completed his first assertion and defence of the norm
towards which human intentionality, once undeceived, strives in the
project of "venturesome thought". He now moves into the quasi-empirical area in which the traces of[28] the "good New" that "is never that
completely new" (*PHI*,7) can be detected, for, Bloch maintains,

> It (the "good New") acts far beyond the daydreams by which
> life is pervaded and of which the figurative arts are full. All
> freedom movements are guided by utopian aspirations, and all
> Christians know them after their own fashion too, with sleep-
> ing conscience or with consternation, from the exodus and mes-
> sianic parts of the Bible. (*PHI*,7)

These "traces" are relatively obvious in comparison with the extraordinary, rich, but highly compressed conglomerate of ideas drawn from
all parts of the Western cultural tradition which fills out and illustrates Bloch's basic hypotheses. There is, in this, however, an underlying structure which it is our aim to unearth and isolate. Thus, for example, Bloch regards Plato's Eros, Aristotle's concept of matter as moving

---

[27]The more likely sources of Bloch's inspiration at this juncture would appear to be the
two pre-Marxian texts: Feuerbach's *Foundations of the Philosophy of the Future* (1846)
and Kant's *Dreams of a Spirit-Seer* (1766). Bloch's inspired eclecticism makes specific at-
tributions a risk-laden enterprise, particularly as regards *The Principle of Hope*.

[28]Bloch's use of the term "traces" is a continuation of the approach recorded in *Spuren*,
G.A.,I, which is a collection of short texts reminiscent of Kafka's *Kurzerzählungen*.
Adorno's notion of the "break" (*Bruch*) is analogous to Bloch's "trace": the seeming seam-
lessness of a reified reality can only be shattered by a subversion based upon the detection
of that which *once was* (Adorno - hence his "melancholy science"), or what *will be*
(Bloch - hence his militant optimism).

from possibility to actuality, Leibniz's concept of tendency (*conatus*), aspects of Kant's postulates of moral consciousness, and Hegel's historical dialectic as all containing a residual utopian glimmer which is extinguished by mere "contemplation" (*Betrachtung*). Above all, Bloch claims, the past overtakes the future in the thought of Hegel.[29] "Thus", he concludes, "the utopian principle could not achieve a breakthrough, either in the archaic-mythical world, despite exodus from this, or in the urbane-rationalistic one, despite explosive dialectics" (*PHI*,8). Both worlds share the "contemplative-idealistic" (*betrachtende-idealistisch*) and thus passive mode of knowing; and they therefore "presuppose a closed world that has already become, including the projected over-world in which What Has Become is reflected" (*PHI*,8). In the archaic world the gods of perfection, just as much as the ideas and ideals of the enlightened, rational world are to be understood as finite objects just as much as the empirical facts of the world. Put more directly, attempts at transcendence, both archaic and modern, are but reflective illusions to be understood, alongside the merely factual, in a single, enclosed world. Without such a realisation, open, processive thought of a kind capable of attempting to change the world might well be nullified. In Bloch's Marxist intellectual dialect: "only knowledge as conscious theory-practice confronts Becoming and what can be decided within it, conversely, contemplative knowledge can only refer by definition to What Has Become" (*PHI*,8). Bloch has put the Marxian transformation of the discussion of theory and practice into a context characterised by a heightened awareness of time and futurity, and this consistently serves as one level of synthesis in *The Principle of Hope*.

The ground-myths of Western culture are consequently pervaded with the past and their rational appraisal in philosophical reflection is conceived of as subject to the ancestral domination of the Platonic doctrine of *anamnesis*, "the doctrine that all knowledge is simply re-remembering" (*PHI*,8), that is a "re-remembering" (*Wiedererinnerung*) of "ideas perceived before birth, of totally primal past or what is ahistorically eternal" (*PHI*,8). According to this view "Being-ness simply coincides with Been-ness, and the owl of Minerva always begins its flight only after dusk has fallen, when a form of life has already be-

---

[29]This assertion needs careful qualification precisely because Bloch's project includes the re-Hegelianisation of Marx. See the discussion of Hegel in *Subjekt-Objekt G.A.*,8, esp. "*die Aufhebung*", pp. 379-520 in which Bloch locates his understanding of Hegel in the context of the subsequent tradition. Bloch's characterisation of the Hegelian dialectic terms is extreme: "What Has Been overwhelms what is approaching, the collection of things that have become totally obstructs the categories Future, Front, Novum" (*PHI*,8). This is an overdetermination produced by an understandable desire on Bloch's part to stress his originality over against that of Hegel.

come old" (*PHI*,8). All philosophies, even that of Hegel, which retain the "phantom of anamnesis" are to be consigned to the "antiquarium" over against which Bloch sets the Marxian innovation grounded in the passion (*Pathos*) of change, that is in the inception of a theory which resists mere contemplation (*Schauung*) and explanatory interpretation (*Auslegung*). In the Marxian method thus conceived the rigid demarcation of the temporal zones of future and past is purportedly dissolved, and in the representation of the past itself, "unbecome future becomes visible" (*PHI*,9). Marxism, thus understood, provides the key not only to understanding history as process but also to the emancipation of the caged contents of past history. Those who grasp the past on its own in the old, contemplative way turn the past into "a mere commodity category, that is, a reified Factum without consciousness of its Fieri and of its continuing process" (*PHI*,9). This is Bloch's dialectical imposition of the method of the "commodity dialectic" upon those elements in history which have lost any reference to futurity.[30]

Bloch is not content, moreover, to let this Marxian insight function as a mere temporal determinant, and the means of access into the future potential of otherwise closed-off historical events. The Marxian inheritance is far fuller; it provides, according to Bloch, an opening into the comprehension of the whole historical process which is the condition of mastery over history itself;

> But true action in the present itself occurs solely in the totality
> of this process which is unclosed both forwards and backwards,
> materialist dialectics becomes the instrument to control this
> process, the instrument of the mediated, controlled Novum.
> (*PHI*,9)

It is passages such as this which indicate the persisting, and tarnished attraction of Marxism residing in its promise not merely of insight but of real historical power. Bloch, however, is more concerned to point out that the anticipations of the explicit materialist dialectic (which eventually provides the means of controlling the total process) are in no way confined to the residual progressivism of the "Ratio of

---

[30]The notion of "commodity dialectic" derived in the first instance from the "fetishism of commodities", in *Capital* I, Ch.1, section 4, is central to the revisionist Marxist view of social reality under capitalism: all relationships appear to lose their human content when concealed by the exchange value embodied in commodities. Bloch does not present his argument primarily in terms of the basis of a critique of the socio-economic process whereby labour value is transmuted in exchange value and ultimately into accumulated wealth (i.e. capital) but uses the conceptual vocabulary of commodity dialectics in the context of a quasi-metaphysical argument related to the totality of the historical process.

the bourgeois era", but can be found in earlier societies and their myths. In effect (and here a theological parallel is evident) these traces in myth "minus mere ideology and particularly minus pre-scientifically preserved superstition" (*PHI*,9) must be "demythologised": the dross of primitive accretion has to be burnt off to expose the progressive gold. So out of "pre-capitalist world pictures" (including varieties of scholastic philosophy) it is possible to rescue teleology, totality, and the category of quality, along with the myths of Prometheus and the Golden Age.[31] This grandiose salvage-operation is informed by, even inconceivable,without Marx's discovery:

> Marxist philosophy, as that which at least adequately addresses what is becoming and what is approaching, also knows the whole of the past in creative breadth, because it knows no part other than the still living, not yet discharged past. Marxist philosophy is that of the future, therefore also of the future in the past; thus, in this collected consciousness of Front, it is living theory-practice of comprehended tendency, familiar with occurrence, in league with the Novum. (*PHI*,9)

Bloch's panegyric has, of course also to be seen in the harsh light of historical enactment and his later personal departure from communist social reality. It should, in reality, be understood equally as implicit, coded protest against the actual social realisation of Marxism as it is an explicit denunciation of capitalism. Beyond any such tactical considerations, Bloch's strategy is clear: he now has a methodological tool (ostensibly forged out of Marxian teaching) capable of being directed towards the decipherment of history and the transformation of social reality. This is characterised as follows,

> ... the light, in whose appearance the processive, unclosed Totum is depicted and promoted, is called *docta spes, dialectical-materialistically comprehended hope*. (Bloch's emphasis)

[31]Bloch expounds a position conceived upon the Hegelian level of abstraction, directed at the goal of totality. The residual presence, indeed the reactivation of "refunctioned" metaphysical concepts and mythological motifs facilitates this. At the same time Bloch disregards those immanent determinations that make the pursuit of "totality" a central but highly contentious issue in Marxist theory. See M. Jay, *Marxism and Totality The Adventures of a Concept from Lukács to Habermas* (Cambridge: Polity, 1984) for a comprehensive survey of the problem.

consequently,

> The basic theme of philosophy which remains and is, in that it
> becomes, in the still unbecome, still unachieved homeland
> (*Heimat*), as it develops outward and upwards in the dialectic-
> materialist struggle of the New with the old.
>   (*PHI*,9)

Two important points can be made which clarify Bloch's *docta spes*
or reflected hope as it is now fused with the materialist dialectic. The
first is this: whilst Bloch calls upon Marx's conception of the class
struggle implicit in the dialectic of the real, this has to undergo modification. The truly terrifying annihilation, the rendering impossible of
a class proposed by Marx and enforced with varying degrees of ruth-
lessness in the history of communist societies, might well be thought out
of place in Bloch's theoretical setting because his highest goal, encounter with the Novum, relies upon a discriminating salvage operation based upon prevenient historical latencies present in *all* social
levels of the historical process. Second, furthermore, Bloch's dialectic
consists of a re-Hegelianisation of Marx, inasmuch as the struggle is not
restricted to that between social classes as such (as the historical em-
bodiments of good and evil) but between the manifestations of the new
and the old. Thus here, as in the *Phenomenology of Mind*, antiquity and
modernity struggle for supremacy in a warfare which Hegel represented in such fecund images as that of Lord and Bondsman.[32] The distinctions Bloch employs ultimately owe more to the ancestral tension
between the "two cities", and its developed cognates in Luther's two
worlds and later secularised variants in German idealism,[33] than to the
brutally identified class identities of the good "new" proletariat and
the bad "old" bourgeoisie. Indeed, putting these two related points together we may again ask if it is not in fact the case that Bloch's variant of the dialectic is far closer to a qualified Hegel than to Marx.
Bloch's repeated intellectual genuflections made before the Marxian

[32] The vocabulary of class extinction expressed in a pattern strongly reminiscent of
Hegel's ontological parable of lordship and bondage in the *Phenomenology of Mind* coex-
ists uneasily here with Bloch's dialectical juxtaposition of past-dominated present and a
liberative futurity. For a wider contextualisation of two such widely differing interpretations of Hegel, see R.H. Roberts, "The Reception of Hegel's Parable of the Lord and
Bondsman", *New Comparison*, No.5, Summer 1988, pp.23-39. Marx translates the dialectic of power in Hegel's *Phenomenology* into class conflict; Bloch, by contrast, transforms
Hegel's retrospective recapitulation of the conflict of eras into a prospective, critical
utopianism.

[33] U. Duchrow's magisterial study of the "two-kingdoms" doctrine, *Christenheit und
Welverantwortung Traditionsgeschichte und systematische Struktur der Zweireichlehre*
(Stuttgart: Klett-Cotta, 1983) adds weight to this assertion, see pp.75-96.

altar, and anecdotal defence of the legitimacy of his position is perhaps best passed over discretely when it is seen in relation to the contemporary context of his efforts (*PHI*,10ff.)[34]

IV. PROSPECT: THE STRUCTURE OF THE DEDUCTION OF HOPE

In the concluding pages of the Introduction of *The Principle of Hope* Bloch summarises the contents of each of the subsequent five sections of the first volume. First, in "Report" Bloch ranges over commonplace experience unearthing from it "daydreams of an average kind". On this basis, second, the actual occurrence of such known material Bloch establishes a hypothesis, a "Foundation" consisting of a conception of "anticipatory consciousness". Central to this second step is the "discovery and unmistakeable notation of the Not-Yet-Conscious" and this is expounded in the context of the discovery of the unconscious in the tradition extending from Leibniz, through the Romantics to Freud. Out of the subsequent phenomenological analysis of "emotion" (*Affekt*) is developed the conception of a "directing act of a cognitive kind "(*Richtungsakt kognitiver Art*) (*PHI*,12). This experiential category of anticipatory consciousness and its intensionality is subsumed under the "utopian function" (*utopische Funktion*) and its contents. In this "Foundation" Bloch constructs what amounts to a descriptive metaphysics and nascent ontology growing out of the phenomenology of anticipatory consciousness formalised, objectively, as the full utopian dimension in which the utopian function is to be recast more broadly in relation to ideology, archetypes, ideals, symbols, and to the categories Front and Novum, Nothing and Homeland. Bloch's allusion to "Nothing and All" will lead the reader into the more obscure recesses of the Western tradition as German dialectical-mysticism is recovered in "transformed" (*unfunktionerte*) form. The "world-riddle"[35] itself is to be found in the inner dialectic of utopian consciousness:

> Utopian consciousness wants to look far into the distance, but ultimately only in order to penetrate the darkness so near it of

[34]It ill behoved Bloch to defend the legitimacy of the dream of an alternative reality suppressed in Marxist-Leninist aesthetics when his lamentable defence of the Moscow trials is taken into account. See S. Markun's attempted justification of Bloch's behaviour, which begins significantly: "Ernst Bloch's apology for the Moscow trials is a stumbling block for many", op.cit., p.58 and Zudeieck's comments, op.cit., pp.153-7.

[35]This term, *Welträtsel*, recalls Ernst Haeckel's immensely successful popularisation of evolutionary monistic materialism in the period immediately prior to the First World War and on a more intellectually elevated level the philosophy of Heinrich Rickert upon which Bloch wrote in his doctoral thesis. See P. Zudeieck, op.cit., pp.31-3 for an informative account.

the just lived moment, in which everything that is both drives and is hidden from itself. In other words: we need the most powerful telescope, that of polished utopian consciousness, in order to penetrate precisely the nearest nearness. Namely, the most immediate immediacy, in which the core of self-location (*sich-Befindens*) and being-there (*Da-Seins*) still lies, in which at the same time the whole knot of the world-secret is to be found. (*PHI*,12)

This distinctive approach to the analysis of the "matter" (*die Sache*) is resolved in phenomenological-ontological analysis of the Not-Yet-Conscious and the convoluted, inter-related linguistic strategies of anticipatory consciousness. Bloch's intellectual tool is now capable of reciprocal application to the anticipatory traces detectable in the total content of human culture.

In the third part of the first volume of *The Principle of Hope*, "Transition", Bloch previews a return to the "wishful images in the mirror", and launches an assault upon the corrupted images of bourgeois culture embedded in fashion, advertisement, fairytale, publicity, popular dance, the "dream-factory (*Traum-Fabrik*) of film" and the theatre itself, which are all subsumed into an all-embracing industry. In contrast to this perversion of formalised utopian insight, in the fourth part, entitled "Construction", Bloch embarks upon an initial outline-survey of a rich range of medical, social, technological, architectural and geographical utopias, besides those reflected in painting and literature. Here Bloch generalises a workable concept, something of a Weberian "ideal type" out of the data presented, which coheres with the future-orientated category of the imagination that is detected and deduced in the central sections of the first volume of *The Principle of Hope*. The very breadth and catholicity of Bloch's vision (though it is critically informed by a recognition of the influence of class barriers) transcends any arbitrary limitations, it purports to be universal; it is out of this that a new "construction" is to be attempted.

Finally, in the fifth section, entitled *Identity*, Bloch takes up the intention comprised under the Faust scheme. "Guiding images" (*Leitbilden*) emerge and in the (for Bloch positive) figures of Don Giovanni, Odysseus and Faust, and (the more questionable) Don Quixote, the concrete images of the utopian Humanum are set forth in the human imagination. The practice of concrete utopia leads inevitably to Marx, and, so Bloch maintains: "Becoming happy was always what was sought after in the dream of a better life, and only Marxism can initiate it" (*PHI*,17). Thus is provided fresh access to a "creative Marxism", a "revision" understood in a rather substantial sense in which are harnessed the fullest fruits of the great cultural tradition, filtered, refined and concentrated. Bloch recapitulates and concludes,

> Only with the farewell to the closed, static concept of being does the real dimension of hope open. Instead, the world is full of propensity towards something, tending towards something, latency of something, and this intended something means fulfilment of the intending. It means a world which is more adequate for us, without degrading suffering, anxiety, self-alienation, nothingness. (*PHI*,18)

Bloch juxtaposes his staged, interwoven and reciprocally self-confirmatory, inductive genesis of formalised conceptions of hope with the condition of their realisation, for "Marxist knowledge means: the difficult processes of what is approaching enter into concept and practice" (*PHI*,18). It is on this front that knowledge will undergo renovative transformation: the immanent Novum will manifest itself.

In the course of this first chapter we have analysed at length the Introduction to *The Philosophy of Hope* and shown how Bloch, over against the apparent victory of the past, proposes the initial principles of a philosophy of the future that will rehabilitate *in toto* the utopian dimension of anticipatory consciousness. At this early stage the emergent formal structure of Bloch's strategy has many elements in it that are analogous to other reconstructions of totality out of categorial survivals of the Kantian critique. Thus both Bloch and, for example, the theologian and hermeneuticist F.D.E. Schleiermacher disclaim the rationalist idealist starting-point, and construct out of anticipatory consciousness, and the sense of absolute dependence, respectively, full-blown systematic interpretations of the fundamental nature of human reality as informed by future-orientated (and atheistic), or God-consciousness-directed (and pantheistic), categorial options.

In the first stages of our reading of *The Principle of Hope* we have become aware of Bloch's indebtedness to central figures of the German idealist tradition, Kant and Hegel, and to this we shall soon add their Romantic counterparts, above all Goethe. This appropriation is expressed, as will become increasingly clear, through Bloch's exploitation in modified form of what Hans Urs von Balthasar has perceptively called the "thought-form" (*Denkform*) of German idealism, a pattern of transcendental argument in which an absolute presupposition is systematically exploited as the source of comprehensive integration.[36] The central feature of Bloch's reworking of this method lies in

---

[36]*Karl Barth, Deutung und Darstellung seiner Theologie* (Einsiedeln: Johannes Verlag, 1951), parts I and II. The present exposition of Bloch's ambiguous and refunctioned

an attempted reversal of the ontological priority of the time order from an emphasis on the past, and present, to the latent future. Upon this categorial foundation and within an expanding framework we shall see how *The Principle of Hope* has a vertebral structure which serves to support copious literary flesh, a texture accumulated not merely through argument, but also through the indirect associative allusion generated by exalted cultural colportage. In this prodigal cornucopia many aspects of the tradition apparently discarded by critical modernity (both "bourgeois" and Marxist) and thus reduced to the status of obsolescent detritus are "refunctioned", transvalued and put to work in Bloch's vision of a militantly optimistic post-modernity. Chief amongst these rehabilitations is not a revision of Marx's teaching as such, but a refunctioned account of religion and myth which is advanced precisely as the correction of a failure *within* Marxism. Marx proposed the *abolition* of religion as the universal and necessary *a priori* of the full emancipation of humankind; Bloch reasserts the religious *a priori*. Congruent with Bloch's atheistic reappropriation of religion and myth is a series of other concerns which add substance to his image as the "scholastic" of the Marxist tradition. Bloch's concerns go well beyond the frontiers of a Marxism narrowly conceived into the negative dialectics of a technological culture that suppresses religion and myth and thereby threatens to extinguish the psychic identity of the human race. Conceived in these terms, Bloch points to a common ground, the rehabilitation of an immanent "beyond", in which all benevolent ideologies, religious or non-religious have a vital and continuing interest.

relationship with Hegel owes much in methodological terms to von Balthasar's technique of comparative, systematic analysis of Barth's analogous dependence upon Hegel.

CHAPTER III

THE UTOPIAN DREAM AND THE CONQUEST OF ANAMNESIS

As we noted at the end of the previous chapter Ernst Bloch divides the first volume of *The Principle of Hope* into five sections. We shall now expand these critically in successive chapters and highlight the structural principles of the work, whilst at the same time showing how Bloch's vision both relates to, and differentiates itself from, the cultural inheritance upon which it draws with eclectic, yet directed energy. There is here to be seen a cyclic development in which we move from the quasi-empirical phenomenology of the dream into the analysis of the transcendental condition of the category of the Front, that is of future anticipation itself.

I) THE PHENOMENOLOGY OF THE DAY-DREAM: 'REPORT'

Bloch begins his explanation of boundary-breaking futurity with a rhapsodic evocation of the growth of consciousness in the child[1] who starts out empty, yet who moves, cries and craves. In searching, the child learns to wait when its wishes are frustrated. Exploration and destruction confront each other; yet the unnamed slips away, "it is not yet here" (*PHI*,21). Later the grasp upon the world is more confident; our wishes are named; identities are not yet fixed, they merge and re-emerge for "Play is transformation (*Verwandeln*), though within what is safe and returns" (*PHI*,27); with a Piaget-like empathy (and lack of hesitation in universalising particular experience) Bloch presents a reflected stream of consciousness, a phenomenology of the passage from infancy into childhood. Characteristically the prime mover is male, "the boy sallies forth, collects from everywhere what is sent his way"

---

[1] It is apparent that this representation of the emergence of order out of inchoate beginnings is a formalisation of personal recollection, see the similarity of this opening passage with "*Geist, der sich erst bildet*" in *Spuren* G.A., I, pp.61-72 and also Markun's comment on the parallel, op.cit., p.8. Bloch frequently initiates discourse with remarks arising out of a stream of consciousness that gradually take on an organised form, see for example the early pages of *Geist der Utopie* (1918) G.A. 16, pp.1ff.

(*PH* I,22);[2] the man recalls the childhood experience of the tree-house and its autonomous freedom. The woman's story, "I wished I could be under the cupboard, I wanted to live there and play with the dog" (*PH* I,22), is not uncharacteristic of Bloch's Romantic preconceptions: the man asserts and explores; the woman reverts, receives or is taken. The archetypal "little day-dream" that the "wishful land is an island" (*das Wunschland ist ... eine Insel*) (*PH* I,24). At the dawn of adolescence "the fellow-travelling ego is discovered" (*PH* I,24), a hatred for the average floods the mind and young boys assert themselves and "aspire to a nobler life than their father might lead, to tremendous deeds" (*PH* I,24); these fantasies are an "escape and return of the conqueror",[3] the construction of castles in the air, but such imagining of things other than they are is influenced by class-position and cultural forces. Extravagent travel and conquest fantasies characteristic of the male child have their representative female counterpoint, "I wanted to become a painter, I dreamed myself into an oriental castle on a mountain, living alone there with my illegitimate child which I had by a very distinguished man" (*PH* I,25), but here the imagery employed is still that of a re-enclosed creativity and a self-elected, impregnated passivity. Moreover the conditioning is explicit beyond mere gender typing,

> These are still excessive bourgeois notions of a juvenile kind, in proletarian adolescents of this age they are much more muted, more grown up, and even more realistic. But even here if the contents have ceased to be so fantastic, their attraction still remains that of a fairytale, sharply transcending the given world. Clearly such fantasies do not only emanate from the depths of the mind, but just as often from newspapers, from adventure books with their wonderfully glossy pictures. (*PH* I,25)

The reader might well imagine what Bloch might have made of more recent entertainment media developments. It is, however vital to Bloch's argument that the will "destroys the house in which it is based and in which the best things are forbidden" and that thus "in timeless history it builds its mountain stronghold in the clouds or the knight's castle in the form of a ship" (*PH* I,25). The image of the castle is

---

[2]The juxtaposition of male assertiveness and female passivity is characteristic; the depiction of the male child setting out to collect and thus to conquer is again Hegelian in undertone.

[3]The depiction of the male dream as *"Flucht und Rückkehr des Siegers"* p.24 is once more reminiscent of Hegel's depiction of the path from unreflected to reflected self-knowledge in the *Phenomenology of Mind*.

paradigmatic in Bloch's implicit, yet clearly intended, typology of dreams. With a sensitivity to the *Sturm und Drang* of adolescent love-dreams, reminiscent of the febrile poetry of the young Karl Marx, Bloch clearly regards this phase of human development as of critical importance. Here at least the dreamed possibility of things is evident before it is quenched in mundane normality: "since wishing does not decrease later on, only what is wished for diminishes," (*PH* I,29). The immature wishful themes may turn sour for:

> The often invoked streak of blue in the bourgeois sky became of course a streak of blood; the stupid or stupified had their very own strong man called Hitler. But the greyness of a young mediocrity has never shone without its capricious figures; the wish itself puts them on his arm. (*PH* I,29)

Out of the disappointment of hopes arises regret; the dreams of regret mostly concern lost money. The dream of revenge, in particular in its petit bourgeois form, is the product of repressed impotence, "men are too cowardly to do evil, too weak to do good; the evil that they cannot, or cannot yet do, they enjoy in advance the dream of revenge" (*PH* I,30). Thus, "the Nazi dream of revenge is also subjectively bottled up, not rebellious; it is blind, not revolutionary rage (*PH* I,30-1). Revenge wreaked upon those at the top and upon Jews betrays this dream; it conveys with it the malice and breathlessness of the mob. Bloch's analysis (if it can be so termed) of the phenomenon of Nazism is inadequate; it is an explanation which combines Marxist apologia with the post-war East German intellectual elite's facile response to events of world-shattering significance.

> The Instigator, the essence of the Night of the Long Knives was, of course, big business, but the raving petit bourgeois was the astonishing, the horribly seducible manifestation of this essence. From it emerged the terror, which is the poison in the 'average man in the street', as the petit bourgeois is now called in American, a poison which has nowhere near been fully excreted. His wishes for revenge are rotten and blind; God help us, when they are stirred up. (*PH* I,31)

It would appear that not only Bloch's experience of National Socialism, but also his American exile colour his vitriolic depiction of the adult petit-bourgeois' private (and effervescent) sexual and business dreams as those of the deprived (and despised) "Babbitt", who compensates for his impotent mediocrity.[4] This "little man... proletarianised, but without proletarian consciousness" hovers on the edge of life imagining in dreams what he knows he has not yet and will never achieve. The bourgeois class as a whole resists and ridicules the "utopian" element of the dream and the rich man seeks to dispel his ennui by a lust for novelty that culminates in the bizarre and the trivial.

The unflattering representations of the petit-and the moneyed bourgeois dreams that emerges out of Bloch's initial depiction of the growth of consciousness and its counterpart in childhood are then contrasted with the "non-bourgeois dreamer" (*PH* I,35). In this class of dreamers it is the proletarian consciousness that is described, but this is not identified in any concrete or exclusive way with that class itself; here is no lazy rotten Babbitt clinging limpet-like waiting for the chance to bring him good fortune. The non-bourgeois dreamer anticipates the possibility of change in the given world both in reality and in the dream. Whilst he, like the Babbitt, might also want his "chicken in the pot and two cars in the garage" (*PH* I,35) his dream nevertheless transcends this vulgarity.[5]

> But the values of comfortable happiness shift in the prospects of the revolutionary wishful dreams, if only because happiness no longer arises out of the unhappiness of others and measures itself against it. Because our fellow men is no longer the barrier to our own freedom, but rather the means by which this freedom is truly achieved. Instead of freedom of acquisition, there shines freedom from an acquisition, instead of imagined pleasures of cheating in the economic struggle, there shines the imagined victory in the proletarian class struggle. (*PH* I,35)

This is our first clear glimpse of Bloch's utopia, a Marxian vision of an unalienated humanity in which other human beings are not manipulated as the objects of conquest on the path to aggrandisement, but are valued as subjects in altruistic association for whom fulfilment is to be attained, concretely, so he argues, under conditions only furnishable

---

[4]"Babbitt", an onomatopoeic play on the word "rabbit", and a generalisation based on the chief character of Sinclair Lewis's novel of that name published in 1922. The "Babbitt" comes to represent for Bloch the lowest human type, the embodiment of anti-heroic mediocrity in the petit-bourgeois.

[5]Part of the violence of Bloch's attack upon the American life might well stem from the unacknowledged ironies in the relationships of his "dream" with the "American Dream" and to entrepreneurial capitalist culture as well as with the rigid, centralised economic and social determinism of the communist societies in which Bloch's "dream" was, supposedly, to be enacted.

through a Marxist philosophy of theory and practice and the application of his consistent and original form of dialectical materialism.

Having examined childhood and its dreams which are only lightly divided by class-consciousness, the growing differentiation of the adolescent, and finally the sharply divergent dreams of petit bourgeois and non-bourgeois maturity, Bloch then turns briefly to old age, in which "we learn to forget" when "exciting wishes recede, although their images remain" (*PH* I,35). The decline into old age can be the occasion of a descent into peevishness; it is unwished for and rarely imagined in prospect. There is, however, a healthy image of old age where it is a "thoroughly formed maturity" that "feels more at home giving than taking (*PH* I,39); silence and rest overtake striving in the representative figures of the aged Goethe and Jacob Grimm who embody a positive quality in old age, but this is an image that has "gone out of circulation economically and in terms of content" (*PH* I,40). It is, Bloch baldly asserts, only a socialist society that can fulfil the wishes of old age for leisure: "Wish and the ability to be without vulgar haste, to see what is important, to forget what is unimportant: all this is authentic *life* in old age (*PH* I,41). This "socialist norm" is to be brought about by power, through hard work, for "the obsession with what is better remains, even when what is better has been prevented for so long (*PH* I,42). This New is not yet pre-defined for "when what is wished for arrives, it surprises us" (*PH* I,42).

No reader could pretend that the first section of *The Principle of Hope* was a passage of devastating profundity; it is, as it were, lightly orchestrated, an early, distant sounding of themes that nevertheless exist close at hand. It is like the jotted folk tunes in the notebook of the composer who will transform through a creative *Umfunktionierung* what he has found by the hedgerows. Into the material in this preliminary and informal scheme Bloch will infuse a massive interpretative and synthetic impulse: thus under heat and pressure the Marxist basal strata and the accumulated overlay of cultural tradition interact and there takes place a metamorphosis of the mundane out of which spurts forth articulate anticipatory consciousness.

II) PSYCHOANALYSIS AND THE PHENOMENOLOGY OF NOT-YET-CONSCIOUS: FOUNDATION

The second, and by far the longest section of volume I of *The Principle of Hope* is concerned with "anticipatory consciousness" (*das antizipierende Bewusstsein*) and consists in a monumental explication and analysis of the residual "obsession with what is better" (*die Sucht nach dem Besseren*) (*PH* I,42) with which the first part ended. It is at

this juncture that Bloch commits himself in earnest to that hypostatisation of phenomenological concepts to which German language and
thought so well lends itself. The internal description of the experience
of the self has been formalised in German philosophical thought at
least since Kant but the origins of this varied genre can be traced far
further back into the mystical tradition. The exploration of
"inwardness" is thus a time-honoured pursuit sanctioned by tradition
and enhanced by the linguistic possibilities of German. This inwardness
tradition is not accepted uncritically, yet Bloch does not hesitate to exploit as fully as possible linguistic possibilities given their fullest
(even notorious) expression by his contemporary Heidegger. The re-util-
isation of inwardness has, however, to be a *transformed* use: the recovery of tradition can never be *mere* reactivation, it must imply recreation.

We experience ourselves as driven inwardly by a non-emergent
"That" (*Dass*) located in our very corporeality. We do not seek it out for
it is always with us; announced but unnamed, an urge and thirst constantly provoke us for, "the nature of our immediate being is empty and
hence greedy, striving and hence restless" (*PH* I,45). The historical antecedents of the description of this state are not hard to find, the theological anthropology of St. Augustine is but one example.[6] Here, however, Bloch naturally does not venture into an anthropology comprising
transcendence as such. Inner "urging" (*Drangen*) expressed as "striving"
(*Streben*) is experienced as "longing" (*Sehnen*). Once this longing ceases
to be restless and achieves direction it becomes conscious "searching"
(*Suchen*), a goal-directed "driving" (*Trieben*). The concept of "drive"
(*Trieb*) so attained is fundamental; in the sphere of feeling it is differentiated into "passions" (*Leidenschaften*) and "feelings" (*Affekten*). In
the act of imagination craving becomes specific in "wishing"
(*Wunschen*). Thus at the root of what it is to be human is the drive to
"fill a hollow space in the striving and longing, to fill something lacking with an external something" (*PH* I,46).

Thus far Bloch has sought to articulate out of the experience of
emptiness a definite conception of the "drive" (*Trieb*). The very existence of this propensity mistakenly suggests something beyond; but
there is nothing "beyond" the body:

> Even the drive-instinct belongs to the economy (*Haushalt*) of
> the individual body and is only employed in so far as it belongs

---

[6]There is a defensible sense in which Bloch's presentation of the early Heidegger's
"being-unto-death" and Bloch's own "longing" are negative and positive reworkings, respectively, of a secularised Augustinian phenomenology.

to it, in so far as the body does its own business, fleeing from what damages it, searching for what preserves it. (*PH* I,49)

Man is, however, a complex of drives, a conscious animal, insatiable yet with the ability to conceptualise his wishes. The acquisitive drive (*Erwerbstrieb*) is itself acquired, and stimulated by its context in late capitalist society, but, further to this, the "fascist death-drive" has intensified itself far beyond Romantic sentimentality under the conditions of imperialism and bourgeois nihilism. In the face of these developments the "religious drive", that is (once purged of its "superstructure") "the drive upwards, the erotic urge towards the changeless" has receded, except where, under the specific conditions of fascism, it reverts to the mythology of Blood and Soil. Thus, the regressive tendency of the religious drive is here understood by Bloch as the product of a secularisation process stated in straightforward Marxist terms. But, given the diverse pressures upon the emergent drives then:

We realize that man is an equally changeable and extensive complex of of drives, a heap of *changing*, and mostly badly ordered wishes. And a permanent motivating force, a single basic drive, in so far as it does not become independent and thus hang in the air is hardly conceivable. The principal motivating force does not even become visible in men of the same time and class, by psychoanalytically dismantling their apparently pure inner clockwork, for example. There are certainly several basic drives; now one, now another emerges more strongly, now they work together, like opposing winds around a ship, and they do not even remain similar to themselves. (*PH* I, 50)

The diversity of drives does not, however, exclude the possible hegemony of any one of them and so in his search for the primal human drive Bloch engages with the originator of this conceptual scheme, that is with Freud and his positing of the sexual urge as the most powerful human drive. There then follows a densely written and absorbing presentation and critique of the stages in the development of Freud's conception of the fundamental human drive in relation to his erstwhile pupil C.G. Jung and disciple Alfred Adler. This discussion is further informed by the wider elements present in Bloch's socio-cultural critique.

Freud regarded the sexual drive as the primal urge; libido thus governs life. It has its positive aspect: pleasurable satisfaction through sexual relaxation, to which Freud later added a tendency towards negative pleasure, the death drive. Thus the "emotion of *Liebestod*" represents the supposed interconnection of cruelty and sexual pleasure. Over

56   Hope and its Hieroglyph

against the "dark id" of the body and its drives the ego "affirms, denies and censors the drives, consciousness depends on it, it is the power which makes our mutual life coherent" (*PH* I,52). The unacceptable sexual surplus undergoes repression, and by these means the libido and its "pleasure principle" (*Lustprinzip*) are subjected to discipline; hence the "bourgeois individual ... wears down his Dionysian horns on 'reality', as Freud calls his bourgeois environment (the commodity world and its ideology)" (*PH* I,52). Over and above the mere ego stands the "super ego" (*Über-Ich*) or the "ego-deal" (*Ich-Ideal*) which represent wider claims, "it represents our relation to our parents; it creates all the surrogate functions of piety", and this culminates, taken all altogether, in what Bloch regards as "an extraordinary superstructure of drives" open to dismantling in the course of analysis. (*PH* I,53). The contents of the super-ego are supposedly composed "*exclusively* of 'illusions' with regard to the outside world" (*PH* I,53). Here Bloch confronts Freud's interpretation of the nature of the super-ego: the unconscious but final hegemony of the "id". Thus the influence of the repressed drives over the ego is not, as Freud would have it, an anonymous being "'lived' by unknown, uncontrollable forces" but the external and highly explicit "alien domination of the capitalist mode of production" which has been turned into the "libido-id" (*PH* I,53).

The above is a skeletal representation of a compound argument, but it is sufficient to show how Bloch brings to bear upon Freud a Marxist critique typical of the later German revisionists.[7] The point of encounter, conducted at a high level of abstraction, is between a set of theoretical constructs developed within the sphere of individual psychology on the one hand, and, on the other, the hypostatised consequences of the "commodity dialectic" of capitalism on the other.[8] This is the meeting place in which two distinct explanational schemata coincide. The psychoanalytic reduction of the repressed unconscious through its rational exposure is a private act within the wider "discontent" (*Unbehagen*) of a "civilisation" Bloch intends to subvert upon other grounds.

Freud's account of the libido, as the "single basic drive and the essential content of human existence" and the mechanism of repression that gives rise to neurotic states and to the renowned complexes, presupposes as its categorial foundation the existence of the unconscious.

[7]H. Marcuse's *Eros and Civilisation* (Boston, 1955) is perhaps the most famous exemplification of this conjunction, fundamental to the school of "critical theory".

[8]There is, consequent upon this juxtaposition, a set of corresponding problems surrounding the crux of freewill-determinisim within Marxist critical theory. Bloch's critique of Freud has a brutal vigour which is salutary in the light of the extraordinarily pervasive diffusion of the latter's ideas into culture at many levels.

The latter is a unsatisfactory medium for the articulation of anticipatory consciousness, for:

> The unconscious in Freud is therefore one into which something can only be pushed back. Or which at least, as id, surrounds consciousness as if this were a closed ring: a phylogenetic inheritance all around conscious man. (*PH* I,56)

In consequence, Bloch argues:

> The unconscious of psychoanalysis is therefore, as we can see, *never a Not-Yet-Conscious*, an element of progression; it consists rather of regression. Accordingly, even the process of making this unconscious conscious only clarifies What Has Been, i.e. *there is nothing new in the Freudian unconscious.* (*PH* I,56)

The denial of future capacity to Freud's unconscious would appear to place a correspondingly greater burden of proof upon Bloch to demonstrate that his own conception of anticipatory consciousness may contain the "New" despite his avowed and uncompromising immanent materialism. It is the regressive aspects of Freud's theory as developed by C.G. Jung that precipitates some real verbal violence on Bloch's part. Jung, the "psychoanalytic fascist" (*PH* I,56), comprehensively reduced the libido and its contents to the primaeval, for, "according to him, exclusively phylogenetic primaeval memories or primeval fantasies exist in the unconscious, falsely designated 'archetypes'; and all wishful images (*Wunschbilder*) also go back into this night" (*PH* I,56).[9] It is apparent that such regression would rule out *a priori* the possibility of "wishful images" reflecting the New rather than merely the accumulated psychological detritus of the past. The sublimation of the self-enclosed libido into "imagination"[10] or the higher virtue of an altruis-

---

[9]Bloch's excessive polemic should not be allowed to obscure the real point of his criticism of Jung, that he locks humankind into regressive identity and makes it a willing recipient of primeval impulses.

[10]Bloch's translators render, *"Phantasie als Ersatz für Trieberfüllung"* perfectly correctly as "imagination is a substitute for the fulfilment of drives", (*PH* I,56) but the semantic richness of *"Phantasie"* as opposed to the relative colourlessness of the contemporary English "imagination" must be borne in mind. Something of the resonance of this term is conveyed in Wilhelm Dilthey's *"Goethe und die dichterische Phantasie"* in *Das Erlebnis und die Dichtung* (Leipzig: B.G. Taubner, 1921) pp.174-267. Given Bloch's pervasive indebtedness to Goethe it is not surprising that Dilthey defines *"Phantasie"* as follows in a way close to what we find in *The Principle of Hope*:

> *"Phantasie ist - so sahen wir - in den ganzen seelischen Zusammenhang verwoben. Jede im täglichen Leben stattfindende Mitteilung bildet unwillkürlich das Erlebte um; Wünsche, Befürchtungen, Träume der Zukunft überschreiten das Wirkliche; jedes Handeln ist bestimmt durch ein Bild von etwas, das noch nicht*

tic *caritas*, and even the pleasures to be derived from artistic creation
by the artist and his audience are, according to Freud, but temporary
and even illusory diversions, for, "art ... works exclusively with the illusions with which the unsatisfied libido allows itself to be fooled"
(*PH* I,57). Freud's conflict with his pupils, and their refusal to submit
to the absolute primacy of the sexual libido in psychoanalytic theory,
either took the form of outright rejection and the subsequent choice of a
different driving force, or the less drastic step of coating the libido
with a "mythical patience" (*PH* I,57). Alfred Adler reverted to the bi-
polar struggle and the will to power,[11] which is seen by Bloch as
quintessentially capitalist; consequently, "unfulfilled power-drive
produces the inferiority complex"(*PH* I,57). Bloch's comparison of the
historical antecedents and the social contexts of Freud's concept of libido and Adler's "will to power" is a small but entertaining masterpiece of compressed, turgid polemic which we leave the reader to enjoy:

> Because Adler therefore drives sex out of the libido and inserts
> individual power, his definition of drives takes the ever
> steeper capitalist path from Schopenhauer to Nietzsche and
> reflects this path ideologically and psychoanalytically.
> Freud's concept of libido bordered on the 'will to life' in
> Schopenhauer's philosophy; Schopenhauer in fact described
> the sexual organs as 'the focal points of the will'. Adler's 'will
> to power' conversely coincides verbally, and partly also in
> terms of content with Nietzsche's definition of the basic drive
> from his last period; in this respect Nietzsche has triumphed
> over Schopenhauer here, that is to say, the imperialist elbow
> has triumphed over the gentlemanly pleasure-displeasure
> body in psychoanalysis. The competitive struggle which
> hardly leaves any time for sexual worries stresses industrious-
> ness rather than randiness; the hectic day of the businessman
> thus eclipses the hectic night of the rake and his libido. (*PH*
> I,58)

So far as Bloch is concerned, Adler at least recognised the rapacious
"will to power" of capitalism and included it in his psychological the-

ist: *die Lebensideale schreiten vor dem Menschen, ja der Menschheit her und
führen sie höheren Zielen entgegen: die grossen Momente des Daseins, Geburt,
Liebe, Tod werden verklärt durch Bräuche, die die Realitäten umkleiden und
über sie hinausweisen.* p.184

[11] This has obvious Nietzschian undertones but its provenance is traceable to Hegel.
How Bloch can distinguish his own conception of the drive towards mediation from the
theory of aggression systematised in Adler is less than obvious, except insofar that it is
conceived notionally in terms of a Marxian mode of fulfilment.

ory of basic human drives;[12] Jung, the "fascistically frothing psycho-
analyst" (*der faschistich schaumende Psychonalytiker*) (*PH* I,59), has,
by contrast, "consequently posited the frenzy-drive (*Rauschtrieb*) in
place of the power drive" (*PH* I,59). Once again Bloch launches himself
into luxuriant polemic best experienced at first hand. In outline his argument runs as follows: libido for Jung is an archaic undivided primeval
unity of all drives, an "Eros" which includes ecstatic states extending
from "eating the last supper, from coitus to unio mystica, from the
frothing mouth of the shaman, even the berserker, to the rapture of Fra
Angelico" (*PH* I,59).[13] Whereas Freud advocated the banal resolution
of the neurotic, "mystified libido" into present consciousness, Jung advocates a descent into the primal "affirmation of a mescalin Dionysus".
Thus as "Nietzsche triumphs over Schopenhauer" so we are invited to
return to Jung's dionysiac-vitalist world of "elemental feel-thinking";
here, Bloch maintains, "the fascist Jung borders on the Romantic reactionary distortions which Bergson's vitalism underwent; as in sentimen-
tal penis-poets like D.H. Lawrence, in complete Tarzan philosophers
like Ludwig Klages" (*PH* I,59). Jung's vision of an "archaic collective
regression" is underlaid by the collective unconscious, a conception developed out of Freud's individual unconscious which has been hypostatised and universalised into a primeval racial resource from which
mankind alienates itself at the risk of persistent neurosis. This is, we
might say, a biologically-conceived organic memory, almost, to use a
term Bloch does not employ, a recoverable "species-being"
(*Gattungswesen*).[14] It is on the basis of this (to Bloch's way of thinking
highly pernicious) regression into the collective unconscious, that Jung's
procedure becomes identical with the function of "religion",[15]

Psychosynthesis - fleeing the present, hating the future,
searching for primeval time - this becomes the same as

[12]Bloch conveniently attributes these tendencies to the capitalist process external to
(but imposed upon) the individual and his drives. He fails to indicate any readiness to
recognise the philosophy of power implicit (and later developed) in his own proposals.

[13]"Frenzy" here implies narcotic intoxication which indicates an identification of the
reductive psychological analysis of "mystical" experience with a single causal agency.
For a careful consideration of such reductionism (as applied to the problem, but not to
Bloch) see R.C. Zaehner, *Mysticism Sacred and Profane* (Oxford: Oxford University
Press, 1957).

[14]We are of course here involved with the problem of the all-pervasive competition of
contrasting human identities created in the context of the fragmentation and pluralism,
both ideological and explanatory evident in the growth of the human sciences.

[15]This is an important crux in Bloch's argument as regards his interpretation of the religious aspect "re-ligio", a "connecting back" is displaced by a refunctioned "connecting
forward" as we see in chs. 8 and 9 below.

"religion" in the etymological sense of the word: namely re-ligio, connecting back (*PH* I,61).

Bloch's declared interest in anticipatory consciousness rather than
the repressed unconscious, together with his perception of the parallel
between the *individual* psychoanalytical return into the collective
memory and the *collective* socio-psychological fascistic regression into
that memory may account in some measure for the ferocity of his attack
upon psychoanalysis which is full of rich insults, brilliant and highly
stimulating. Bloch succeeds in penetrating the self-referential, non-al-
lusory literary style of Freud and places him in his cultural setting in a
way both complex and illuminating, despite the ad hominem overlay.
So far as Bloch is concerned, both Freud and Jung are on the same plane,
despite their different conceptions and resolutions of the tensions of the
subject in relation to the unconscious; they "both understand the unconscious solely as something past in historical development, as something
that has sunk down into the cellar and only exists there" (*PH* I,64).
Freud and his "perverted pupil" recognise "no pre-consciousness of the
new" (*PH* I,64) inasmuch as they idolize the libido, albeit in different
ways. The power of the libido understood as sexual drive (Freud), the
will-to-power (Adler) and primeval Dionysus (Jung) is rendered absolute; it is, Bloch argues, "never discussed as *a variable of socio-economic
conditions*" (*PH* I,64). With commendable clear-sightedness Bloch
recognises that not only must basic drives vary in accordance with class
and epoch but he further asserts that the psychoanalytical conception
of the sexual drive is not really fundamental at all. Ultimate finality
is to be found in the simple drive to preserve life; so it is therefore
ironic that hunger is always left out of psychoanalytical theory. It is
therefore against this critical account of psychoanalytic theory that
Bloch develops his own account of the basic drive: hunger.

It is typical of Bloch's down-to-earth mentality that he places the
cry of hunger over that of lovesickness. With a few unmystified thrusts
he pushes to one side the psychoanalytic process of exposure that would
appear to ignore class and national limitations[16] for, "the fear of losing
one's job is hardly a castration complex" (*PH* I,66). Questions of sexual
hygiene apart, Bloch sets against each other the conflicting explanatory models:[17]

[16]Bloch remarks with refreshing candour: "The French bourgeois thus has alone a
smaller reserve of cant than the average German, let alone the average Englishman; consequently he shows less sexual stuffiness, fewer libidinal repression complexes" (*PH* I,
p.66).

[17]In this passage Bloch retreats from polemical overdetermination and gives a relative (but not exclusive) priority to an evolutionary-materialist, rather than a sexual explanation of the historical process. Again his juxtaposition of possibilities is readily un-

Obviously, however, there is no erotic conception of history to replace the economic one, no explanation of the world in terms of libido and its distortions, rather than in terms of the economy and its superstructure. Here too then we should ultimately stick with the real expression of the matter (*Auspruch der Sache*): with *economic interest*, not the only, but the fundamental interest. The self-preservation which manifests itself within this interest is the soundest among the many basic drives and, despite all temporal, class-based modifications which it is also subject to, surely the most universal (*PH* I,66-7).

Here Bloch has liberated himself from the thrall of psychoanalytic schemata and he thus makes contact with the most primitive and pervasive basic drive, that of self-preservation. By these means he thus places himself in direct contact with elements in the prevenient philosophical tradition and with dominant trends in contemporary sociobiology:[18]

'Suum esse conservare', to preserve one's being, that is and remains however, according to Spinoza's unerring definition the 'appetitus' of all beings. Even if capitalist competitive economy has made it individual beyond all measure, it still runs, however modified, remorselessly through all societies (*PH* (I,67).

We may therefore conceive this initial critique of Freud as a retreat from post-psychoanalytical fragmentation *back* into a tradition now thought to contain intellectual tools more adequate to the task of encountering and grasping the contemporary condition in both theoretical and practical terms.

Bloch broadens his critique of psychoanalysis by setting the emergent argument in the evolutionary context. Attempts made to recover "primal man" out of the multiplicity of evolved "basic drives" fail and the products of such ventures (be they by Rousseau, Nietzsche, Freud or Jung) are contextually bound to the circumstances of their authors: "all definitions of basic drives only flourish in the soil of their own time and are limited to that time (*PH* I,69). Bloch's determinative assumption of the Marxist dimension is maintained: "Economic interest fans the final instance in the historically existing framework of drives, but

derstandable in the context of early twentieth century German culture in which the scientific materialism was challenged by the psychoanalytic "discovery" of the unconscious.

[18]The philosophical and cultural consequences of evolutionary insight have been more readily recognised in recent American rather than British sociology and philosophy.

even this, precisely this once again, as we know, has its changing historical form, the changes in the mode of production and exchange" (*PH* I,69).[19] Despite the metamorphosis of man through history, hunger and the drive towards self-preservation are constants; the self remains "with its hunger and the variable extension of this hunger still open, moved, extending itself" (*PH* I,69). This basic drive with its expression in the emotions has to be analysed from the standpoint of the act of intending,[20] that is in a mode of being depicted by Kierkegaard as "existential".

Once more Bloch has to distinguish between healthy and degenerate developments in the existential tradition that he wishes to appropriate. What began as the "highly emotional" *Confessions* of Augustine in which the "becoming conscious of consciousness emerged here in the self-reflection of a man of intensive will-power" was sustained by Kierkegaard against Hegel, but this genre later collapsed into Heidegger's "animal, petit-bourgeois experiential phenomenology" (*PH* I,72). Bloch cites Descartes and Spinoza in order to inject a measure of rationality into his nascent method without at the same time losing touch with the emotion out of which intentionality arises. Even Hegel (in his early masterpiece, the *Phenomenology of Mind*) recognised the motivatory power of passion (*Leidenschaft*). Rather than being caught up into the categorisation of emotions into strong or weak, Bloch distinguishes emotions of rejection or inclination and then asserts what is for him most basic distinction, a division of the emotions into "filled and expectant emotions" (*PH* I,74). So here are juxtaposed categories of emotion which build humane discriminations into the basis of Bloch's analysis. The "emotions of rejection" (*Abwehraffekte*) such as fear, envy, anger, contempt and hate are contrasted with the "emotions of inclination" (*Zuwendungsaffekte*), contentment, generosity, trust, admiration and love (*PH* I,73). Such a distinction is imperfect in that the duality of displeasure-pleasure may manifest itself in mixed forms. Bloch makes a further distinction of the emotions above and beyond this preliminary division, that is between "filled emotions" (*gefüllte-Affekte*), such as envy, greed, admiration with short term intentionality, as opposed to "expectant emotions"

[19]Bloch's use of Marxist historical materialist (i.e. economic) determinism is *polemical* rather than *constitutive* in his later argument. Bloch does not argue for a systematic correlation between human drives and his own "philosophy of the future" on the one hand, and, on the other, socio-economic forces, that is in Marxist terms the material "basis" of the ideological "superstructure".

[20]Whereas Bloch specifically refers at this juncture to Brentano his position is eclectic and ambiguous with regard to a range of thinkers whose concerns are primarily located in the phenomenological analysis of "inwardness": Augustine, Kierkegaard, Hegel and Heidegger have all to undergo a dual process of appropriation through partial negation..

(*Erwartungsaffekte*) like anxiety, fear, hope, belief with long term, anticipatory intentionality. These emotions are then explicated in terms of time, that is with regard to the future. By these means Bloch conditions his initial affective anthropology by a temporal analytical schemata thereby transforming it into the starting-point of the wider, positive project. Using the "mode of the future" (*Modus der Zukunft*) Bloch maintains that,

> whereas the filled emotions only have an unreal future, i.e. one in which objectively nothing new happens, the expectant emotions essentially imply a real future; in fact that of the Not-Yet, of what has objectively not yet been there. When they are banal, fear and hope also intend unreal future, but secretly or deep down even then a more total fulfilment has entered the banal fulfilment, one which, quite unlike the filled emotions, lies beyond the available given world. Thus the urge, the appetite and its wish usually break out frontally in the expectant emotions. (*PH* I,75)

Out of the foregoing passage and its series of discriminations there emerges *hope*, the most important and authentic emotion which sets itself against passive passion[21] as the "most human of all mental feelings", and which is exclusively attributable to men yet it retains the most wide-ranging, as-yet unachieved point of reference.

Bloch is now in a position to re-unite for the first time in his argument a newly-wrought conception of "theory" (the basic hunger drive expressed in self-extension forwards) with "practice" understood as *active* expectation (*tätige Erwartung*). Persisting hunger therefore demands change, it expresses a "revolutionary interest" directed against the "prison of deprivation" (*PH* I,75) and is no mere self-preservation but a self-extension. In the interim, however, the drive generated by hunger, a drive towards satisfaction, becomes a drive that "survives the available world in the imagination" (*PH* I,76). So it is (as Marx pointed out)[22] that the human worker (as opposed to the ant) realises a

---

[21]Bloch's negation of fear and his appropriation of the inwardness of expectation implies a critique of religious self-negation, or so he appears to argue: "For the negative expectant emotions, of anxiety and fear are still completely suffering, oppressed, unfree, no matter how strongly they reject. Indeed something of the extinction of self announces itself in them, and something of the nothingness into which ultimately the merely passive passion streams" (*PH* I, p.75).

[22]*Das Kapital* (East Berlin: Dietz, 1947) I, p.186. The slender textual basis of Bloch's re-utopianisation of Marx is evident to a reader with an informed knowledge of the texts. Bloch's attitude to Marx is primarily focussed in his exegesis of the *Theses on Feuerbach* as already noted.

purpose conceived primarily in the planning of the imagination. Now
we can appreciate the reason for the importance with which Bloch in-
vests the notion of the daydream: it is the "wishful element" (*das
Wunschhafte*) in the expectation that arises from hunger which can
divert from, yet also galvanise humanity towards a better life. The
earlier distinction between enervating escapist dream and sustaining,
progressive dream is now set in a more concrete context, beyond, as it
were, the rearwardly obsessed orientation of psycho-analysis, firmly
grounded in Bloch's version of the materialist critique of Marx. Thus:

> the venturer beyond does not occupy a shaft in the ground be-
> neath existing consciousness, with a single exit either into the
> familiar daylight world of today, as in Freud, or into a roman-
> ticised diluvium, as in C.G. Jung, and Klages. What hovers
> ahead of the self-extension drive forwards is rather, as will
> have to be shown, a Not-Yet-Conscious, one that has never been
> conscious and has never existed in the past, therefore itself a
> forward dawning, into the New. It is the dawning that can sur-
> round even the simplest daydreams; from these it extends into
> the further areas of negated deprivation, and hence of hope
> (*PH* I,77).

Bloch has now laid the foundations of a position upon which he is
to erect the huge structure that we outline in the ensuing chapters of
this book. As Bloch himself remarks, such a positive and critical intellectual construction calls for the generous outlay of energy as each facet
of his comprehensive view of the world and human destiny has to be
reworked so as to refract the future light of the Novum. There are many
unanswered questions, the assertions are numerous, yet the justifications
are so far limited. Out of this adumbrated matrix of ideas, and
supremely out of the intersection of human intensionality with an as
yet undefined future, the "philosophy of hope" proper is to arise. As
the initial framework is now apparent Bloch can revert to his
"empirical" shared category, the "daydream" out of which so much
has to be unfolded if he is to sustain the connection between what humanity is, and what, in his critical utopian vision, he would wish it to
become.

III) THE DIFFERENTIATION OF THE DREAM: NIGHT AND DAY

Bloch returns to the discussion of the dream and juxtaposes the
night-and the daydream. Despite his previous attack upon Freud,

Bloch is obliged to return to the dream; it is because the latter discovered that "dreams are not just foam" (*PH* I,78), nor are they prophetic oracles, but they subsist somewhere between the two, that is between utterly groundless fantasy and definite prediction of the future. Day- and night-dreams are both components in the vast field of utopian consciousness, but they must be carefully distinguished.

The night-dreams hallucinate wishful ideas by easing internal censorship, by exploiting the loosened association of ideas inherited from the conscious state, and by exploiting the separation off of the practical demands of the outside world. In the night-dream the ego reverts to childhood but continues, in a reduced and distorted way, to censor the dream wishes that, consequently, reappear in symbolic disguise. The interpretation of dreams (and equally the analysis of the symptoms of neurosis) experience resistance (*Widerstand*): the day-ego disapproves of its nocturnal counterpart. Bloch draws freely upon the fruits of the cultural and psychoanalytical tradition as he unfolds critically the power of the dream-symbols in the context of regression and the genesis of fear through the namelessness of disorientated "libido", with the result that, "all repressed wishful emotions turn into phobias in this realm of the unconscious (*PH* I,83). Bloch recalls that even Freud became dissatisfied with this mono-causal account of the genesis of anxiety and admitted positive and objective "hunger, subsistence worries, economic despair, and existential anxiety (*PH* I,84). This criticism is pursued with the purpose, consistent with the earlier analysis, of retaining the *formal structure* but purging and transforming the *content* of the Freudian conception of the unconscious and its power:

> If therefore the Freudian libido-subjectivisms of anxiety are untenable, the correlation he established between phobias and repressed wishful emotions still remains important and true; nor is it orientated around narcissistic fantasies, but around the objective content of the wishful emotions. Anxiety and its dreams may have their initial origin in parturition, just as they have their final biological content at the moment of death. But where anxiety arises not merely in a biological sense, but in a way which is only to be found in human beings, especially in the form of an anxiety dream: then it is essentially founded on *social* blockages of the self-preservation drive. In fact, it is simply the *annihilated content* of the wish, *a content actually transformed into its very opposite*, which causes anxiety and ultimate despair. (*PH* I,85)

Bloch both recovers and purges Freud in the interests of preserving his fundamental commitment to the assertion that "every dream is wish fulfilment" (*PH* I,86). Correlating with, but distinct from the night-dream, is the daydream which purportedly enjoys a higher degree of purposive organisation: "the daydream can furnish inspirations which do not require interpreting, but working out, it builds castles in the air as blueprints too, and not always just fictitious ones" (*PH* I,86). The emphasis Bloch places upon the daydream leads not unnaturally to an attack upon the tendency within psychoanalysis to downgrade daydreams to the level of the night-dreams to which they are, as it were, the mere preliminary. Against this reductive transposition Bloch sets his decisive image of the castle, arguing that, "the castle in the air (*Luftschloss*) is not a stepping-stone to the nocturnal labyrinth, if anything, the nocturnal labyrinths lie like cellars beneath the daytime castle in the air" (*PH* I,87).

In positive terms, the daydream has certain distinct advantages over the night-dream: first, it is under the control of the daydreamer'; and second, the ego remains intact;[23] and, third, it is world-improving. The conserved assertiveness of the ego that orchestrates the daydream, preserves, in turn, its content against the onslaught of the censoring moral ego, hence the "utopistically intensified ego builds itself and what belongs to it in a castle in the air in an often amazingly carefree blue"[24] (*PH* I,91). The emergence of the daydream into social utility demands in the first instance "least of all the altered ego as in the night-trance, but rather an ego with taut muscles and (sic) a concrete head (*mit konkretem Kopf*)" (*PH* I,91).

The gradual process of the definition of the dream then encounters a further danger connected with its capacity to conceive of world-improvement. As with the mutual classification of night-and daydreams with opium and hashish, so on the level of mental illness schizophrenia and paranoia (understood by Bloch as regression and projective delusion, respectively) are likewise unwelcome possibilities. Whilst these conditions cannot in reality be neatly separated, and both represent an "extreme turning-away from the current or available reality" (*PH*,92), they are in fact distinguishable in terms of Bloch's temporal criterion. Whilst paranoia may culminate in schizophrenia the former

---

[23]Bloch sets the contrast of the night-and daydream apart from drug-induced states of which with Walter Benjamin he had some passing personal experience. Thus Bloch could write that "*opium* appears to belong to the night-dream, hashish to the daydream" (*PH* I, p.89).

[24]Bloch's colour symbolism is pervasive. The "often invoked streak of blue" was first encountered on p.29, here the "*oft verbluffend umbeschwertes Blau*" indicates that "blue" is the colour of open, expectant hope towards which the intensified ego (having undergone the process of *Steigerung*) directs itself.

ventures into a fantasy of world-improvement whereas the latter succumbs to regression into the archaic. Bloch's problem is, then, how to sift out the sound utopian grain from the mound of chaff thrown up by the undoubted madmen possessed with utopian ambition.

The positive appraisal of the daydream as world-improving impinges directly upon the explanation of artistic creativity. Here again Bloch has simultaneously both to appropriate and partially to negate Freud. Freud reduced the truth of utopian creativity, that is "consciousness directed into the good New" (*PH* I,94), to the "merely diluting concept of 'sublimation'" which obscured its character. The daydream as "common property extends into the non-sublimated, but in fact concentrated expanse, into that of the utopian dimension" (*PH* I,94). Whereas Bloch does not pre-define the form or content of the work of art as such, he does argue that a Faustian self-extension is indispensable, for the "waking dream with world-extension is always presupposed for the accomplished work of art, *as the most imaginative experiment of perfection possible*" (*PH* I,95). This capacity of the daydream and its world-extending role is not confined in its effects to art but is of universal significance:

> Anticipations (*Vorwegnahmen*) and intensifications (*Steigerungen*) which refer to men, social utopian ones and those of beauty, even of transfiguration, are really only at home in the daydream. Above all revolutionary interest, with knowledge of how bad the world is, with acknowledgment of how good it could be if it were otherwise, needs the waking dream of world-improvement, keeps hold of it in a wholly unheuristic, wholly realistic way in both its theory and practice (*PH* I,95).

The fourth, and indeed decisive characteristic of the waking, open dream is that it will not renounce its fulfilment through a relapse into fictitious fulfilment or spiritualization. Bloch, once more drawing upon his erudition, illustrates this by reference to the childhood imaginative worlds of Clemens Brentano and the poet Mörike, both of which are mistakenly reduced by the psychoanalytical critique when understood as mere chimera or genre. Yet again Bloch confronts Freud and attempts to defend the validity of the daydream against the psychoanalytic reductionist who considers that "nothing at all corresponds to these contents in the outside world" to whom "art as a whole is false appearance, religion as a whole illusion" (*PH* I,96-7).[25] It is precisely

[25]Bloch's treatment of art has initially to be understood in the context of the *Expressionismusdebatte*; but the relation of aesthetics and religion, and the displacement of the latter by the former is a tension pervasive in German thought from the Romantic period

at this point that Bloch inserts the sharp-ended wedge of his major positive proposal:

> What is essential for the daydream, particularly in the journey to the end, is: the seriousness of a pre-appearance of the possible Real. (PH I,97)

This first statement of the major theme outside the earlier prolegomenic Introduction has immediately to struggle for its survival in the face of the further formalisation of the Freudian reduction of the "spiritual realm of imagination" to a "conservation area withdrawn from the reality principle" (PH I,97)[26]. Freud was committed, falsely in Bloch's judgment, to the immutability of reality in an outdated mechanistic world-picture, whereas Jung located the source or the introverted material in the archaic myth and the archetypes. Over against both of these alternatives Bloch sets out the future as the place of fulfilment, in effect he inverts the temporal structure of the doctrine of archetypes. So, even conceding the "really archaic basic ground of memory" this ought to be sought out in the images of hope, in the positive archetypes of the Golden Age and of Paradise. Thus for Bloch great art is to be understood as the true bearer of utopian consciousness in that the world-improving imagination imbues it with its obvious character besides carrying it "towards a latency of its coming side" (PH I,98). In sum, Bloch sets the regressive night-dream over against the day-dream,that "projects its images into the future, by no means indiscriminately, but controllable even given the most impetuous imagination and mediatable with the objectively possible" (PH I,99). Whereas longing is common to both forms of dream, the daydream does not direct

---

onwards. It is central to Adorno's work as seen, for example, in the relation of his second doctoral dissertation, *"Kierkegaard Konstruktion des Aesthetischen"* to the posthumously published *"Aesthetische Theorie"*.

[26]The basis of Bloch's observations upon Freud at this juncture are taken from the *Vorlesungen* of 1922, cited on pp. PH I, p.97. The passage in question is masterly and worthy of citation, it indicates that both Freud and Bloch engaged with issues only now impinging to some effect upon the popular mind.

> In the exercise of his imagination, man thus continues to enjoy the freedom from external compulsion which he has long since renounced in reality ... The creation of the spiritual realm of the imagination finds its complete counterpart in the laying-out of conservation areas, nature reserves in those places where the demands of agriculture, of traffic and of industry threaten to change quickly the original face of the earth beyond recognition. The nature reserve preserves this old state which we have elsewhere regretfully sacrificed to necessity. Everything may thrive and grow as it wants, even what is useless or harmful. The spiritual realm of imagination is also such a conservation area, withdrawn from the reality principle. (Freud, *Vorlesungen*, 1922, p.416).

itself into excavation and interpretation but towards concretion and rec-
tification.

In the ensuing discussion of the emergent dream in Romanticism,
Expressionism and Surrealism, and particularly in James Joyce's *Ulysses*
Bloch recognises the impracticality of trying to separate the regressive
from the progressive dream. Thus it is obvious that in such a militantly
modernist work as *Ulysses* the waking dream communicates through archaic material. Archaic brooding can be utopian, and in so far as it succeeds night-and daydreams may issue in a "merging of the dream-
games" (*PH* I,102); so it is that, undischarged, undeveloped dreams
may open up in a utopian way. Therefore, Bloch argues:

> only the daylight opens up the wonderfully relevant material
> of night-dreams, of the archaic in general, and it is this mate-
> rial only because and in so far as it is still itself utopian, trans-
> posed in a utopian way. Regression therefore occurs artistically
> only with profit when something that has not become, a future
> possible, is also still encapsulated in the archetype. (*PH* I,103)

In his typical way Bloch wants to regain access both to the tradition
and the contemporary context by re-orientating each towards the as yet
unfulfilled future. To make this possible it has first been necessary to
clear a trail through the psychoanalytic jungle in order to locate the
foot of the rock-face of reality itself. Henceforth the real climb begins
with a struggle against the weight of prevenient traditions obsessed
with the past. Thus we are invited to scale and explore Bloch's positive hermeneutic of existence; that is anticipatory consciousness itself.

Bloch pauses briefly in an intriguing interlude in which he considers "mood" (*Stimmung*) as the medium of daydream. Mood is indicative
(despite its variety) of a pervasive ego-grounded unity as opposed to
"states-of-being" (*das Befinden*) which in turn implies a more organic-
based condition. This distinction, which is justified through musical
metaphor and references to Theodor Lipps (Bloch's early teacher), is a
further step in the clarification of Bloch's distinctive approach to the
analysis of the inwardness of anticipatory consciousness that is found in
the next major section of Part II. Recognising that Heidegger had already trodden this ground in *Sein und Zeit* (1927), Bloch maintains that
the latter failed adequately to distinguish and separate state-of-being
and mood. For Heidegger, mood is the product of our finding ourselves in
a situation as "being has become manifest as burden".[27] Thus the
Heideggerian "boredness (which) reveals That-Which-Is in the

---

[27]Bloch cites *Sein und Zeit* (1927) p.134.

whole"[28] is summarily disposed of by Bloch's ad hominem critique of class consciousness: "not the misery of all mankind, but solely that of the unilluminated hopeless petit bourgeoisie strikes us when we come to this sentence in Heidegger, concerning the 'abysses' of this kind of state-of-mind" (*PH* I,105). This moribund mood, that of a declining class, lacks entirely a wishful character; again Bloch invokes his colour symbolism and pushes Heidegger back into the morass underlying his boredom:

> What is missing is precisely the colour for waking dreams, with which the mood can picture its blue hour, without it of course becoming uninteresting in existential-ontical terms and sinking down into existentialist-ontological terms into nihilism (*PH* I,106).

As with Freud, so with Heidegger,[29] Bloch is engaged upon the difficult enterprise of recovery: on the one hand he needs to appropriate an insight or the elements of a category, on the other he has to negate and purge so as to render what he finds suitable for re-use. The "blue" dimension of the mood has previously been disregarded in relation to the daydream, and it is precisely at the place of transition from the "black" to the "blue hour" that Bloch finds the *"medium in which waking dream images develop most comfortably"* (*PH* I,106). This is staged in the context of passages of exalted writing in which wide-ranging allusion to the shortcomings of Impressionism and developments in musical style compliment each other.[30] Even pathos, an "anti-mood" characteristic of certain works of art, provides evidence through the quality of the imagination for its counterpart: "the bright-dark mood provides the medium in which all daydreams begin, even those with hardness, and especially those with arousing blue (azure)" (*PH* I,107). The exposition of expectant emotion is continued, this time in dialogue with Husserl and again with characteristic critical appropria-

---

[28]Bloch refers to *Was ist Metaphysik?* (1929) p.16.

[29]Bloch here redraws Heidegger's own classic distinction between the "ontic" (that which pertains to existent particulars) and the "ontological" (that which relates to being as such). See J. MacQuarrie, *An Existentialist Theology* (London: SCM, 1955) pp.30ff. for a fine discussion of this distinction.

[30]As Wayne Hudson indicates, the extraordinary breadth of intellectual and cultural sensitivity and the diverse talents of the brilliant group of Marxist revisionist intellectuals with which Bloch was associated lost its last representative with his death. On the one hand Bloch had a comprehensive vision, on the other his particular interpretation of this or that cultural artifact is frequently criticised, especially by those with a narrow and unforgiving conception of expertise. Thus with regard to *Geist der Utopie*, the musicologist Paul Bekker attacked *"Blochs Unkenntnis sowohl musikwissenschaftlicher wie musikästhetischer Schriften"*, see Zudeieck, op.cit., p.68.

tion. Whereas Husserl posited a "set horizon" in the memory idea, as opposed to hope in "real imagination, and the 'real' future of its Object (*PH* I,108), he nevertheless retained the connection between expectation and intention.[31] Husserl thereby redeemed himself and his phenomenological method because the relativisation of memory set bounds upon regressive analytical tendencies. Granting the inclusion in Bloch of this method and its openness to intension and expectation, then the "first and fundamental negative expectant emotion, *anxiety* begins as the most mood-based and undefined" (*PH* I,109).

The ascription of primacy to "anxiety" (*Angst*) places Bloch once more in a confrontational stance with Freud and Heidegger. Freud characteristically advances a regressive and subjective account of psychological causation (anxiety as derived from the constriction in breathing, *angustia*, at the point of separation from the mother) which is reflected in all later feelings of anxiety. Heidegger so generalises anxiety as to make it into the "simple, undifferentiated 'Thusness' in everything, the existential 'basic state-of-mind'" that is the "Being-Subject-to-Death of all Being-in-the-World" (*PH* I,110) which, according to Bloch, merely reflects this writer's petit-bourgeois mentality.[32] In contrast to anxiety (and its extensions into "fear" - *Furcht*, "fright" - *Schrech*, and "terror" - *Entsetzen* (*PH* I,110)); Hope, although also mood-based, reflects the "dawning-decanted element of the auroral" (*das Dämmernd-Ausgegossene des Aurorahaften*) (*PH* I,111). Hope is, in contradistinction to *both* anxiety *and* memory, "a relation to a purely cognitive process and system of ideas which benefits no other emotion", and indeed Bloch argues that such is its power that "hope drowns anxi-

---

[31] Bloch alludes specifically to Husserl's *Zur Phänomenologie des inneren Zeitbewusstseins* (1928), "Every originally constituting process is animated by protensions (*Protensionen*) which emptily constitute and collect what is coming as such", p.410.

[32] In another polemical aside Bloch makes some sound points which should not be obscured by too great attention being given to the rhetorical heightening:

> Heidegger thus reflects and, with his ontology of anxiety, clearly only makes absolute the 'basic state-of-mind' of a declining society. From the standpoint of the petit bourgeoisie, he reflects the society of monopoly capitalism, with permanent crisis as its normal condition; the only alternatives to permanent crisis are war and war production. What was for primitive man still the 'Not-at-home' in impenetrable nature, has become for the unsuspecting victims of monopoly capitalism their society, the gigantic alienated enterprise into which they are placed. Heidegger however - with a sociological ignorance which matches his metaphysical dilettantism - makes this anxiety into the basic state-of-mind of man in general, including the nothingness into which he is supposedly always, everywhere and irrevocably thrown. All that remains of Heidegger's anxiety - 'hermeneutics' is at best a kind of familiarity, acute in the petit bourgeosie, with anxiety as unsuspectingness. (*PH* I, p.110)

The ludicrous attribution of "petit-bourgeois" status to Heidegger contrasts with Bloch's sound and salutary awareness of the reality, all too often ignored, of the displacement of "impenetrable nature" by a socially-constructed reality.

ety" (*PH* I,112). With a somewhat forced optimism Bloch takes up
Hölderlin's line "Where there is danger, rescue also grows"[33] as an
indication of the "positive dialectical turning point in which fear of
the place of death disappears" (*PH* I,112).[34]

IV) HOPE AND DISPLACEMENT: THE HERMENEUTIC OF REFUNCTIONING

In this chapter we have seen how Bloch has developed a conception of the dream that depends upon a dialectical conjunction of negative purgation and positive appropriation of context and tradition informed by the as yet largely implicit demands of anticipatory consciousness. Here Bloch hovers on the secularised fringe of a displaced
religious consciousness, as is indicated by the introduction of the word
"faith" (*Glaube*) at this critical juncture.[35]

> Danger and faith are the truth of hope, in such a way that both
> are gathered in it, and danger contains no fear, faith no lazy
> quietism. Hope is thus ultimately a practical, a militant emo-
> tion, it unfurls banners. If *confidence* (*Zuversicht*) emerges from
> hope as well, then the *expectant emotion which has become ab-
> solutely positive* is present or as good as present, the opposite
> pole to despair. (*PH* I,112)

A dialectical passage of despair into hope is fundamental; the only
language capable of expressing Bloch's intentions has to draw upon religious conceptuality. As will become increasingly apparent, Bloch's
optimism becomes *forced* and strident where it is generated paradoxically through the dissolution of the theistic postulates of theism into
the human and historical process. Whether, and in what sense, Bloch's
argument can be said at this stage to have force beyond that invested in
it by the optimistic energy of its author is open to question, given the
often expressive rather than evidential character of the assertions.
Bloch's imagery is aesthetically compelling in its beauty, but the precise origin of the sustaining force of the vision is questionable:

---

[33]In the original: "*Wo Gefahr ist, wächst das Rettende auch*".

[34]The rendering of the dative pronoun in the phrase "*dem die Furcht der Todesstelle
verschwunden ist*" as "*for which* fear of the place of death disappears" is problematic in
the Plaice translation.

[35]It becomes increasingly apparent that the re-working of religious conceptions, their
"refunctioning" (*Umfunktionierung*), is not peripheral but utterly central to Bloch's project of renewal.

But whereas the expectant intention in the emotion of despair only appears as a corpse, in confidence it gives up and yields itself up like a wise virgin, who, in going into chamber of the bridegroom, offers up (darbringt) as well as gives up (aufgibt i.e. surrenders) her intention. Despair touches almost completely that Nothing which all the negative expectant emotions are approaching; confidence, on the other hand, has in its horizon almost that All to which the weakest hope, even that transposed by unreal future, essentially refers. Despair transcends, in that its Nothing defeats the intention in the certainty of extinction, confidence, in that its All allows the intention to enter into the certainty of salvation (Heilsgewissheit) (PH I,112-3).

This powerful, if highly paradoxical, passage can be understood as a representation of the ancestral German dialectical tradition[36] within the affective and phenomenological context developed in reliance upon, and in critical dialogue with Freud, Heidegger and Husserl. Here we encounter for the first time the full expression of Bloch's "recursive modernism",[37] the refunctional transformation (Umfunktionierung) of conceptions drawn methodologically not only from the nascent human sciences but also expressively from the religious tradition. The further characterisation of negative and positive expectant emotions as "informal" and "paradisal", respectively, is consistent. Given that mood provides the medium of daydreaming then expectant emotion gives its "direction" (Direktion). Both emotion and ideas, linked together on the positive "wishful road" (Wunschstrasse) will issue into what we regard as Bloch's transcendental deduction of the category of the New and its attendant phenomenological epistemology to which we now turn:

Both future-orientated intentions, that of expectant emotions and that of expectant ideas, accordingly extend into a Not-Yet-Conscious, that is, into a class of consciousness which is itself to be designated not as filled, but as anticipatory. The waking dreams advance, provided they contain real future, collectively into this Not-Yet-Conscious, into the unbecome-unfilled

[36] Seen in the light of Thomas Münzer, Bloch is here infusing the dialectic of Nichtigkeit with the vision of the nature of faith conveyed in the life of the radical reformer, as we saw in chapter 1.

[37] Hudson's term "recursive modernism" is, perhaps, unnecessarily obscure: "refunctioning" is odd but right, it describes the process whereby the past is recovered, purged, and re-applied in the context of modernity and we shall use it freely in what follows.

or utopian field. Its composition, which is in the first instance psychological, must now be investigated; certainly cum ira et studio, with partiality for the already understood forward imagination, for the object-based Possible in psychological approaches to it. For only in the discovery of the Not-Yet-Conscious does expectation, above all positive expectation, attain its proper status: the status of a utopian function, in emotions as well as in ideas and in thoughts. (PH,113)

So, then, with passion and application Bloch sets out into the realm of Not-Yet-Conscious; his intellectual vessel is launched onto the ocean of futurity, the dimension of Noch-Nicht-Sein. Here, and consistently throughout *The Principle of Hope*, religious conceptions, albeit displaced and refunctioned, prove indispensable in sustaining Bloch's voyage towards a universality and totality that transcends the contingencies of class and purports to encapsulate human destiny itself. Confrontation with the ultimate definition of religion itself is thus finally inevitable and, we shall argue, the point of integration of Bloch's visionary philosophy as it is consummated in *The Principle of Hope*.

CHAPTER IV

THE MARCH INTO THE BLUE: THE AESTHETIC OF THE NOT-YET-CONSCIOUS

We have now reached a point of transition in Bloch's *The Principle of Hope* analogous to that in the *Critique of Pure Reason* where Kant passes beyond the extended Introduction to the Transcendental Aesthetic. Thus Bloch's preliminary outline at one level of analysis has cleared the ground and provided the intellectual paradigms for a more profound investigation into the very condition of the possibility of the inquiry itself. So Bloch directs his attention to "Not-Yet-Conscious as a New Class of Consciousness and as the Class of Consciousness of the New" (*PH* I,114) in a passage consisting largely in the phenomenological description (besides the continuing critical contextualization) of the category of anticipatory consciousness, the initial reality of which was outlined in the opening passages of volume I of *The Principle of Hope* explored in the preceding chapters.

I. THE EMANCIPATION OF THE NOT-YET-CONSCIOUS

The ponderous full title of the section in which Bloch unfolds at length the "Discovery of the Not-Yet-Conscious or of Forward Dawning"[1] (*PH* I,114) indicates nevertheless with fair precision the direction of the argument: it moves from the intimation of such consciousness into its abstracted, phenomenological foundation and then into the occasions of its occurrence and finally into an account of its manifestation. Consciousness, with which Bloch begins, is dependent upon the degree of stimulation and thus not wholly uniform. The "edges of consciousness" (*PH* I,114) are on the one hand where consciousness fades into that which is forgotten, but also, more significantly, where consciousness

---

[1]With characteristic prolixity Bloch continues: "Not-Yet-Conscious as a New Class of Consciousness and as the Class of Consciousness of the New: Youth, Time of Change, Productivity, Concept of the Utopian Foundation, its Encounter with Interest, Ideology, Archetypes, Ideals, Allegory-Symbols", (*PH*,p.114). "*Bewusstseinklasse*" is a deliberate word-play on "*Klassenbewusstsein*" as used in Lukács' work *History and Class Consciousness*. See "*Aktualitat und Utopie zu Lukács' 'Geschichte und Klassenbewusstsein'*", *GA* 10, pp. 598-620.

dawns there is also an "edge", a "threshold in consciousness" (*PH* I,115). Underlying both the edge and the threshold lies "relatively unconscious material", and "the attentive glance must first make an effort, often a painful effort to focus on it" (*PH* I,115). This material is in a sense recoverable, it is "certainly capable of being preconscious, both in the depths of the no longer perceptible and especially where new material rises which has never occurred to anyone" (*PH* I,115). The possibility of the recovery and elucidation of such material is the sine qua non of the whole subsequent argument: without the Freudian formalisation of the discovery of the unconscious Bloch's project would fail at the outset.

For Freud, however, the "preconscious" (*Vorbewusstsein*) is not "new" in Bloch's sense but the sediment deposited, as it were, at the rim of constantly receding consciousness. Freud concentrated, insofar as he wrote about the preconscious, upon its regressive and retrospective emergence out of the forgotten and the repressed materials of consciousness. There is even in Freud a further kind of unconscious that resides "in the ego itself"[2], which he grants to be the source of significant intellectual production and this will not readily fit into the repression model. Bloch focusses upon this as the source of material that is not repressed, but that which "comes up" (*ein Heraufkommendes*) (*PH* I,116). The nightdream is associated with regression and the No-Longer-Conscious, but the daydream is by contrast borne towards that which is, both as regards the subject, and the objectively new. In the daydream, the "crucial definition of a Not-Yet-Conscious reveals itself (*eröffnet sich*), as the clan to which the daydream belongs" (*PH* I,116). This is indeed sensitive ground and Bloch himself is aware of it: whereas the daydream now has a "final psychological definite feature" which can be clarified, there has, up until this point, been no such "psychology of the unconscious of the other side, of forward dawning" (*PH* I,116). Bloch presents us with such a "discovery":

> This unconscious has remained unnoticed, although it represents the actual space of receptivity of the New and the production of the New. The Not-Yet-Conscious is admittedly just as much a preconscious as is the unconscious of repressedness and forgottenness. In its way it is even an unconscious which is just as difficult and resistant as that of repressedness. Yet it is by no means subordinated to the manifest consciousness of today, but rather to the future consciousness which is only just beginning to

---

[2]Bloch's exposition of Freud's categories is detailed and illuminating, his reference to *Das Ich und das Es*" (1923) p.17, would appear to reflect a dimension analogous to Kant's noumenal ego.

come up. The Not-Yet-Conscious is thus solely the preconscious of what is to come, the psychological birthplace of the New (*PH* I,116).

This analysis is, as we have seen, to a very considerable degree dependent upon Freud, who in turn owes much (in his case wholly absorbed and unacknowledged) to the intellectual tradition Bloch has himself reviewed. What is remarkable here, however, is not a consistent development of Freud, nor even merely a partial purgation of his method (although, as we have seen it is this in part) but an *inversion* of the temporal structure of his theory of the unconscious. Whereas, analogously, Marx can be said to have turned the Hegelian dialectic on its head, Bloch has, as it were, turned Freud's scheme through 180°: we are to investigate and unfold a repressed *future*, through a consistently worked out leap of intellectual imagination. Is this, are we to suppose, more or less valid than the original Freudian scheme of the unconscious? Is it in the final account more than an intellectual sleight of hand reliant upon a logical misuse of the category of time? If wholly negative answers to these questions are accepted at this juncture then the structure of *The Principle of Hope* would appear not so much as a bridge linking the New with the Not-Yet-Conscious as a plank extended into the void of the Not-Yet. It would, in reality, be a naked exercise in intellectual projection, a thought experiment open to brutal reductive criticism.

As we saw in chapter one, the dialectical-materialist critique directed at Bloch's philosophy in the intellectual purge in East Germany is commensurate with our account: he was accused of re-idealising Marxism. Even so, this is no mere covert repristination of Hegel or Schelling because the distinction Bloch employs between the conscious and the unconscious, is, as it were, modern and not metaphysical. Yet critical assessment of *The Principle of Hope* seen in the context of Bloch's development and the wider background, has to recognise the philosophical (and, indeed, the metaphysical) issues that inform the psychological and temporal matrix of this body of thought.[3] We are obliged then, to grant *provisional* validity to Bloch's category recognising that its status is both psychologically and philosophically ques-

---

[3]One of the fascinating aspects of Bloch's work (as indeed with that of such creative theological thinkers like Karl Barth) is the mode of recovery of the tradition and its attendant transformation, through *"Umfunktionierung"* which results in a highly complex "structure" and "textuality" in their literary productions. Thus the recognition of the critical hiatus results in the involuted co-existence of pre-modern, critical, and post-modern proposals. The premature resolution of these stages of complexity through monocular, hermeneutical fundamentalism of any kind destroys the essential integrity of any such venture. See ch.10 below.

tionable, given that it is based upon the hypostatisation of the language concerned with what is *not* because it is *not yet*. Can Bloch's apparent suppression of the past in favour of the future be consistently sustained, and, if not, what might be the consequences of the re-admission of tradition, albeit represented by means of its ingestion into the unconscious? It becomes increasingly clear that these questions are underlaid by universal problems concerning the nature of truth and the representation of reality itself. Recapitulating in summary terms all these questions in a Hegelian dialect, we may ask if, in the final analysis, Bloch's *essai* is a true, or a false "mediation" (*Vermittlung*) directed at the intellectual articulation of the human condition.

Bloch's approach to the investigation of the Not-Yet-Conscious is, in the first instance, characteristically indirect. In youth, times of change and of creative expression the hidden power of the New manifests itself; the young Narodniki are prophetic figures presaging the "red dawn" of the city workers.[4] In the pre-revolutionary Russian novel, in *Sturm and Drang* and the *Vormärz* prior to the revolution of Marx 1848, Bloch sees youth and forward movement united. The effect is again cumulative rather than historical as such, Bloch is seeking to evoke an alternative way of looking at culture as latent with futurity rather than as the mere bearer of identities originating in the past. Society is heavy, premonitory, pregnant with a new order, as in the Renaissance and the transition from feudal to modern bourgeois society.[5] Bloch applies his category universally and does not limit his exposition of the New to a "good" Marxist New emerging exclusively in a messianic proletariat. The "Not-Yet-Conscious as conscious premonition" and as "Incipit vita nova ... also designated psychologically the aurora quality of the age" (*PH* I,118) also manifested itself in the then progressive entrepreneur, in individualism and in the emergence of national consciousness; the effect of these two latter was felt upon the feeling for nature and landscape and in the opening up of new continents and knowledge of the cosmos. For Bloch, Bacon's words in the *Novum Organum* sums this all up as follows: we should not fear the "faint and uncertain breeze of Hope". The anticipatory element in these representative events is apostrophised in prodigal terms:

---

[4]Needless to say Bloch takes liberties with history here in implying a uniform socialist progression. The Narodniki were an aristocratic and bourgeois student "back-to-the people" activist movement whose agitation in the 1870's foreran the later, self-consciously Marxist-proletarian revolutionary movement.

[5]Bloch, like the other Marxist revisionists, saw history in terms of a series of epochal transformations utilising a method and outlook originally derived from *The German Ideology* (1846) and other Marxian texts.

All times of change are thus filled with the Not-Yet-Conscious, even overfilled; a Not-Yet-Conscious which is caused by a rising class. The expression of this state which recaptures the experience of the Renaissance is the monologue in Goethe's Faust, here too satiety, waking dreams, dawn-red are the ingredients of the onward. (*PH* I,119)

Bloch wishes at all costs to preserve the sense of "hot dark roaming" of youth uninfected by the "putrefaction of yesterday" (*PH* I,117) and at the very core of his argument lies the phenomenon of creative work, supremely that of the genius, for: "*Intellectual productivity, creation* proves to be particularly full of Not-Yet-Conscious material, that is, of youth that potentiates itself in creative work" (*PH* I,119). Here Bloch's sympathies are indulged without restraint; he cites Goethe, Klopstock and Hölderlin at length. We select so as to transmit something of the effulgent enthusiasm Bloch injects into his text. In Goethe's *Faust*:[6]

> Then give me once again the time,
> When I was still becoming strong,

in Klopstock's ode "To Friend and Foe":

> The hot soul of the youth was thirsting
> After immortality!
> I woke, and I dreamed
> Of the bold voyage on the ocean of the future.

and in Holderlin's "At the Source of the Danube":

> ..., so the word
> Came to us out of the East/
> She comes to us
> A stranger, awakening
> The voice that shapes humanity.

Bloch brings to his readers the burgeoning, compulsive energy of the German Romantic quest for new life in which "*youth, time of change,*

---

[6]Parallel with Bloch's transformatory recovery of Hegel's *Phenomenology of Mind* and of "religion" and the partially de-mythologised conception of future-orientated existence is his treatment of Goethe's *Faust* as the cultural world-conquering human ideal that is, however problematically, synthesised with a Marxist basis for its realisation. See chs. 8 and 9 below.

productivity simultaneously coincide in talents which get off to a felic-
itous start" (*PH* I,121-2). Above all it is in the colossal creativity of
Goethe, the "vast intention-dimension" of the Prometheus fragment,[7]
Faust (and even *Urfaust*), besides the later *Wilhelm Meister*,[8] that
mastery of the future, the translation of prospect and expectation into
reality has taken place in a "first crossing of the water" (Dante). The
intensely Germanic quality of Bloch's treatment of the perception and
realisation of the anticipatory consciousness of the New is striking and
unambiguous. This national cultural impulse is further reinforced when
the nature of its productivity is clarified. Bloch's account of creativity
has to be understood not only in the Romantic context, but also in relation to the discussion of "work" (*Arbeit*) within Marxism and thus as
part of Marx's critique of Hegel.[9]

Bloch's approach to the question of productivity (*Produktivität*) is
uninhibited, the great unrest (*Unruhe*) associated with formal dream-
ing is:

> An active unrest, with its new origin opposed to rigidity, de-
> veloping full of premonition. Even in the unusual form in which
> it appears, this premonition is the feeling for what is on its
> way. When it becomes creative, it combines with imagination,
> particularly with that of the objectively Possible. This premo-
> nition with its potential for work is intellectual productivity,
> understood here as *work-forming*. (*PH* I,122)

The presentation of intellectual productivity as "work-forming"
(*werk-bildend*) contains an oblique challenge both to the Marxian (and
Marxist) conception of "work" (i.e. *Arbeit*) in the material, industrial
context, and to the merely abstract intellectual activity (*Tätigkeit*) of

---

[7]The Prometheus motif is a recurrent motif in the evolution of the German spirit from
Romanticism through to the "Left-wing" Hegelians. Whereas, however, Marx put a
negative stress on Prometheus' words "I hate all the gods" in Aeschylus' text, Bloch returns to the self-assertiveness of Romanticism. For Marx's use see the doctoral dissertation of 1841, *Differenz der demokratischen und epikureischen Naturphilosophie*, Karl
Marx - Fredrich Engels *Werke* (East Berlin: Dietz Verlag, 1977), *Ergänzungsband* I, p.262.

[8]There is no full-length study of the relation of Bloch to Goethe. The background is
explored with unrivalled largesse in Hans Urs von Balthasar's *Prometheus Studien zu
Geschichte der deutschen Idealismus* (Heidelberg: F.H. Kerle, 1947), see esp. pp.407-514
devoted to Goethe. This provocative study, originally published under the title *Apokalypse der deutschen Seele* in 1937 is an indispensable, even if diffusely-written, source for
the comprehension of the displacements of aesthetic, eschatological and religious ideas
in German Romanticism. This book awaits "reception" in the Anglo-Saxon world.

[9]See, for example, Reinhold Grimm, *Arbeit als Thema in der deutschen Literatur vom
Mittelatter bis zur Gegenwart* (Königstein: Athenäum, 1979) and in relation to Marx,
Helmut Klages, *Technischer Humanismus, Philosophie und Soziologie der Arbeit bei
Marx* (Stuttgart, 1964).

Hegel. Bloch, by his direct appeal to, and restatement of, the Romantic theory of creativity[10] cannot but be seen as putting himself into a state of conflict with Marx whose emphasis (along with later Marxist thinkers) upon the causal role of material relations and the reductive implications of the theories of alienation and objectification (*Verdinglichung*) was such as to neglect and even denigrate the act of individual creation and self-sacrifice.

Bloch conceives of three stages in the process of creative production: "incubation" (*Inkubation*), "so-called inspiration" (*Inspiration*) and "explication" (*Explikation*) (*PH* I,122). Thus first in "incubation" an intense propensity informs our as yet unfulfilled interaction; we are in unresolved contradiction, we are not yet what we would be. This is followed, second, by abrupt clarification termed (misleadingly according to Bloch) "inspiration"; creation seems to come from outside or above. Here Bloch directly confronts the question of transcendence which, in accordance with his consistent (but as yet unstated) materialism, he is bound to reformulate in terms compatible with his vision:

> The productive creator is no showman, nor is he a psychological relic from primeval times; he is neither a sooty flame from the abyss, but nor is he, no matter what Nietzsche may coquettishly have wished to remind us, a mouthpiece of higher powers. The transcendental mythicization of inspiration, as if it descended from above, really is without substance; it is superior to the magic-archaic version only in so far as it does at least attempt to do justice to the transcendence, that is: that is the surpassing expanding element in intellectual creation, and does not distort this creation into a sinking down, into a language of the night. (*PH* I,123)

Having, as we have seen at some length, put a strict limit upon the past as the source of anticipatory hope and its practical correlate, productivity, Bloch now closes off the possibility of ascribing creativity to a transcendent represented in terms of myth. The justification for this comes in a specific allusion to Descartes, whose "discovery" of the principle of the *cogito ergo sum* was an experience of paradigmatic lucidity undergone at an exceptional highpoint of consciousness. Over against such superstition Bloch posits an interaction between individual and context:

---

[10]The whole Romantic discussion of creativity and imagination is of relevance here. See, for example, M.H. Abrams, *Natural Supernaturalism: Tradition and Revolution in Romantic Literature* (New York: W.W. Norton, 1971), chs. 3 and 4.

The kindling place of inspiration lies in the *meeting* of a specific content which has become ripe for expression, forming and execution. Not only the subjective, but also the objective conditions for the expression of a Novum must therefore be ready, must be ripe, so that this Novum can break through out of mere incubation and suddenly gain insight into itself. And these conditions are always socio-economic and of a progressive kind: without the capitalist mandate, the subjective mandate towards cogito ergo sum would never have found its inspiration; without an incipient proletarian mandate, the discovery of the materialist dialectic would have been impossible or would have remained merely a brewing apercu, and neither would it have struck like lightning into the no longer naive popular soil. (*PH* I,124)

It is thus the genius who (Bloch here cites the Hegelian Karl Rosenkranz) "accomplishes what is objectively necessary in a particular sphere" (*PH* I,125); thus Marx, "began to accomplish the objectively necessary in a particular sphere as his individual destiny, and who experienced the inspirational breakthrough of his work as no other could in fully grasped concurrence with the socio-historical tendency of his time" (*PH* I,125). This heroic conception of genius[11] is generalised in the following terms which leave us in no doubt as to Bloch's estimate:

Thus inspiration as a whole, whenever it is work-forming, emerges from the meeting (*Zusammenkunft*) of subject and object, from the meeting of its tendency with the objective tendency of the time, and is the flash with which this concordance begins. (*PH* I,125)

In the third, final stage of the act of production the "agonising, blissful work" of "explication" takes place. Genius may, as Bloch indicates, be hard work,[12] but it should in a relentless (yet lively) way translate vision (*Vision*) into work (*Werk*). Bloch's wholehearted appropriation of, and dependence upon a heroic Romantic aesthetic is virtually unqualified as he proceeds to build upon the distinction drawn by Schopenhauer:

---

[11]The German discussion of the nature of genius is likewise here relevant, see Jochen Schmidt, *Die Geschichte des Genie-Gedankens in der deutschen Literatur, Philosophie und Politik 1750-1945* (Darmstadt: WBG 1985) Vol.II for a comprehensive presentation.

[12]"Genius ist Fleiß", pp.141-2.

Talent resembles a marksman who hits a target which others cannot reach; genius resembles one who hits a target so far away they are not even able to see it. (cited *PH* I,126)

The genius as "pioneer on the borders of an advancing world" (*PH* I,126) has, in psychological terms, a peculiar sensitivity to the Not-Yet-Conscious, besides the energy to project and explicate it and an enhanced sensitivity to change in the temporal and material process. Bloch's approval of Carlyle's conception of the "spiritual hero"[13] is consistent with this. There is no touch of ironic self-distancing in Bloch's conception and, given the nature of his project, it is scarcely possible to resist an implied identification of his own efforts with the ideal he represents. Bloch recapitulates the position towards which he has worked, indicating that the anticipatory consciousness is crystallised in the Not-Yet-Conscious; thus:

the Not-Yet-Conscious as a whole is the psychological representation of the Not-Yet-Become in an age and its world, on the Front of the World. The making conscious of the Not-Yet-Conscious, the forming of the Not-Yet-Become, exists only in this space, a space of concrete anticipation, only here is the volcano of productivity to be found pouring out its fire. Mastery in the work of genius, a mastery which is foreign to what has normally become, is also comprehensible only as a phenomenon of the Novum. Every great work of art thus still remains, except for its manifest character, impelled towards the latency of the other side, i.e. towards the contents of a future which had not yet appeared in its own time, if not towards the contents of an as yet unknown final state.(*PH* I,127)

Such works as *The Magic Flute* or the *Iliad* are both such great works, historically localised and yet possessing "eternal youth". Productivity on the Front, emerging from the depths, yet at the peak of consciousness, is driven into the "blue", the colour of distance and the symbol of creative emancipation. We are now in a highly-charged intellectual environment which for the average, even the informed Anglo-Saxon reader, is both alien and intoxicating. This is a theory of the

[13]"It is ever the way with the Thinker, the spiritual Hero. What he says all men are not far from saying, were longing to say. The Thoughts of all start up, as from painful enchanted sleep, round his Thought; answering to it, Yes, even so!", *Heroes, Hero-Worship and the Heroic in History*. It is, of course, no accident that Carlyle was much influenced by German thought.

creative act in terms of which the human agenda ought to be rewritten and undergo revolutionary enactment.

II. RESISTANCE

It is not surprising that Bloch, having appropriated the psycho-analytical model of the unconscious in temporarily inverted form, and given his need to "discover" the Not-Yet-Conscious is now ready to assimilate and refunction a further feature of Freud's scheme, that is, "resistance" (*Widerstand*). Resistance to the Not-Yet-Conscious is different from that directed at the No-Longer-Conscious; the former is not a neurotic resistance, but arises "only when a discrepancy between power and will arises in the willingness to produce" (*PH* I,128), although, as Bloch notes, such a discrepancy can give rise to acute suffering. The transposition of the psycho-analytical model needs to be assessed with care because its present field of operation is not merely the temporally reversed sphere of the subconscious and its emergence but also the act of imaginative creation. To what degree and in what precise way the status of the model as a mode of explanation changes under the condition of assimilation is a matter of some importance, and the *difference* becomes stark once Bloch moves from explanation of the preconscious to that of resistance. The subject which produces does not, according to Bloch, experience resistance in himself to the will towards the Not-Yet-Conscious and its contents, whereas the recipients of his work and their blocked receptivity do; they exemplify the "resistance of the uncomprehending world" (*PH* I,129). This involves a decisive modification of the Freudian model in that the resistance whilst in the intractable recipient is also ascribed to the nature of the Novum itself. Here Bloch passes beyond normally accepted bounds of sense and treats the Novum, the hypostatised future, latent in the Not-Yet-Conscious, as a dimension of understanding open to analysis:

> But the psychology of producing itself reveals no sign of inner resistance to the acts of illumination under discussion here; instead, the resistance which belongs to production and is endemic to it is not present in the human subject at all. It is to be found instead in the matter treated by the subject and is only mirrored by the specific details of explication. It is to be found in the hazardous straights of the Novum, in the still inchoate, utterly habit-free character of the *new material*. (*PH* I,129)

The exemption of the heroic "producer" from resistance and the displacement of resistance exclusively onto the receiver of the work and to the intrinsic character of the Novum itself obliges Bloch to explain at some length how the resentment against the New arises. The real reasons for resistance (and the consequent psychological resentment - *Ressentiment*)[14] lie "exclusively in the terrain of the matter, itself a terrain which is not yet enclosed, let alone rounded off" (*PH*, I,129-30). Bloch's explanation of the guardianship of the New against its production is *not*, however, in the first instance in terms of the "matter" (*Sache*) of the New itself but in the "material" (*Material*), the historical context of the appearance of the New.[15] The important passage that follows (*PH* I, pp.130-1) contains clear indication of how Bloch conceives of the interaction between the temporal onset of the New (and the nature of its "matter" or *Sache*) and the socio-historical blockage, more specifically the "socio-economic barrier to vision" (*ökonomisch-soziale Blickschranke*) unscaleable by even the most daring mind. There is a level beyond which no researcher, however able, may go because of the "social barrier" (*gesellschaftliche Schranke*) that confronts all such efforts. The resistance implicit in the wisdom of Minerva is caused by social and historical limitations; thus:

> No Greek mathematician would have understood differential calculus, not even Zeno, close though he came to it. The infinitesimal, the variable quantity, lay totally beneath the horizon of Greek society; only capitalism caused what was previously fixed and finite to enter such a state of flux that rest could be conceived as infinitesimal movement, and non-static notions of quantity conceived at all. (*PH* I,130)

Whether this historiographical remark is in fact true does not immediately concern us,[16] it is important to note that Bloch once more

[14]The use of the word *"Ressentiment"* indicates another dimension of Bloch's qualified recovery of Nietzsche. See Walter Kaufmann, *Nietzsche Philosopher, Psychologist, Antichrist* (Princeton: Princeton University Press, 1974) pp.371-8, and the references indicated in K. Schlechta, *Nietzsche - Index* (Munich: Hanser Verlag, 1965).

[15]At this point Bloch plays off the "matter" (*Sache*) against "material" (*Material*). Unfortunately the translators' footnote relating to this distinction does not appear until *PH* I, p.225 but it is relevant to pp.129-130. Bloch's juxtaposition of "matter" and "material" bears a strong resemblance to an idealist distinction of "reality" and "appearance" now refunctioned within a forward-orientated, temporal, rather than a present-structured ontological scheme. It is central to our understanding and critique of Bloch's thought-experiment that temporal categories cannot be used thus without ontological consequences.

[16]The postulation of direct socio-economic determinants in the evolution of mathematics, is the product of the inexact science of *Ideologiekritik* and one of the more problematic aspects of the history of ideas as informed by Marxist insight. See, for example, A. Koyré, *From Closed World to Infinite Universe* (New York, 1958) for a classic historical account without ideological bias.

conveniently uses his Marxist polemic so as to exculpate, in this case, the subjects that "resist" the Not-Yet-Conscious. It is, in effect, a secularised re-working of historical causality in which the socio-economic course of history governs, limits (and indeed provokes) the growth of consciousness and knowledge. Bloch goes on to argue (again on Marxian precedent) that the notion of work was alien to Greek, slave-owning society and thus did not feature in their epistemology. "History has its timetable" (*PH* I,130) and this limits the intention and execution of works within its epochs. This boundedness is based on the state of the *material*, whereas the *matter* enjoys (and this word can be imposed upon Bloch here without misrepresentation) a form of transcendence immanent within the socio-historical matrix:

> The thing which ultimately determines the productivity-re-sistance remains the hazardous straits of the matter itself, remains the sealedness, clearing only sparingly, of the Novum in the overall process, which proceeds as world. The by no means fundamental, but rather historically temporary resistance in this is still noted even where it is claimed that it has been overcome, namely through courage. (*PH* I,130-131)

Bloch appeals in a not wholly convincing way to Hegel in support of a conception of knowledge that renders itself in the "nature of hard work sharpened by the very difficulty of the resistance" (*PH* I,131) but which is at the same time to be conceived in materialist terms tinged with the limited, consciousness-based transcendence of a pregnant futurity. For the first time in *The Principle of Hope* a refunctioning of materialism itself becomes apparent; without the admission of the latency of matter the whole structure would lack a rational dynamic capable of sustaining it. The fulness in the process may resist, but it is not a world-mystery lying in a "kind of cosmo-analytic rubbish pit", but a reality that is to be sealed in a "Not-Yet-Appearance of itself" (*Noch-Nicht-Erscheinung*);[17] Hegelian tools are used to produce a "work" restructured from the standpoint of time and being.

Bloch now once more traces the history of the identification of unconscious processes from Leibniz' "*petites perceptions insensibles*" through the *Sturm und Drang* movement into Romanticism and thus to J.G. Hamann and the intimidating imagination of Jean Paul. Romanti-

---

[17]The presentation of a latent future in these terms depend simplicitly upon the capacity of the German language to represent truth in terms of self-revealing virtuality. Thus, for example, Heidegger's essay, *Vom Wesen der Wahrheit* (Frankfurt am Main, 1943) provides a formal presentation of these possibilities.

cism, as the precursor of psycho-analysis, elevated *anamnesis*[18] over and above the vision of the utopian condition despite the movement's pretence to innovation. Thus seduced, the Not-Yet-Conscious was betrayed by Romanticism and further impeded by the ascendant bourgeoisie in triumphant capitalism, a class for whom "coming events merely cast their *shadow*, nothing but shadow" (*PH* I,137). The wilful contemporary hostility of the bourgeoisie toward the future is now attributed to an awareness that capitalist society senses itself negated by its own possibilities; thus psycho-analysis was devised to manage the retrospective mechanism of repression that developed in a superannuated class subsisting in a society without a future. Bloch, as before, launches himself in rich polemic when encountering Freud, and yet riper diatribe when directed at Jung. The exaggeration of the libido of "these parasites" and their dreams given by "the Lord, now called Eros" (*PH* I,137), compounded by the anxiety and resignation of the bourgeoisie lead to the wholly regressive, repression model of the unconscious; so, Bloch maintains:

> The barrier in front of the Novum in the great progressive work of Leibniz becomes a guillotine for the Novum in the final bourgeois psychology of the unconscious. (*PH* I,138)

This pungent yet somewhat opaque statement summarises Bloch's negative response to the practicality of using psycho-analysis as the jumping-off point for the rehabilitation of resisted anticipatory consciousness, despite his own carefully constructed categorical reworking of the unconscious as the preconscious of the Not-Yet-Conscious. This results in a further change of level in the argument: a shift from the explicit psychological explanation of the phenomenon of the Not-Yet-Conscious to the philosophical and quasi-metaphysical explanation of its active dimension, the utopian function. Thus the failure of the bourgeoisie is not to be put down entirely to its misappropriation of the category of the unconscious inherited from Romanticism, but to the "continuing spell of static living and thinking" (*PH* I,139). The formal expression of the expanding daydream, registered in the unconscious but developed philosophically by Marx, Campanella, Bacon and Fichte, lacked a psychological basis and epistemology capable of explaining

[18]Bloch's presentation of the struggle within Romanticism between "anamnesis", recourse to memory, albeit suppressed on the one hand and a utopian, Promethean future-orientated intentionality, on the other, is brilliant but somewhat impressionistic. For a detailed contextually-related and theoretical study of the "inwardness" of the Romantic epoch see P. Sprengel, *Innerlichkeit Jean Paul oder das Leiden an der Gesellschaft* (Munich: Carl Hanser, 1977) written specifically as a reply to Wolfgang Harich's book on Jean Paul.

its possible-real place in the world. The continued intellectual life of
the "concept of a pre-ordained, ultimately finished world (ordo sem-
piternus rerum)" was the anachronistic continuation of "feudal statics"
that "inhibited the concept of newness" (*PH* I,139) in Leibniz and even
Hegel.[19] Ultimately it is Plato's theory of knowledge grounded in
anamnesis, a "re-remembering of something seen before" (*PH* I,140)
that, through its repeated reproduction succeeds (even in the case of
Hegel) in stifling access to the Not-Yet-Being.[20] Even Bergson's vitalist
philosophy is "impressionistic", and "liberal-anarchistic, not anticipatory" (*PH* I,140) because it is caught in a formula of infinite repetition rather than a venturing beyond.[21] Consequently, Bloch maintains
that in comprehensive terms:

> A vast mental realm of the Not-Yet-Conscious, one that is con-
> stantly travelled, has so far remained undiscovered, or its dis-
> coveries have remained unnoticed. Similarly, a vast realm of
> the Not-Yet-Become, which form the corelate of the Not-Yet-
> Conscious, remained stationary, and the closely related real
> categories: Front, Novum, Objective Possibility, which are
> inaccessible to anamnesis, remained without a theory of cate-
> gories in the world before Marx.(*PH* I,141)

It is this purported ultimacy of the work of Marx, the creation of
categories that emancipate the Not-Yet-Conscious and its practical enactment, which Bloch regards as an epochal historical turning-point in
the aftermath of exhausted, ultimately reactionary Romanticism. Thus
it is that affirmation of "experience of the modern age, as a positive
age"[22] is now possible because it is only this present age that possesses

[19]See R.H. Roberts "The Reception of Hegel's Parable of the Lord and Bondsman",
loc.cit., which confirms Bloch's representation of the *Phenomenology of Mind* as a key
work in the evolution of nineteenth century thought embodying in an unresolved, dialectical textuality many aspects of the conflict of pre-critical ambiguity with critical modernity and its consequences.

[20]Whether this is a fair or adequate interpretation of Hegel is open to question.
Bloch's presentation of Hegel in *Subjekt-Objekt GA*, 8, pp.473-488, and the last volume of
the posthumously-published *Leipziger Vorlesungen* vol, 4, pp.337-352, contains more
measured justification.

[21]Bergson is truly a *bête-noire* for Bloch, this is probably because the *affinities* between their views are so close that an equally sharp *differentiation* is required in order to
avoid any danger of a superficial identification. Both, notably, work under the influence
of Nietzsche; at issue is the interpretation of the basis of vitalism.

[22]Hans Blumenberg's *The Legitimacy of the Modern Age* (Cambridge, Mass: MIT, 1985)
provides an important and illuminating parallel to Bloch's positive estimation of
modernity, without the latter's attempted re-mythologisation of human experience. This
discussion continues in Jurgen Habermas's *The Philosophical Discourse of Modernity*
(Cambridge, Mass: MIT Press, 1987).

the "socio-economic prerequisites for a theory of the Not-Yet-Conscious and whatever is related to it in the Not-Yet-Become of the world" (*PH* I,141). It is therefore Marxism that initiates for the first time an epistemology not dependent upon the past, that is upon the "Becomeness" (*Gewordenheit*) of the world. Whereas Romanticism failed to understand utopia, Marxism accorded it a definitive status and "rescued the rational core of utopia and made it concrete as well as the core of still idealist tendency-dialectics" (*PH* I,141). So Bloch has freed himself for an extended discussion of the utopian function: Romanticism provided the key to the subject but Marxism has so exposed and conceived the socio-historical conditions of the object (and thus of the subject as object) that when subject and object coincide in the illuminative tension of anticipatory consciousness, there then opens up the utopian function and the idea-into-reality of the Novum. This is a central feature of Bloch's *revision* of Marxism in the light of the utopian principle and it requires immediate defence and consolidation if it is not to succumb in principle to Marx's own attacks upon utopian socialism.[23]

III. THE APPLICATION OF THE UTOPIAN FUNCTION: THE REBIRTH OF ALLEGORY

How is mere wishful thinking to be avoided? For Bloch the Heideggerian act of self-projection proclaims its own impotence; it is exclusively in the purported power and truth of Marxism that the cloud-castle in our dreams has, as it were, been driven forward and strengthened with concreteness. In this the present context the "utopian function is ... the only transcendent one which has remained, and the only one which has deserved to remain: the only one which is transcendent without transcendence" (*PH* I,146); at its root is the Ratio of militant optimism. It was Marx's achievement to open up and delineate the Novum, in sum:

> the *act-content* of hope is, as a consciously illuminated, knowingly elucidated content, the *positive utopian function*; the *historical content* first represented in ideas, encyclopaedically explored in real judgements, is *human culture referred to its concrete-utopian horizon*. (*PH* I,146)

---

[23]Bloch again risks running counter to the received wisdom of the Marxist tradition's negative view of "utopian socialism" as classically represented in the *Communist Manifesto* and Engels's *Socialism: Utopian and Scientific*.

That this might in fact be a revision of and no mere development of Marxism is a difficulty that Bloch must later confront. Here Bloch proceeds to set his conception of the utopian function against the development of the transcendental ego in German Idealism and, following this, to relate the question of ideology to ideals, archetypes, symbols, allegory and symbols. Bloch accepts outright Marx's designation of ideologies as the ruling ideas of each age yet he sees ideology as penetrable by the utopian function. Indeed without the latter function, the "spiritual surplus" that goes beyond static normality and provokes change would be inconceivable. Even within the "selfish system" of Adam Smith's political economy and its handling of interest (and the coincidence of conflicting interests) the utopian strand is evident, despite the phenomenona of "false consciousness" Bloch does not therefore appear to share the Manichee-like and near apocalyptic dualism between historical evil and revolutionary emancipation characteristic of Marx, who denigrated all convictions lying outside his own definition of social and historical truth. On the contrary, Bloch, consistent with his position outlined earlier, detects traces of the utopian function (as indeed anticipatory consciousness) in every area of the human condition. Bloch's drive towards universality once more triumphs over the limitations and pre-commitments of Marx himself. The detailed discussion of ideology (PH I,153ff.) is finely-wrought and informative; Bloch takes as his starting-point Marx'statement made in a letter to Arnold Ruge in 1843:

> Our matter must therefore be: reform of consciousness not through dogmas, but through analysis of mystical consciousness which is still unclear in itself. It will then become apparent that the world has long possessed the dream of the matter, of which it must only possess the consciousness in order to possess it in reality. It will become apparent that it is not a question of a great thought-dash between past and future, but of the *carrying-through* of the thoughts of the past. (PH I,156)

This passage admirably prefigures Bloch's approach,[24] whilst at the same time indicating that the "dream" is always the future qualified by the past, interpreted here so as specifically to preserve the worth-

---

[24]Again it is impossible to escape the impression that Bloch has to represent Marx's thought in terms of its periphery as distinct from its central thrust when it comes to the question of "mystical consciousness". It is unsurprising when Jameson, op.cit., p.116 cites the same letter in a different translation - Bloch himself offers little other textual evidence apart, as we shall see, from the *Theses on Feuerbach*.

while past in the cultural inheritance mediated through texts and artifacts:

> Even the class ideologies, within which the great works of the past lie, lead precisely to that surplus over and above the false consciousness bound to its position, the surplus which is called continuing culture, and is therefore a substratum of the claimable cultural inheritance.(PH I,156)

It is the utopian function which not only produces the "surplus" that constitutes culture over and above "false consciousness" but also endows ideology with its capacity to permit the premature harmonization of social contradictions.[25] Thus the surplus (*Überschuss*), a sort of *donum superadditum* over and above mere ideology, stems from the utopian function, and this constitutes the "substratum" (*Substrat*) of cultural inheritance (PH I,157) towards which it was Bloch's life-work to direct attention. As a result of his perception of the anticipatory utopian function as a universal category, Bloch's attitude to the cultural inheritance is far more positive than that of Marx in the nineteenth century or, in his own generation, of those members of the Frankfurt School, most notably T.W. Adorno, whose participation in the "lament over reification" and whose theory of the total alienation implicit in "objectification" (*Verdinglichung*)[26] generated an intensely paradoxical attitude towards the cultural inheritance. Thus, whereas Bloch argues that there is a "spirit of utopia in the final predicate of every great statement, in Strasbourg cathedral and in the Divine Comedy, in the expectant music of Beethoven and in the latencies of the Mass in B minor (i.e. by Bach)" (PH I,158), Adorno wrote in somewhat sour tones of Beethoven's *Missa Solemnis* as an "alienated masterpiece".[27] Bloch's images are telling when he asserts that,

---

[25]Bloch would here appear to be drawing upon Lukács' conception of ideology as "false consciousness" (*falsches Bewusstsein*) that endows ideology with the capacity to resolve conflict prematurely. See Edgar Thaidigsmann, *Falsche Versöhnung Religion und Ideologiekritik beim jungen Marx* (Munich: Kaiser, 1978) for an account of the origins of these conceptions in the thought of the early Marx.

[26]Both Bloch and Adorno recognise the obfuscation of reality that results from "reification"; Bloch is essentially an optimist, Adorno a pessimist when it comes down to the question of transforming reality rather than constructing a response in terms of the patient suffering of the burden of alienation in "hibernation". See Gillian Rose, *The Melancholy Science*, loc.cit., for insight into Adorno's strategy.

[27]See T.W. Adorno, "Missa Solemnis: an alienated masterpiece", *Telos*, 28, 1976, pp.121 ff. This is but an aside, there is a complex history associated with the three volumes of Adorno's music-theoretical writings in the collected works.

It is in this despair which still contains an unum necessarium
even as something lost, and in the Hymn to Joy. Kyrie and
Credo rise in the concept of utopia as that of comprehended
hope (*der begriffenen Hoffnung*) in a completely different way,
even unless the reflection of mere time-bound ideology has been
shed, precisely then. The exact imagination of the Not-Yet-
Conscious thus completes the critical enlightenment itself, by
revealing the gold that was not affected by aqua fortis, and the
good content which remain most valid, indeed rises when class
illusion, class ideology have been destroyed. (*PH* I,158)

It is inconceivable that Marx could have written in such affirma-
tory (even if qualified) terms about these cultural artifacts, that is on
the basis of their bearing a utopian universality transcending class origin and ideology. The utopian function is thus a mighty instrument capable not only, on the one hand, of bringing great and true culture out of
a class-based tradition but, on the other, it also contains and negates
the extremity of the dismissive Marxist reduction of any given cultural
artifact to its class basis.

Having come to a reckoning with "interest" and "ideology", Bloch
now turns in the concluding passages of this consideration of the utopian
function to "archetypes", "ideals" and "allegory-symbols" and it is
here that inspired eclecticism enjoys almost unfettered exercise within
the limits dictated by immense erudition. So from Goethe's Helen in
Faust, from Plato, Romanticism and (even) from the work of the "arch-
reactionary" C.G. Jung, Bloch gathers materials which he distinguishes not in terms of what they refer to, but, using the early categori-
sations of Bachofen and Creuzer, selects once more in terms of the
utopian principle. Thus Bloch maintains that Romanticism showed
that "despite their original Augustinian consonance with prototypes in
the sense of Platonic Ideas, archetypes have little or nothing in common
with these and their pure, ultimately even transcendental idealism"
(*PH* I,161).

Bloch takes a step further away from Marx when he argues that
archetypes held back in the repressive form are even more dangerous
than ideology when they divert attention away from the open future.
Indeed "expired feudal archetypes" exerted a perverse influence upon
Romanticism and turned it in a reactionary direction. Employing what
now amounts to the full utopian hermeneutical principle Bloch teases
out the material that has an "elective affinity" (*Wahlverwandte*)[28]

---

[28]Once more Bloch's reworking of a motif from Goethe is apparent in his use of the
highly suggestive literary trope of "elective affinity", drawn from the title of Goethe's
programmatic novel, *Wahlverwandtschaften*.

with it. Such material is "extra-territorial" (*extraterritorial*);[29] it is recoverable as "undischarged" (*unabgegoltenen*) utopian elements to be distinguished from the rotten archetypes. The healthy, utopian tending archetypes can be regarded as a "new point of logic, to the categorical table of the imagination" (*PH* I,162).[30] Into this category of the utopian imagination fall the archetypes of the Lord of Cockaigne, the fight with the dragon[31] (St. George, Apollo, Siegfried, St. Michael), the master demon riding out to kill the sun (Fenriswolf, Pharoah, Herod, Gessler), the release of the virgin (Perseus and Andromeda) and the theme of a dragon-land (Egypt, Canaan, the kingdom of Antichrist before the beginning of the New Jerusalem). Bloch has an especially high regard for Beethoven's *Fidelio* and for the modern archetype of dancing in the ruins of the Bastille. Even archaic archetypes are capable of a utopian "refunctioning" (*Umfunktionierung*) that can liberate archetypally encapsulated hope, here again the example is operatic, Mozart's *Magic Flute*. The utopian function not only discovers its own "cultural surplus" but, more profoundly, may fetch "back from the double-edged archetypal depths an element of itself, an archaically stored anticipation of still Not-Yet-Conscious, Not-Yet-Achieved Material (*PH* I,164). In other words an archetype can be brought to life, this time dialectically, once the utopian function *refunctions* its lost or suppressed utopian and progressive side.

In a similar and parallel manner Bloch rehabilitates "ideals" in the way prescribed by the utopian principle now allegedly earthed in Marxism. The doctrines of the "ideals" in Freud, Kant, Hegel, Schopenhauer, Grisebach, and their subversion in Ibsen are all reviewed. The later, degenerate presentation of ideals can be demysti-

---

[29]One of the few writers working in English who has openly drawn Bloch's ideas into his perspective is George Steiner, whose collection, *Extraterritorial, Papers on Literature and the Language of Revolution* (London, 1968), is explicitly indebted: "It will take a long time before the revolutionary structure of Ernst Bloch's *Das Prinzip Hoffnung*, which is part epic voyage, part imaginary memoir, part ontological treatise, and language experiment throughout, will have been grasped, let alone exploited", pp.168-769.

[30]Bloch's postulation of a "categorial table of the imagination" puts him squarely in the tradition of post-Kantian thinkers who attempt to rehabilitate a dimension of human existence unreduced within Kant's first *Critique* and use it as the basis of categorial reconstruction. Here we distinguish our position from that of Fredric Jameson who emphasises the formal disjunction between Bloch's literary method and that of the great idealists. It is our contention that Bloch retains the structure of transcendental analysis, albeit overlaid by deconstructive unfinishedness. See *Marxism and Form* pp. 158 ff.

[31]There is a truly remarkable parallel here between Bloch's remythologisation of his future-orientated phenomenology and the Swiss theologian Fritz Buri's *Dogmatik als Selbstverständnis des christlichen Glaubens* (Bern: Paul Haupt, 1978), see vol.3, pp.457-576, "*Die Zukunft der Antwortung*". Both Bloch and Buri begin with the failure of the Parousia and reactivate eschatological futurity as the primal dimension of human existence.

fied on the basis of mere critical realism, "no research into ideology, let alone utopian function is necessary (*PH* I,171). The powerlessness of ideals, especially in Luther's Germany, is manifest, but inasmuch as an ideal contains "intended perfection" it then becomes accessible to utopian treatment and, indeed, to the testing implicit in material mediation:

> The lonely island where Utopia supposedly lies may be an archetype, but more strongly at work within it are the ideal form of perfection which is striven for, as either free or ordered development of the content of life. Utopian function therefore has to prove itself through the ideal basically along the same lines as through utopias themselves: along the lines of concrete mediation with material ideal-tendency. (*PH* I,173)

So Bloch concludes that the Marxian anathema against ideals (as expressions of mere bourgeois class interest) applies only to abstractly-originated rather the concrete-tending goals. Supreme amongst the latter is, of course, the highest good of a classless society embodied in socialism, which is itself a concrete ideal.

Lastly, Bloch turns to the allegory-symbols which also deserve recovery. Inspired by Goethe's literary metaphor, "poems are painted windowpanes", Bloch argues against the Romantic devaluation of allegory as an artificial and undesirable distancing from immediate experience. On the contrary, allegory at its height was no mere "Allegory decoration of abstractions but the attempt to convey a thing-meaning through other thing-meanings'" (*PH* I,175), that is on the basis of coordinated archetypes. Bloch offers readings of texts, here drawn from Goethe, in which allegory and symbol are reinterpreted in the light of the universal utopian function. Rather than reading such literary material as shot through with a quasi-idealist distinction between image and idea in a dualistic Platonic sense, Bloch interprets along the temporal axis:[32]

> Thus this cipher also exists in reality; not merely in allegorical and symbolic designation of this reality: and such real-ciphers exist precisely *because the world-process itself is a utopian function, with the matter of the objectively Possible as its substance.* (*PH* I,177)

---

[32]The recovery and reworking of the idea of reality as "cipher" owes much to Bloch's relationship with Walter Benjamin, see *Über Walter Benjamin* (Frankfurt am Main: Suhrkamp, 1968), pp.17ff. and S. Markun, op.cit., p.33.

Longing, anticipation, distance, and hiddenness, all elements in the utopian function determine the allegorical-symbolic dimension, they point to the great "public mystery" it is Bloch's initial task to unearth, and by exposure in the congruent socio-historical conditions, his goal to realise. Through the relentless application of the utopian function Bloch works towards a positive appropriation of *all* the dimensions of concrete anticipatory consciousness. The utopian function serves as a "principle of significance", a touchstone that once more draws out the future-promising gold out of the static and regressive mythological dross. Without doubt Bloch has here enlarged the sensibility of modernity and widened the perceptions of "narrow-gauge" Marxism.

Having rehabilitated archetypes, ideals and allegory Bloch then looks for the "utopian image trace" (*utopischer Bildrest*) in the "surplus" that has become culture. In a way analogous to the "vestigia trinitatis" that Augustine found in the constitution of the human and in the form of the cosmos, Bloch searches for the utopian image in the cultural representations of human sensibility that he wishes to recover and safeguard for a positive Marxist posterity. This is an important passage in that it contains the first extended references to the religious influence upon the emergence of modernity as Bloch is to appropriate and interpret it. The supplementary discussion begins with a sensitive analysis of the often disappointing relationship between the dream and its fulfilment. Thus from Stendhal (who advocated immediate possession of a woman and satisfaction of desire without intrusion of imagination as the guarantee of happiness) and the Romantics (who were reluctant to allow their exalted images of femininity to relapse into actual sexual experience) Bloch builds up the contrast between the ideal, idolized objective imagination and the mundane "row over a smashed soup-dish" (E.T.A. Hoffman) that attends the dream as it were desecrated by reality. Out of this primarily Romantic dilemma between the retention of dream and the risk of sexual fiasco and disappointment, Bloch builds a further element of his philosophical anthropology. Interestingly, in Kierkegaard and his rejection of his fiancee Regine Olsen, Bloch finds not merely a corresponding expression of the Romantic refusal of the actual but the extreme representation of the ancestral, Platonised Christian ideal, "not only is the unconditional present of love very difficult to attain, but also, wholly in keeping, that of Christian imitation, Christian love: There have been no Christians since the days of the Apostles'" (*PH* I,182).[33] This cultiva-

---

[33]The contemporary dilemmas of Christianity were represented, so far as the Marxist revisionists were concerned, primarily by Kierkegaard's analytic of Christian existence. Further to this see Bloch's *Leipziger Vorlesungen* vol,4, pp.360-367; T.W. Adorno, *Sören*

tion (event cult) of the extreme and difficult was out of step with a "resigned" bourgeois ethos, with its merely final commitment to ideals, shows Kierkegaard to have had a distinctly unromantic aspect to him which teaches mistrust in hope. Bloch rationalises this (in a wide-ranging discussion linking the Odyssey with Romanticism) into an argument for the persisting beyondness of the utopian hope. So, he argues, "in each fulfilment, in so far and in so much as this is even possible totaliter, there remains a peculiar element of hope whose *mode of being* is not that of the existing or *currently existing reality*, and which is consequently left over together with its content" (*PH* I,186); there is, then, an image of the object which persists over and beyond the attainment in the *"real-utopian possibility of the object itself which points even further"* (*PH* I,186). Bloch develops this through a reduplication of the intensionality of the act of appropriation for: "victory is properly grasped as *task* and thus *the happy present is simultaneously grasped as pledge for the future"* (*PH* I,188); this amounts to an argument for a kind of "permanent revolution".

All the foregoing is preparation for an extremely forceful presentation and analysis of the nature of realization in Hegel, Aristotle, Schelling and, beyond that, in Marx. Bloch has carried us into the formal dawning of the Not-Yet-Conscious and explored its cultural traces and he is now finally in a position to move on to a yet higher plane of abstraction in which we are confronted not merely with the psychological and literary artifacts that represent to us the impinging "blue" of anticipatory consciousness, but, beyond this, to unfold its elements, the categories within the experience of hope itself. Thus having first passed through an "aesthetic" we are now in a position to comprehend, in dialogue with the whole western philosophical tradition, and supremely in concert with Marx, the transcendental "deduction" of the category hope in an "analytic" of very considerable power. This progression requires, as it were, a measured suspension of disbelief for, as we have indicated primarily in footnotes, Bloch's enterprise both presupposes a vast cultural panorama and, more problematically, the resolution of a series of questions philosophical, historical, theological, but above all linguistic and epistemological, any one of which pressed to excess could disrupt the thought-experiment it is our primary purpose to adumbrate.

Kierkegaard Konstruktion des Ästhetischen G.S. vol.I, and Lukac's pre-Marxist study of Kierkegaard in *The Soul and its Forms.*

CHAPTER V

THE TRANSCENDENTAL DEDUCTION
OF THE CATEGORY OF THE FUTURE

In this, the third of four expository chapters devoted to the first volume of *The Principle of Hope*, we encounter the centrepiece of the whole trilogy from which flow in consequence the exploratory applications of the second and third volumes. If we pursue the analogy with Kant we may see the first volume as a "First Critique" followed by repeated applications which rework the basic discovery in new contexts. The statement and explanation of the "real possibility" in the "categories of Front, Novum, Ultimum and the Horizon" is Bloch's attempt to fix philosophically and in structural terms the mighty extended leap of intellectual imagination he has made in the location and exploration of antipatory consciousness and its correlate in the utopian function.

Bloch's justification of the "utopian trace-images" with which we concluded the previous chapter calls for some understanding of the nature of the synthesis between literary and philosophical material superimposed on the intellectual substructure of the utopian imagination. Bloch's first and second reasons for their being trace-images lie in the hesitance and quiescence of the subject, respectively; the third carries over from the subject (i.e. the analysis of consciousness and intensionality) into the object and then into the relation of "cognition-ground" with "real-ground" (*PH* I,190), or, to put it into terms which relate Bloch to Marx more directly, the question of the nature of matter itself. On this basis we then encounter the centre-piece of *The Principle of Hope*; the deduction of the category of hope in its full splendour.

I. THE PROBLEM OF REALIZATION: ORIGIN, ENTELECHY AND FUTURE GOAL

Bloch first argues for a philosophical rehabilitation of the concept of the act of realization itself.[1] The neglect of this, stem he argues,

---

[1]The distinctions drawn between *"Real"* and *"Realitat"* and *"Wirklicheit"* and their respective cognates is of central importance in recent German thought, see J.P. Stern's initial exploration of the ideology and literature of "reality" in "'Reality' in Early

from the denigration of work (*Arbeit*) in antiquity where it was seen as the prerogative of slaves and manual workers. The depiction of creating and knowing as the reproduction of an ideal given, together with the supremacy of the interpretative model of passive contemplation, retarded the conceptual representation of the act of generation in other than rationalistic terms until the modern period. The "panlogic ideology" took mathematical (Kant), artistic (Schelling) and natural forms (Hegel), but all reduced the process of realization to the appearance of an automatically unfolding logos related to the ultimate identity of subject and object. This, in Bloch's terminology, is a relation between "cognition-ground (*Erkenntnisgrund*) and "real-ground" (*Realgrund*) (*PH* I,190). Against this logocentric tendency Bloch sets Aristotle, according to whom "realization is solely the self-realization of the form-idea or entelechy which is inherent in things; the entelechy is thus itself the energy (or the action) towards its Realization" (*PH* I,191). The problem of realization (*Realization*) as such arises when the self-consistency of the entelechy is ruptured by reference to mechanical matter as this impinges as contingency upon nature and capricious fate in history. Thus the motive power of realization is shifted in Aristotle onto mechanical matter, or, in the case of Hegel to the "Being-beside-itself of the whole of nature itself" (*Aussersichsein der ganzen Natur selbst*), where it persists as "unresolved contradiction" (*PH* I,191).

Into the setting of this juxtaposition of Aristotle and Hegel, Bloch introduces the later Schelling who extracted the problem of "Realization" from its rationalist context and re-assigned the "That-existence" (*Dass-Dasein*) and "entry-origin" (*Eintritts-Ursprung*) to the mythology of the Fall of Man and of Lucifer.[2] So the "That-existence" and "entry-origin", the quest for the entity, does not follow from the *quid*, that is the rationally grasped essence of matter,[3] but is transferred into a dimension beyond the mere idea. The conception of impetus informing the idea of Realization breaks open the circle of ideality, but in a direction wholly unacceptable to Bloch: contingency then becomes the manifestation of evil which opposes the good universal. This posi-

---

Twentieth-century German Literature" in the A. Phillips Griffiths (ed.) *Philosophy and Literature* (Cambridge: Cambridge University Press, 1984), pp.41-57.

[2]Bloch here refers to Schelling's "Philosophy and Religion" *Werke* VI, p.38. One of the most important and relatively unexplored areas in nineteenth and twentieth century German religious thought is to be found in the nature and degree of the latter's indebtedness to the later Schelling. See, W.R. Corti *"Die Mythopoese des Werdenden Gottes'"* in A.M. Koktanek (ed) *Schelling Studien Festgabe fur Manfred Schröter* (Munich: F. Oldenburg, 1965), pp.82-112.

[3]It is not for nothing that Bloch has been referred to as the "Thomas" of Marxism, he uses scholastic and Aristotelian distinctions with considerable freedom, "refunctioning" them in a way of crucial importance for his overall intellectual venture, fundamental to which is the *atheistic* reappropriation of religion.

tion was attained by the later Schelling and it remains a kind of hideous philosophical caricature against which at least two other earlier major figures, Kierkegaard and Engels,[4] reacted equally strongly.

In a brief passage (I, 189-195), Bloch passes from examination of the cultural expression of anticipatory consciousness in its least explicit trace form to the central philosophical issues of the whole work: the motivation, the *"Realization"* of what is, and even more significantly, of what is to be. This takes us from the margin - into the heartland of Bloch's philosophical reflection. For Bloch, Schelling is seen as pointing to a dead-end: he "tore the realizing element and the idea apart and ... senselessly and totally he made the appearance of realization itself absolute to the point of dependability" (*PH* I,192). Neither Schelling's negative solution nor the one produced by the "optimists of the incarnation" is satisfactory; in essence, the problem of realization has remained effectively uninvestigated and, more particularly, the problem should, and will be investigated *within* the context of the utopia complex.[5]

Bloch's own attempted solution is highly individual (as we would now expect) and proceeds along the following lines: first, he assumes the controlling factor of the utopian function as interpretative key: second, more specifically, he works in terms of the tension between present and future as a form of the immanent-transcendental (as opposed to an ontological-idealist) scheme; and, third, he employs a mode of argument and an intellectual and linguistic genre which is both concrete and yet involves the hypostatisation of the logic of the temporal Front. We might with irony describe Bloch's expository style as the "ordinary language" of German philosophy, as such it is strictly-speaking inimitable and resists repetition in terms which do not deflate unmercifully. The passage that we cite at length is presented as the culmination of the preceding argument (which we have subjected to extended critical exposition) and as the threshold to the subsequent categorial exploration:

---

[4]The reception of Schelling's 184/42 lectures is outlined by Manfred Franck in his illuminating introduction to the recent paperback edition, *F.W.J. Schelling Philosophie der Offenbarung* (Frankfurt am Main: Suhrkamp, 1977), pp.9-84.

[5]The question of the reception of Schelling as regards twentieth-century thought is complex and less well-explored than, say, in the case of Hegel. An adequate interpretation of the relation of Bloch and Schelling would depend upon this broader context. A significant parallel is the relation of Karl Barth with the latter, see Kurt Lüthi, *Gott und das Böse Eine biblisch-theologische und systematische These zur Lehre vom Bosen, entworfen in Auseinandersetzung mit Schelling und Karl Barth* (Zurich-Stuttgart: Zwingli Verlag, 1961). We do well to keep in mind Lüthi's remark that, *"Parallelität der Denkform bedeutet nicht-ohne weiteres inhaltliche Übereinstimmung"* p.7. In other words form and content are distinguishable in post-idealist appropriations of Schelling.

We said that even in the entrance of something there was still something that remains behind itself. Something about it darkens and cannot completely free itself from this Not, this Not-there in the midst of immediate nearness of occurrence. We have already identified above the dimming of the just lived moment, and precisely this dimness makes it difficult, in the most immediate way, to experience something that has entered wholly as such. At the same time, however, this most immediate thing in itself is nothing other than the driving force, the That-factor, consequently the intensive aspect of the realizing element itself. And this realizing element still stands squarely in the Not-Having of its act and content: the darkness of the just lived moment illustrates precisely this Not-Having-Itself of *the realizing element*. And it is in fact this still unattained aspect in the realizing element which primarily also over-shadows the Here and Now of something realized. Therein therefore lies the ultimate, the principal solution of the Not-, Not-Yet-Carpe diem, definitely without romanticism: what is realized is brilliant and slightly in shadow at the same time, *because in the realizing element itself there is something that has not yet realized itself.* The unrealized Realizing element brings its own most peculiar minus into the plus of the Realization as soon as the latter occurs. (*PH* I,193)

In this passage Bloch moves out of the ideal-real problematic and into the new logic of anticipatory consciousness, in terms of which the quiddity of the object is to be reconceived. We noted earlier how Bloch first effected this translation of categories; his brief, confident reiteration in terms of the real-possible interface is characteristic, henceforth the legitimacy of his position has for the purposes of exposition to be assumed. The outworking of the "real possibility" (*reale Möglichkeit*) now takes on the form of a transcendental argument within the context of which a deductive unfolding of the inner logic of the category may take place.

On the one hand Bloch's argument relies upon the utopian function (we use this term broadly to include the whole process of transposition from "anticipatory consciousness" and imagination to the "real possibility" of the categories of future hope), on the other it is determined by a specific charge laid against Schelling as the last representative of the tradition that is to be transformed. In Schelling's philosophy (and implicit in the slaughter of the World Wars) there lies the possibility that Nothing (*das Nichte*) just as much (as in Hegelian pan-logism) the All (*das Alles*) is ultimate truth. Absolute nihilism, this "circulation of Nothing ... which Aristotle wrongly laid to the charge of mechanical matter" (*PH* I,194) corresponds in structural terms with Schelling's attempted displacement of Satan into the primal ground (*Urgrund*) of the world. There is evidence that "both were looking for a scapegoat for imperfection in their completed world, that is, a world already statically defined to an end" (*PH* I,194).[6] The search for a scapegoat could be understood (but Bloch does not put it in this way) as the partly secularised extension of the theodicy argument into fundamental philosophy. Against Aristotle thus understood and Schelling (and, we may assume, much that lies between), Bloch argues conversely that,

> insight into process as something undecided-with Nothing or All in its real end-possibility - needs no scapegoat, either with regard to the existing unfinished piece of work onto the not wholly redeemed goal image in its best conceivable fulfilment. (*PH* I,194)

This "end-possibility" is to be understood as the "not yet emerged real-izedness of the realising element" or, in the language of the philosophical tradition, the "not yet discovered, positively manifested, realized Absolute and Essence"; both modes of expression are, we may say, aspect of the structure of the "aporias of realization". In a passage of daring synthesis Bloch identifies the reworked philosophical problematic with the utopian quest and with this puts the keystone of his massive intellectual arch in place and renders the structure capable of load-bearing:

> Only if a Being were like utopia, if consequently the still completely outstanding kind of reality of successfulness had made the driving-content of the Here and Now itself radically present, would the basic stock of this driving: hope be wholly included in the realized reality. The content of what has been realized would then be the content of the realizing element itself, the What Essence (*quidditas*) of the solution would be precisely the opened That-ground (*quodditas*) of the world. *The Essence -* most highly qualified matter - has not yet appeared, therefore missing represents its not yet manifested Absolute in every previously successful appearance. (*PH* I,194)

---

[6]Schelling's recourse to *Urgrund* raises important questions relating to the mystical antecedents of German idealism, see, for example, Ernst Benz, *The Mystical Sources of German Romantic Philosophy* (Pennsylvania: Pickwick,1983), esp. chs. 2 and 3.

So, then, when Bloch asserts that there is space in the world on the Front of concrete anticipatory consciousness in which the most fundamental ontological discontinuities will cohere in the future goal, he is postulating nothing less than the following: first, a solution to the problem of nihilism; second, a resolution of the theodicy issue by the demonstration that it is a non-problem; and, third an elucidation of the nature of being itself. Consequently any accusation of lack of ambition on Bloch's part would be to do him a grave injustice, indeed this is the point at which his thought passes from a descriptive phenomenology into a form of revisionary metaphysics.

II. The "Real Possibility": the Deduction of the Categories - Primum, Novum and Ultimum

In the foregoing pages we have encountered the highest degree of abstraction so far apparent in *The Principle of Hope*. Characteristically, in the exposition of the real "possibility", that is of the correlation of the categories of "Front," "Novum," "Ultimum" and "the Horizon" with the utopian imagination, Bloch reverts to a more leisured, accessible style. Repetition, repeated climaxes and developments and a refusal to concede strict, or rather *constrictive* form are characteristic. The total effect is cumulative but the demands on the reader are nevertheless considerable for there can be no relaxation of concentration on the part of those who intend a positive response to *The Principle of Hope* and wish to enter that aspect of the world-experience it is Bloch's objective to articulate.

The key to the comprehension of Bloch's exposition of the categories of the "real possibility" is provided by the last sentence in his quotation from Marx's correspondence with Ruge of 1843

> It will then become apparent that the world has long possessed the dream of the matter, of which it must only possess the consciousness in order to possess it in reality. (*PH* I,195)

This is the "real possibility," the general constituent elements of which are to be understood in terms of "categories" open to further specification. Grounding his argument once more in the depiction of human experience, in the latency of youth and the capacity to dream, Bloch distinguishes between the incomplete triumph of what has Become (*das Gewordene*) and the Real (*das Wirkliche*). The Real is "process", the "widely ramified (*weitverzweigte*) mediation between present, unfinished past, and above all: possible future" (*PH* I,196). Being presents itself as "dialectical-material" with an "enclosed capability of becoming" (i.e. it is open to the future), and so, in full congruence with the overall preceding argument, the "really Possible", the object of categorical investigation, is the "*sufficiently mediated, i.e. dialectically-materialistically mediated newness*" which "gives utopian imagination its *second, its concrete correlate*" beyond the mere confines of consciousness (*PH* I,197). If reality is open in this way, that is not completely determined, then utopia cannot be dismissed by virtue of the nature of reality as given. A discrimination must be made: Bloch's "concrete utopia" corresponds to the "mediated Novum" that breaks through in reality understood as process, and it is by this latter, "process-reality", and not a (falsely) reified and absolutised factual reality, that utopian dreams are to be judged. Bloch thus sets "Factum" against "Novum", and appeals to the renewed consciousness of contemporary man who is:

> thoroughly acquainted with the frontier-existence outside the previous expectation of Becomeness. He no longer sees himself surrounded by ostensibly completed facts, and no longer considers these as the only Real; devastatingly, possible fascist Nothing has opened up in this Real, and above all, finally and overdue, socialism. (*PH* I,197).

This position clearly indicates Bloch's open attitude towards modernity and the basis of an aesthetic which he consistently set out and applied in the eras of inter-war fascistic capitalist and post-war communist society. Bloch distinguishes his position both from the ossified late nineteenth century alternatives of positivism and idealism, and within socialism, from "schematic" Marxism. In the latter, history is reduced to fixed episodes in the dialectical process which can even appear as "totalities" [7] closed in upon themselves, thereby excluding anticipatory consciousness and submerging the interpretation of the imagination into processual reality itself. So, Bloch concludes, "the will towards utopia is entirely compatible with object-based tendency, in fact is confirmed and at home within it" (*PH* I,197-8); in other words, to be a real socialist, and therefore a real dialectical materialist, is to admit the openness and undetermined nature of the future, the Novum, in the terms in which Bloch has defined it.

---

[7]Martin Jay's *Marxism and Totality The Adventure of a Concept from Lukács to Habermas* (Cambridge: Polity, 1984) once more provides an essential introduction to the problem of "totality" within twentieth century Marxism. Consideration of this question provides clear ground for a conjunction of philosophical and more strictly theological interests.104

The attitude out of which the encounter with the "real possibility" and its categories of Front, Novum and Ultimum springs is that of "militant optimism". Courage, knowledge and work are required to confront and overcome the future, rather than submit to it as fate. The old contemplative mode of knowledge is inadequate to this supreme task as it refers only to the past; it is, furthermore, impotent in the face of present and blind to the future. The new mode of knowledge interacts in a discriminating way with the "Real in history": namely the "events produced by working people together with the abundant interweaving process-connections between past, present and future" (PH I,198). Against quietism of any kind in the face of historical inevitability (whether generated by theological conceptions of providence or mechanical Marxist misunderstandings of the dialectic as self-sufficient, as autarchy)[8] Bloch advocates a militant optimism ostensibly correspondent with Marx's thought. Marx maintained, so Bloch claims, that "no abstract ideals are realized, but rather the repressed elements of the new, humanized society, that is, of the concrete ideal, are set free" (PH I,199). Bloch identifies this tendency[9] with the "revolutionary decision of the proletariat which today commits itself to the final struggle of liberation, a decision of the subjective factor in alliance with the objective factor of economic-material tendency" (PH I,199).

Bloch's "militant optimism" is expanded in a highly individual way, for unlike Kant or Hegel, who took up the discussion of categories originating with Aristotle in a more or less formal manner, Bloch develops what amounts to a secular via negativa.[10] Whilst the twin loci in the dialectical materialist process, man and process, subject and object, stand before the category of the Front this is as yet as little thought out as the concept of the New. The anticipation of the New is

[8]The introduction of this term indicates one of the most fundamental areas of disagreement between Bloch and Marxist orthodoxy as expressed in DIAMAT. Is the dialectic independent of human agency and does it constitute the human condition? Bloch re-idealizes Marxism inasmuch as for him the creative impulse is not derivative from or constituted by material relations, but is, on the contrary, constitutive of the condition of transformation of the human condition.

[9]A most deep seated implausibility in Bloch's re-Hegelianisation and cultural enrichment of Marxism lies in his rhetorical commitment to the proletariat as the likely bearers of his vision of human renewal. Bloch's ideal is only attainable upon the basis of the separation and concentration (and consequent Steigerung) of the exceptional individual who by heroic efforts refracts the demands of an open future into the deficiencies of the present. This is in the the first instance an intellectual and aesthetic, not a "practical" task in the immediate political sense.

[10]The mastery of the past and the organisation of the present in conformity with the exigencies of the future involves a dialectical critique of human pretensions similar in structure (despite its transcendental reorientation towards the future) to the ontological critique in the "via negativa" and its contemporary, atheological reappearance in Adorno and, to a lesser extent, Lukács.

present in youth and in the expectation inherent in most religions. In particular it pervades the whole of the Bible, where it is consummated in the Son of Man who renews all things in a new heaven and a new earth; but this is inadequately represented and has "found no place in any pre-Marxist-world-picture" (*PH* I,201). So in Art Nouveau or the philosophy of Bergson the New appears but not as it ought; it is bounded, for example, in Bergson's case by a restricted and abortive dialectical juxtaposition of class ritual and mechanicism leading to a mere frenzy[11] rather than appearing as the dawning of new life, Bloch's Incipit vita nova. Bergson's Novum is *not* the genuine article, it is a "capitalistic fashion-novelty" concocted out of "sheer excess" and then stabilized: "elan vital and nothing more is and remains itself a Fixum of contemplation "(*PH* I,202).

Characteristically, when faced with a philosophical figure and a position in certain respects dangerously close to his own, Bloch resorts to his class-reduction ploy: "the social reason for Bergson's pseudo-Novum lies in the late bourgeoisie, which has within it nothing new in terms of content" (*PH* I, 202). Such class-based ad hominem accusations are a sign of weakness in Bloch, but this should not divert us from the real climax of his argument which is both important and interesting, with implications for reflection across a wide range of disciplines. Bloch does, however, show the affinity between Bergson's philosophy and that of the Megarian philosopher Diodoros Chronos and he emerges with the conclusion that Bergson forecloses the real concept of the Novum by regarding "*finality* simply as the establishment of a rigid final goal, rather than as the goal-determination of the human will" (*PH* I,202). Mere abstract opposition to mechanical repetition is less than adequate to the reality of the Novum, which itself issues in the form of a finality formalized in the "*category Ultimum*" in which the repetition ends. Thus out of the negative presentation, even the *negation* of Bergson, Bloch introduces the last of his categories of "real Possibility", the Ultimum.

The introduction of the Ultimum precipitates a climax in Bloch's argument (*PH* I, pp.203-5) which demands careful, reflective examination on the part of the reader; this passage contains the most damaging criticism of the Western philosophical and theological tradition to be found in the whole of *The Principle of Hope*. Bloch combines Nietzsche and Hegel and integrates them into a contextualising polarity from which vantage point he is in a position to criticise the whole tradition in a passage of truly virtuoso brilliance. Taking up the theme of "repetition" (*Wiederholung*) from his discussion of Bergson, Bloch

[11]Bloch would appear to have here in mind Bergson's appropriation of Nietzsche and his juxtaposition of the Apollonian and Dionysian principles.

transposes this into a total critique. Given the designation of the totality of the Novum as the Ultimum Bloch puts the latter forward as the
"last, i.e. the highest newness, the repetition (the unremitting repre-
sentedness of the tendency-goal in all progressively New) intensifies
(*steigert*) to the last, highest, most fundamental repetition: of identity" (*PH* I,203). We are on the brink of Bloch's own totalistic
"*Aufhebung*" [12] or supercession of the tradition, implicit within which
is his inversion of the meaning of the temporal order. The triumph of
the Ultimum consists in its "total leap out of everything that previously existed", which is at the same time, "a leap towards the newness
that is ending or identity" (*PH* I,203). Such an Ultimum has not been so
neglected as the Novum that precedes it, for the Last Thing (the eschaton) has been characteristic of religions that set a limit to time, especially the Judaeo-Christian tradition. The absence of the Novum, (in
effect, a functioning goal-centred anticipatory anxiousness) has resulted
in a kind of short-circuiting of the whole conception of the historical
process, it has relapsed into a cyclic pattern:

> Because in the whole of the Judaeo-Christian philosophy, from
> Philo and Augustine to Hegel, the Ultimum relates exclusively
> to a Primum and not to a Novum; consequently the Last Thing
> appeared simply as the attained return of an already com-
> pleted First Thing which has been lost or reliniquished. (*PH*
> I,203)

Into this pattern fits the "pre-Christian form of the self-combusting
and self-renewing Phoenix" and the Heraclitean and Stoic doctrine of
world-conflagration. Thus the "*cycle* is the figure which the Ultimum
attaches so firmly to the Primum that it nurtures logically and metaphysically within it" (*PH* I,203); hence the short-circuited interpretation of the whole world-process. The most grandiloquent expression of
this conception of the world-process is found in the thought of Hegel,
who,

> saw in the Being-for-itself of the idea, which is its Ultimum
> and in which process dies away as in an amen, the Primum of
> the Being-in-itself not only reproduced but fulfilled: the
> 'mediated immediacy' is attained in the Being-for-itself,

---

[12]Bloch does not actually use the term *Aufhebung*, as this word would be unacceptable
as a direct bearer of Hegelian resonance, but what he does postulate is equivalent to the
negation and passing beyond to a higher level, usually rendered in English translation as
"supercession"; it is in fact *Aufhebung* refunctioned in real, if not nominal terms.

rather than the unmediated immediacy in the beginning of the
mere Being-in-itself. (PH I,203)

This passage, being interpreted, means that the first stage in the
dialectical process, unreflective "Being-in-itself" (Ansichsein) passes
into the fulfilment of "Being-for-itself" (Fürsichsein)[13] in such a way
that its reality fades on its inclusion into the second stage: the Ultimum
effectively absorbs and suppresses the Primum. So is constituted an integrated cycle in which the Novum, the active, life-determining encounter with the new in anticipatory consciousness and the utopian function, is itself suppressed. So, in the words of the mature Hegel,[14]

Every part of philosophy is a philosophical whole, a circle
which closes in upon itself, ... the whole it is presents itself as a
circle of circles (Enzyklopädie, par.15).

Not only, however, is the Primum thus denigrated but the Ultimum
also loses its power in the all-embracing arms of a conception of a
"primal being to which process returns almost as a prodigal son and un-
does the substance of its Novum" (PH I,203-4). This is, it need scarcely
be said, a powerful attack on the Hegelian conception of mediation, de-
tecting within it a mutual reduction of beginning (Alpha) and end
(Omega) that destroys the real meaning of both. The correct response is,
Bloch argues, an outright attack upon the whole traditional scheme of
Western thought: the philosophical appropriation of an "anti-re-
remembering, anti-Augustine, anti-Hegel" conception of the Novum and
the Ultimum is imperative; this can then be directed against the ring-
principle and its proponents from Hegel, through Eduard von Hartmann
to Nietzsche. Correspondingly, Bloch appears to deny the whole traditional scheme of a departure from and return of the human to nature,
that is a cyclic voyage of mediation and transformation of subject-object
relation culminating in identity.

Having as it were stated the negative, pursued as a "via negativa"
with regard to the "real possibility", Bloch is now ready to state the
positive aspect of his position in terms of an expansion and extension of

[13]Here the parallel with Hegelian distinction and his dynamic understanding of dialectic is directly reflected in Bloch's future-orientated refunctioning of the an sich/für
sich distinction drawn classically from the Phenomenology of Mind, see pp.218-227 and
justified in detailed textual terms in Subjekt-Object, G.A. vol.8, pp.59-108 (esp. pp.75-77).

[14]Bloch's citation implies a critique of Hegel in terms of the juxtaposition of the
Phenomenology with the later, more rigid and schematic work. See Subjekt-Objekt,
loc.cit.

Marx's conception of the "humanization" of nature.[15] Hope itself disposes of the enclosed circle; its dialectic, driven by unrest and the nature of its goal (which is not, however, a pre-defined essence) breaks open the circle; the "tension-figures" (*Spannungsfiguren*) and "tendency-forms" (*Tendenzgestalten*) are its provisional subversion in cipher-form. Consequently, the goal is not contained or realised in either the Primum (Alpha or beginning) or the Ultimum (Omega or end) but in the terms of their utopian-dialectical conjunction: in the Novum. The Novum is neither a relic of the beginning nor an encapsulated fulfilment of the end but a "Novum of the end", that is "an origin still essentially unrealized in itself" (*PH* I,204). This conception of reality is incomprehensible apart from its roots in the structure of Judaeo-Christian eschatology: it is no distortion to see Bloch's Novum in its secularised form as an "earnest of things to come". It will become increasingly apparent that this total thought experiment has to be understood *within* rather than as standing outside the parameters of possibility afforded by the theological tradition and its eschatological potential.

The latency, the proleptic consciousness of the Novum generated in life lived on the Front is, notwithstanding, grounded in history, that is the "self-apprehension of the historical doer, working man". To this are subordinated the previously established notions of natura naturans and material motion; the self-apprehension of working man enjoys a priority, but this and the "humanization of nature" are located in the "Front of the process of history" at which point the "only mediated-possibility", which *corresponds to exact anticipation; concrete utopia as objective-real correlate*", is encountered. So on this basis Bloch concludes with a consequent re-definition of the nature of human freedom: "the thus designated realm of freedom develops not as return, but as exodus - through into the always intended promised land, promised by process" (*PH* I,205). So ends Bloch's initial characterisation of the categories of real possibility: Front, Novum and Ultimum, which he now proceeds to set in the context of the assumed conditions of their realization (that is, their "real possibility"). It becomes apparent here that Bloch's position is only sustainable in terms other than pure assertion by the "fore-existence" of a real transcendence; hence the extraordinary distance Bloch has to go in asserting the re-functioned religious dimension within a consistent and atheist position. The breaking of the circle

---

[15]Bloch's relationship to the *Paris Manuscripts* of 1844 is not wholly clear, but his position here approximates in important respects that of Marx in "Private Property and Communism" in D.J. Struik (ed) *The Economic and Philosophical Papers of 1844* (New York, 1964), pp.132-146.

with the "exodus" motif has to imply a real future transcendence if Bloch's proposal is not to relapse back into cyclic self-assertion.

III. THE "REAL POSSIBILITY": ITS CONDITION OF REALIZATION

Bloch shows a distinct realism when he surveys the relationship between goal-images and their realization in the actual matrix of history. Recalling his earlier appropriation of part of the Aristotelian conception of matter Bloch elaborates, laying particular emphasis upon the, "What-Is-in-possibility", that is in Aristotle an as yet passive *"womb of fertility from which all world-forms inexhaustibly emerge"* (*PH*, I,207). The, "left-wing" [16] interpretation of the development of this conception which Bloch traces through (amongst others) Avicenna, Averroes, and Giordano Bruno down to Hegel, provides the philosophical tool which allowed Marx to prise apart the dialectic of process from the world-spirit, thus providing a concept of matter commensurate with the demands of dialectical materialism. The concept of matter that emerged has despite its inclusion of "dialectic, process, expropriation of expropriation, humanization of nature" (*PH* I,208), both a "warm" and a "cold" side to it. This "warm" Marxist materialism stresses the humane, liberating intention and the mutuality of realization of man and nature in developing matter, whereas the "cold" stream merely unmasks ideologies and disabuses metaphysical illusion. It is clear by now where Bloch's sympathies lie, that is with the utopian drive towards "Being-in-possibility" and the new, "warm", materialism of latency.

Bloch's account of the possibilities of the dialectic implicit in a concept of matter inherited and developed from the dynamic side of Aristotle is supplemented by a substantial digression into "artistic appearance as visible pre-appearance" in which he translates the abstract, ontological analysis of the dialectic into concrete aesthetic terms, with the result that "beauty is the sensory manifestation of the *idea*" (*PH* I,211). In this way Bloch immediately confronts the potential objection that having chosen "matter" (however conceived) over and above the ancestral and intrinsic primacy of the "idea", he would be unable to sustain a consistent seeking out and portrayal of beauty as the manifestation, within culture, of a primal and legitimate human

---

[16]One of the most valuable and indeed fascinating aspects of Bloch's work is his consistent materialist interpretation of the whole tradition, including scholastic theology. The revisionary account that emerges in "Avicenna und die Aristotelische Linke", *Das Materialismusproblem G.A.* vol.7, pp.479-546 is crucial to Bloch's argument as a whole: matter has to be represented as "non-mechanical", a dynamic source of life.

drive. This discussion serves as the foundation of, and context for
Bloch's final categorial designation, the "Horizon". Having defined
the first three categories Front, Novum and Ultimum in negative terms,
that is in the form of a secularised via negativa, against their philosophical non-appearance or distortion, Bloch now continues his indirect
approach for the fourth and final category and expands this through an
analysis of the aesthetics of beauty and of realism. Simultaneous with
this categorial expansion Bloch is with typical German philosophical
ambition striving to overcome a further polarity: as the Novum is
posited as experiential and proleptic focal point of Primum and
Ultimum so it is crucial that the Enlightenment antithesis between art
and truth be likewise formally overcome.[17]

It is apparent that Bloch sees beauty devalued by its association
with mere appearance but he is obliged to ask the question as to what
philosophical "cash value" good art might have. "What is", Bloch
asks, "the *honest* status of this finish (*Ende*), of a ripeness (*Reife*) in
which only invented material ripens?" (*PH* I,211). What is to be the
contemporary response to the consensus extending from Plotinus to Hegel
that "beauty is the sensory manifestation of the 'idea?' " (*PH* I,211), a
view which in its turn provoked Nietzsche's assertion that all poets
lie? This view of the artist as one in league with appearance reinforced
the Enlightenment antithesis between art and truth once it was openly
confronted with the rational objections to art generated in the new bourgeois age. In both rational and empirical terms the aesthetic dimension
became alienated, and correspondingly in Descartes, Spinoza and
Leibniz only technical aesthetic theories tended to survive. Even in the
latter the beauty of world harmony is a secondary factor. The partial
recovery of aesthetics in rationalism (Baumgarten) was nevertheless
inhibited by the denigrated status of the object of aesthetics and a
"lower cognitive faculty" corresponding to it. A profound iconoclasm
stemming both from Plato[18] and from the Old Testament[19] reinforces
from a "spiritual" (*spirituell*) and religious standpoint hostility towards art. Bloch links this denigration of the aesthetic as against the
drive towards complete clarity of conceptual vision (the pursuit of the
conceptual logos) with a more general moral "turning away from all too
great visibility of 'works' (*Werke*) and the turning towards the invisi-

---

[17]The influence of Goethe's conception of the relation of poetry to truth is evident
here, as it is seen, for example, in *Dichtung und Wahrheit*.

[18]Plato, "What good is there in imitating the shadow of shadows? *Republic*, Book 7.

[19]Bloch cites the prohibition of images: "Thou shalt not make unto thence any graven
image, or any likeness of anything that is in heaven above, or that is in the earth beneath, or that is in the water under the earth", Exodus 20,4.

ble, genuine dimension of 'convictions' (*Gesinnung*)" (*PH* I,213). Bloch's resonant conclusion is that:

> Puritanism in this extensive sense (reaching back as far as Bernard of Clairvaux) finally culminated in Tolstoy's monstrous hatred of Shakespeare, of the lascivious work of beauty in general. Even in Catholicism a horror pulchri led, under Pope Marcellus, to the planning of a ban on elaborate church music, and this horror, applied to what is visible, gave to Protestantism the bare (*kahlen*) God who wishes to be worshipped in moral belief, in the word that is the truth. (*PH* I,213)

The claim to truth in empirical, rationalist, spiritual and religious forms then conversely re-presented beauty as the game of appearance (*das Spiel des Scheins*) and this drew forth a corresponding counter-response in serious artists who sought through realism to represent beauty in truth. The significant realism of Homer, Shakespeare, Goethe, Keller and Tolstoy eschews extravagance and strives for concreteness; this, however, does not settle the aesthetic question.[20] Accordingly, art is not simply realistic portrayal, but, above all a "fantasizing" (*eine Ausfabelung*) in which invented material completes the structure of what has been concretely observed. Art sometimes goes beyond realism in that it strives towards "great appearance" (*grosser Schein*) and this has a "surpassing" (*überbietend*) effect because such works either "consciously romanticise alongside or beyond available existence", or, "far beyond a mere 'subject', they fructify - myth, which is the oldest sustenance of art anyway" (*PH* I,214).[21]

The reason for Bloch's digression into the "visible pre-appearance" of art now becomes apparent. If art decidedly transcends realism (Bloch here refers to Giotto's "Raising of Lazarus", Dante's "Paradiso", and Goethe's portrayal of Heaven in the final part of *Faust*) then in what possible sense can it be said to be "true"? In terms of merely representational realism these images are clearly not true and thus the French mathematician's question is irrefutable when we are *forced* to consider

---

[20]Erich Auerbach's magisterial study *Mimesis The Representation of Reality in Western Culture* (Princeton, 1933) would appear largely to confirm Bloch's estimation of the problem of realism at this point, see ch.1, "Odysseus'scar".

[21]Bloch's critical refunctioning of "myth" is fundamental to his project and can be regarded as the benign converse of the self-conscious and malignant resuscitation of myth in National Socialism. The remythologisation of human experience is vital to the refunctioning of a living tradition; the ethical and political control of this process is another matter.

the question of appearance, *despite* the drive towards realism. So, Bloch argues:

> the question as to the truth of art becomes philosophically the question as to the possibly available depictability of beautiful appearance, as to its degree of reality in the by no means single-layered reality of the world, as to the location of its object correlate.

thus,

> Utopia as object-determination, with the degree of existence of the Real Possible, thus encounters in the simmering phenomenon of art a particularly fruitful problem of probation (*Bewahrung*). (*PH* I,214)

On this basis Bloch can provide an answer to the aesthetic question of truth that emerges as the direct consequence of the ramified argument into which he has integrated anticipatory consciousness and its correlative Novum:

> ... artistic appearance is not only mere appearance, but a meaning, cloaked in images and which can only be described in images, of material that has been driven further, wherever *the exaggeration and fantasizing represent a significant pre-appearance, circulating in turbulent existence itself, of what is real*, a pre-appearance which can specifically be represented in aesthetically immanent terms. (*PH* I,214-5)

As in the discussion of the Primum, Novum and Ultimum, Bloch now develops his discussion into a heightened critical synthesis by means of which he confronts and attempts to overcome what he understands to be the most fundamental defects of the tradition as a whole. Art renders pre-appearance visible as it drives its material (the diverse representation of the world) towards a "stated resolution (*ausgesagten Austrag*) in suffering, happiness and meaning" (*PH* I,215). The aesthetic representation of the Object (*Gegenstand*) is achieved through the "driving-to-the-end that occurs in dialectically open space" (*PH* I,215) and this creates in the artifact an intensified representation, albeit virtual, of the truth. Here "objectivity is thought through from the standpoint of the Object which has not yet become. This "pre-appearance, in contrast to religious pre-appearance, remains immanent despite all transcendence"; in terms of Schiller's comment on Goethe's aesthetic realism, "it

expands 'nature, without going beyond it'" (PH I,215). So, Bloch concludes, artistic, as opposed to religious pre-appearance "remains immanent despite all transcendence": beauty and the sublime itself represent
the existence of the Object that has not yet become.[22] This articulation
of the sublime *within* immanence impels Bloch to a further question,
indeed into confrontation with the tradition, an engagement first explored in *Geist der Utopie*.[23]

If, expanding Bloch, aesthetic pre-appearance is intrinsic within
immanence alone, then all such aesthetic endeavours are attended by
this persistent problem: "how could the *world be perfected without
this world being exploded and apocalyptically vanishing as in
Christian-religious pre-appearances?*" (PH I,215). Bloch then carefully juxtaposes the goals of art and of religion (that is, in the Judaeo-
Christian tradition). Art locates perfection, the Total in the
Particular; religion, by contrast, locates utopian perfection in totality
and places (in Bloch's terms it is almost to be seen as *dis*places) the
"salvation (*Heil*) of the individual matter (*Sache*) completely in the
Totum" (PH I,215).[24] The declaration "I make all things new"[25] of
Judaeo-Christian apocalyptic issues in the tradition of immanent spiritual rebirth, the transformation of society into the *Civitas Dei* and the
transfiguration of nature into the celestial. Art (other than music
which does work explosively (*sprengend*)), is "rounded", "balanced"
and "homogenised" and does not seek to "explode the world" but drives
forwards towards more perfect representation.

These tendencies lead in turn to a conflict within realism, where
the ideal of penetrative concentration is opposed to reproductive naturalism. So Goethe, an advocate of the former, could comment on
Diderot's "Essay on Painting" as follows: "And thus the artist, grateful

---

[22]Bloch's analysis of Romantic latency draws upon the discussion associated with the
late eighteenth century Berlin circle of the Schlegel brothers.

[23]In the second (and from Bloch's point of view definitive) 1923 edition of *Geist der
Utopie* we find the following, p.141: "*Hier siedelt, mit klärendem Geplauder, der selb-
staufriedene Pfahlburger, der nicht nur etwas gesagt zu haben, sondern auch alles ins
Reine gebraucht zur haben glaubt.... Bekker hat die Hilfsmittel, mit denen der
Klavierlehrer die lahme Phantasie seiner Zöglinge zu verbessern sucht, zur exegetischen
Wissenschaft der Musikpoesie erhoben*".

[24]Here the theme of totality and the nineteenth century German preoccupation with
salvation through art are developments that can, so far as Bloch's argument is concerned,
be seen to culminate in the prematurely foreclosed work of Walter Benjamin. See R.
Wolin, *Walter Benjamin An Aesthetic of Redemption* New York: Columbia University
Press, 1982).

[25]"Behold I make all things new", Rev.21,5. Whether Bloch has here, or elsewhere,
adequately or satisfactorily grasped the full complexity of the eschatological and apocalyptic motifs within the Judaeo-Christian tradition and the subsequent "de-eschatologisation" of dogma in the context of ecclesiology is a matter open to further discussion, see
chs. 8 and 9 below.

to nature, which also produced him, gives her a second nature in return, but one that is felt and thought and humanly perfected" (*PH* I,216). Bloch's underlying intention in citing Goethe is, however, to juxtapose the Hegelian and Aristotelian perspectives he first distinguished in the initial articulation of the category of the "Real Possibility." Unlike some of the other aesthetically-informed Marxist revisionists who create an all-comprehensive doctrine out of "second nature" (thereby drawing heavily upon Hegel), Bloch sets himself against the latter and remains consistent with his previously enunciated position. The humanization of nature throughout effects the perfection of nature, but, "not of course in the manner of sensory appearance of an idea which is finished anyway, as Hegel teaches, but rather in the direction of increasingly entelechetic expression as Aristotle states" (*PH* I,216). This distinction is absolutely crucial; it is, this writer believes, the single most profound intellectual decision which puts Bloch into the Marxian camp understood as materialism and distinguishes him from those revisionist Marxists who as it were retreat further, and less critically into an explicitly Hegelian position.

Bloch's commitment to Aristotle has far-reaching consequences not the least of which is the principled retention of atheism rather than any form of covert theism. Bloch's immediately following allusion to Engels (the architect of DIAMAT) comes as no surprise; he cunningly extracts the completed form of his Marxist aesthetic out of Engels' statement that: "realistic art is representative of typical characters in typical situations" which he regards as the equivalent of Aristotle's entelechic conception of "typically resolving force", and not as indicative of the mere average, but of the "significantly characteristic", that is, the "essential image of the matter, decisively developed through exemplary instances" (*PH* I,216). Once more it is *work* that will lead to the solution of the aesthetic question of truth: *"Art is a laboratory and also a feast of implemented possibilities"* (*PH* I,216) and in real art "beauty and even sublimity is that which mediates a premonition of future freedom" (*PH* I,217). Only through the active control of history can the relatively limited pre-appearance of art become part of the broader pattern of life. The "godless prayer of poetry" has limited practicality; but the breaking of images, that is a breaking *into* them with a view to their exemplary fructification, constitutes the struggle towards future freedom latent within the art that Bloch regards as a serious contribution to the human condition.

Bloch's application to art of the Goethian maxim that life is often rounded, but never closed, leads him into a consideration of the nature of completion. The image of completion and finished coherence, drawn from the symbolism and mythology of Pan, can lead to a false finality, that is "Great balance as secularised form of the totally pagan, i.e. *crackless world-picture: the astral myth*" (*PH* I,218). Thus it is possible for art to exist as a "false autarchy" which masks and subdues its immanent pre-appearance. In great art this homogenity is, as it were, subverted from within by its own iconoclasm, "whenever immanence is not driven to closeness of form and content, wherever it still poses as fragment-like" (*PH* I,219). The very character of the mighty engagement implicit in such great art is such that "completion itself, driven so deeply into the Absolute, becomes a fragment" (*PH* I,220). So, in Michelangelo, in Beethoven's late quartets, in Goethe's *West-östlichen Divan* and in *Faust*, the ultimate takes on a fragmentary quality: "unfinishability lacks greatness in finishing" (*PH* I,221).

These observations, set in the rich fabric of an allusive exposition lead Bloch to the appropriation of the contrary of what has just been purged. Whereas the aesthetic attempt at pre-appearance initially involved the perfection of the world "without this world being exploded and apocalyptically vanishing, as in Christian pre-appearance" (*PH* I,215), now the argument is reversed: the reason for the "internal iconoclasm in greatly completed art", and the source of its real pathos is to be found in the "eschatological conscience that came into the world through the Bible" (*PH* I,221). This subversion of the pretentions of completion, a force encountered in great art, is complete and uncompromising:

> Totality in the religion of the Exodus and the Kingdom is solely
> of a totally transforming and exploding kind, is utopian; and,
> confronted with this totality, not only our knowledge, but also
> the whole of what has previously become, to which our con-
> science refers, then appears as unfinished work. (*PH* I,221)

The "explosion" implicit in the apocalyptic statement "Behold, I make all things new" indicates that man is not solid, the future is undecided and enclosed, and this applies likewise to the aesthetic information borne by art. These remarks once more emphasise Bloch's dependence upon the Romantic displacement of the salvific goal from religion into aesthetics, but it is now clear that the latter cannot then survive without the "refunctioned" recovery of the former.

Bloch concludes thus, recognising the explicit internal conflict in the position outlined: "this utopian factor is the paradox in aesthetic immanence, the most fundamentally immanent paradox in this immanence itself" (*PH* I,221). In this aesthetic there is both a protest against the apocalyptic dissolution of Christian re-appearance *and* a recognition of the ultimate grandeur of the Exodus and the kingdom which relativises all artistic pretension, an effect clearly seen in the fragmentary character of great art. Accordingly, the world conceived as the matrix of art is a process full of ciphers, allegories and symbols which, unclosed, advances through dialectic towards further fragmentary forms. The symbol itself is such by virtue of its reference to the "unum necessarium" within it (that is its anticipatory character) and not because it is conceived as a finished truth bearing a disguise. Above all there must be no toleration of platonic-idealist modes of representation. The fragment be it artistic or otherwise, belongs to the subject matter of the world; its witness, we might say, is indirect and enacted through a future determination, not through a regressive and immanent disclosure of a static essence.

Having conquered the paradoxes in aesthetic immanence, Bloch then finds it possible to derive from realism the conclusion that "everything real has a horizon" (*PH* I,222). Having begun his discussion of the aesthetic dimension with a consideration of the Enlightenment antithesis of art and truth, Bloch concludes with a briefer account of the "flat empiricist" and the "effusive enthusiast" (that is the poetic sensibility unconcretely applied). The empiricist reifies the individual moments of the process and freezes them into facts; conversely, the enthusiast sails over the facts yet sometimes remains, by virtue of the use of the imagination, teachable. Imagination, once it grapples with the concrete, does not merely engage with the sensory evidence but is capable of visualizing the "mediation-relation in and behind the immediacy of raw experience" (*PH* I,222). Bloch pulls together the strands of his lengthy discussion and re-locate the Enlightenment dichotomy in the context of the relation between art (*Kunst*) and science (*Wissenschaft*):

> Instead of the isolated fact and the superficial context of abstract immediacy which is likewise isolated from the whole, the relation of appearances to the whole of their epoch and to the utopian Totum located in process now emerges. Art becomes knowledge with the help of imagination of this kind, namely through telling individual images and overall pictures of a characteristically typical kind; it pursues the 'significant aspect' of appearances and executes it. Science, with the help of imagination of this kind, grasps the 'significant aspect' of appearances through concepts, which never remain abstract, never allow the phenomenon to fade, let alone be lost. (*PH* I,222-3)

This 'significant aspect' in both art and science is the "particular aspect of the general", the actual, present engagement within the dialectically open context[26] and the "characteristically typical figure of the Totum" (*PH* I, 223). The "Totum", the "dimension in which even the epochally grasped whole of all epochal moments is itself again a moment" (*PH* I,223)[27], is apparent in great works only on the "horizon", that is in a reality as yet unformed. This horizon is both inward, it extends down vertically within, and external, it lies on the rim of the processual world; both horizons skirt the utopia beyond, both are, Bloch maintains, "consequently identical in the Ultimum" (*PH* I,223). A world conceived without this horizon as the correlate of objective imagination would be a dead reality; realism includes the prospective horizon, it encounters the real as a network of dialectical processes and conceives the world as changeable in the face of an enormous future of "real possibility".[28] Bloch sums up in aphoristic terms,

Concrete utopia stands on the horizon of every reality; real possibility surrounds the open dialectical tendencies and latencies to the very last. (*PH* I,223)

This, and here Bloch reverts once more to Aristotle, is the unfinished movement of unfinished matter, the "uncompleted entelechy"; it is the very nerve thread of his world-view.

IV. ONTOLOGY REGAINED: THE OBJECTIVITY OF THE CATEGORY POSSIBILITY

Bloch has, successively, deduced the categories of the "Real Possible", initially Primum, Novum and Ultimum, and then the Horizon that bounds all significant human endeavour. Following these extensive intellectual mediations which have rendered concrete the objective correlates of the subjective anticipatory consciousness traced out earlier in *The Principle of Hope*, Bloch now restates in formal and gen-

[26]The rendering in the translation of *"die jeweilige Instanz"* and *"die jeweilige charakteristich-typische Figur"* as "the respective characteristically typical figure (*PH* I, 223, orig. 257) is an odd formulation: "present" or "actual" would seem to make more sense of *"jeweilige"* than "respective".

[27]The term "Moment" is clearly Hegelian in inspiration, despite its refunctioned context, see *Phenomenology of Mind*, pp.229-240, "Lordship and Bondage" for a classic presentation of this notion.

[28]In what follows Bloch's relationship with Engels is ambiguous in the extreme, it involves a reversal of the generally accepted view of the latter's role in the evolution of "socialist realism". This is one more place in which Bloch's critical "refunctioning" comes into play despite the ostensibly *direct* relationship.

eral terms the wide-ranging ontology that is implied by the objectivity
of the "real possible of the Novum" as a whole. This reintegrates com-
paratively, again in a highly characteristic manner, the product of intense, imaginative thought with the orthodoxies of the dominant traditions. The formal, theoretical reintegration which we shall now
sketch out briefly in the conclusion of this chapter precedes the bid for
realization that follows. In the latter Bloch re-engages with Marx and
his demand for a total renewal of philosophy as a sequel to its
"abolition". The engagement with the *Theses on Feuerbach* constitutes
the content of Bloch's claim to theoretical Marxist orthodoxy; it will
form the core of the next chapter and provide us with some indication of
the degree to which Bloch can in reality be regarded as a Marxist.

Bloch returns to the ontology of the category first explicated and
refers to its "layers" (*Schichten*). This figurative expression refers to
the actual diversity of the concrete "Can-be" (*Kannsein*) that inhabits
the Possible. In an extremely demanding discussion Bloch attempts to
distinguish "nonsense" from "counter-sense" and to outline the truth
condition for the Possible which is not "strictly fact-based" but a
"factual one, i.e. a cognitive, fact-suited one" (*PH* I,225).[29] Bloch's aim
is to direct attention at the "grounded *assumption*" of a statement, that
it is capable of being. This creative extension of the logic of future-
grounded statements leads into a consideration of future-conditionals
and axioms; Bloch works towards a relation between cognitive and real
ground that forces logical necessity into retreat and posits process as the
prime characteristic of human existence.

On the basis of this discussion Bloch then advances into a discussion
of the Object (*Gegenstand*)[30] and its factual relations referring to Ob-
ject-theory in Meinong and Husserl, concluding that the "fact-based ob-
ject-suited Possible, grasped and defined in terms of Object theory,
therefore definitely constitutes a separate differentiation of possibility and is not ... a superfluous doubling of the object-based real Possible"
(*PH* I,231). By these means Bloch fights off the potential charge that
he is re-creating a new (albeit temporally refunctioned and inverted)
form of idealism with regard to the Object. His eventual goal is the
restatement of the Real Possible as the substitutions for the Being-Into-
Possibility which Aristotle defined as matter. This, worked out in the
pantheistic-materialistic philosophies of the Middle Ages and no-

---

[29]The following passage on pp.229-235 is of exceptional difficulty and merits further
analysis: the move from the consideration of reality and its transformation in *aesthetic*
terms to its evaluation in relation to the question of *truth* raises complex issues, not least
those provoked by the reworking of Aristotle within a refunctioned Hegelianism.

[30]Here the translators belatedly recognise the problem involved in the linguistic representation of the object, *PH* I, p.225, see ch.4 note 15 above.

tably in Giordano Bruno, provided the foundation for a dynamic, potent materialism (as opposed to its allegedly static, Christian scholastic impoverishment). The task of correctly understood dialectical materialism is to rehabilitate materialism by extracting it from the neglected and suppressed patrimony of Aristotle, so as to provide the elements for a re-union of extremes in effect held apart in the tradition: "future and nature, anticipation and matter - chime together in the overdue groundedness of historical-dialectical materialism" (*PH* I,237). On this basis Bloch formulates the quasi-Kantian epigram: *"Without matter no basis of (real) anticipation, without (real) anticipation no horizon of matter is ascertainable"* (*PH* I,237) and then, beyond this, draws out the conclusion that follows from the whole structure of the argument:[31]

> Real possibility thus does not reside in any ready-made ontology of the being of That-Which-Is up to now, but in the ontology, which must constantly be grounded anew, of the being of That-Which-Is-Not-Yet, which discovers future even in the past and in the middle of nature. (*PH* I,237)

In consequence matter itself is explained in the following terms:

> real possibility is the categorial In-Front-of-Itself of material movement considered as a *process*; it is the specific regional character *of reality itself, on the Front of its occurrence.* (*PH* I,237)

Inasmuch as such dynamic attributes feature in the theistic tradition (which Bloch is later to appropriate and refunction), then they are qualified by the inner dialectic of the One and the Many, rest and motion, eternity and time, which tend to resolve process into stasis. Again in contrast with Bloch's position the relation of divine and human being in the main Christian theological traditions is normally qualified by a relation of analogy which mediates the qualitative discontinuity between the two. Bloch's concept of processual, future-laden matter is likewise given a cosmic, totalistic role when it is expanded to include man and cosmos in a vision reminiscent in certain respects of that of Teilhard de Chardin.[32] Thus Bloch outlines an "ascent of man" analo-

---

[31]Again the reworking of ontological questions and the evolution of a conceptual vocabulary to embody its consequences (a task more easily accomplished in German than in English) depends upon Bloch's consistent "Left-wing" materialist interpretation of the scholastics.

[32]Whilst the future-orientated philosophy bears some superficial resemblance to Teilhard's vision, a closer affinity as regards structure and creation of conceptual vocabulary might exist between Bloch and A.N. Whitehead's *Process and Reality An Essay in*

gous to the activity of dynamic matter and these linked together through the *tertium quid* of the Real Possible, the universal Utopian category. This materialism is unaffected by any displacement of its central ontological role through the intrusion of a divinity or an incarnate principle (as in the Christian theology of the Latin Western tradition). Thus in an extraordinary, even rhapsodic passage[33] Bloch traces out the evolution of the Real Possible from its seed in the future which drives on to unfold its latent form through undetermined open leaps from the *"potentia-possibilitas"* into appearance. The historical location of this becoming human is the worker,[34] who is transformed and developed as he "walks upright"; he is an "alpha" who, moving through revolutions comes to his "omega" in classless man, the highest human type.

The light on the horizon of human existence is reflected, so Bloch argues, in almost all social utopias where it presents itself *"psychologically* as *wishful image* forwards, *morally* as human ideal, and *aesthetically* as natural object-based *symbol"* (*PH* I,238). In effect such social utopias constitute the total ideological world of a progressive humanity and they function as the latent invitation to the "more or less realized Possible of an attempted perfect humanity, of perfect social conditions; they are therefore, in their guiding images and guiding panels, galvanizing and exemplary" (*PH* I,238).[35] This, as we noted earlier, tends to become a salvific theory when it culminates in the appearance within the framework of the categories and the manifestations of the Real Possible of the "undistorted and unreified (*unerdinglichte*), beautiful human type and the classless relationship in which there is room for him" (*PH* I,238).

In the utopian human condition the distance between the symbols or ciphers of the utopian possibility and their "full appearance", that is the contrast between what is actually happening in the present and the future, is proleptically overcome by both literature and philosophy. Both work, when progressive, towards an end that is understood as

Cosmology, (New York: Macmillan, 1929). This, like Bloch's, has proved difficult to assimilate into the English (as opposed to the American) cultural sphere.

[33]*PH* I, pp.237-238.

[34]Such heroic depictions of the worker combining a Marxian predeliction for the proletariat with a Nietzschian prediction of the new *"Übermensch"* are not an entirely socialist prerogative, see, for example, Ernst Jünger's *Der Arbeiter Schicksal und Gestalt* (Hamburg, 1932) for a conservative presentation of the new humanity that is to triumph in the age of technology (*Technik*) and to embody a reality that transcends the polarisation of class.

[35]There is here apparent a residuum of the influence of Neo-Kantianism which draws upon the later passages of Kant's *Critique of Pure Reason*, that is upon the "heuristic fiction" of the *"Transcendental Dialectic"*, which likewise inform the position of Hans Vaihinger's *The Philosophy of "As If"* (London: RKP, 1924), an outlook that has distinct affinity with Bloch's presentation. This is not surprising given their mutual indebtedness to Neo-Kantianism.

some kind of uniformity of meaning and convergence of goals. In a direct repudiation of the Kantian separation of the figurative and the logical, Bloch now explicitly brings together disciplines that have functioned in an implicit interconnection throughout the formulation of the philosophy of hope:

> Literature has understood the symbolic region of the real Possible more clearly than previous philosophy owing to its figurative nature, but philosophy incorporates this region with strictness of concept and seriousness of correction. But both realistic literature and philosophy reveal that the world is full of real ciphers and real symbols, full of "signatura rerum" " in the sense of things which contain a central meaning. (*PH* I,240)

These, then, are the tools with which an adequate consciousness of the possibility of the future, the "real Possible" can be forged; the ultimate goal towards which all this works that is, as we have seen, the transformation of man, in what Bloch holds to be specifically Marxian terms. This hermeneutic of the human condition is crowned by a return to the utopian vision of the so called early Marx, the fulfilment of the "real Possible" itself:

> according to the most concrete of all Man's anticipation, the essence of the perfectible is the naturalization of man, the humanisation of nature. That is the abolition of alienation in man and nature, between man and nature or the harmony of the unreified object with the manifested subject, of the unreified subject with the manifested object. Such a perspective of absolute truth, that means here, of complete real being in the Real itself. (*PH* I,240)

All of this stands as it were behind the as yet unturned page of the present, in a future Real universally latent. At this juncture the sheer momentum of Bloch's intellectual imagination carries him once again (*PH* I,241-246) into a compressed and involved exploration of the philosophy of time modality and a critique of the near universal predeliction of class-determined philosophers for "static thinking" (*PH* I,242). Even Bloch's favourite mentors, Aristotle, Nicholas of Cusa, Giordano Bruno and Hegel, posit a "completed One and All" and therefore obstruct the "space of the Open Possible" (*PH* I,242). So, Bloch argues, reinforcing earlier assertions, the categorial concept of possibility is an almost virgin land: "it is the Benjamin among the great concepts" (*PH*

I,242)[36]. The whole orthodox philosophical tradition is liable to abortion and self-stultification by virtue of its almost total suppression of the utopian "real Possible". On this basis Bloch concludes (for reasons not wholly identical with those of Marx) that a new beginning in philosophy is an absolute necessity and thus he begins with Marx's critique of Feuerbach:

> The truth is however the Marxist one, contrasting with all previous philosophy, that the point is to change the world as a correctly integrated world, that is, precisely as a dialectically-materialistically processive world, as an unenclosed world. Changing the changeable world is the theory-practice of the realizably real Possible on the Front of the world, of the world process. And at this end the real Possible, which is homeless in every contemplative-static philosophy, is the real problem of the world itself: as the still unidentical character of appearance and real essential being, ultimality of existence and essence within it. (PH I,246)

According to Bloch, we face a stark choice: either we allow the merely possible to turn into nothing or we regard it as the real Possible, the free and unconditional future, and turn it into Being. This latter assertion is the ground rule of a strategy directed against the all-pervasive threat of nihilism that Bloch recognised with stark and exemplary clarity in the chaos of German thought following the First World War, but which, as we have argued, consistently pervades his work. Man, so freed from false consciousness, must concentrate upon the "central potency in the potency=actuality of processive matter" (PH I,248). The very hinge of history itself (Die Angel in der menschlichen Geschichte) is its producer, working man, without dispossession, alienation, reification or subjugation for purposes of profit. "Marx", Bloch argues, "is the realized teacher of this resolution of the proletariat, of this possible mediation, which is becoming real, of men with themselves and their moral happiness" (PH I,249). So in consequence we now turn to the enactment of the vision, and Bloch's first attempt at a fuller integration of his own thought with that of Marx, a convergence located precisely in the latter's realization that the philosophy of Germany had to give way to a philosophy of the future, a philosophy of

---

[36]Bloch here alludes to Benjamin's tragic suicide on the Franco-Spanish frontier in 1940. This prematurely cut off the productivity of a highly gifted and original thinker with whom Bloch had had a passionate intellectual partnership. See S. Markun, op.cit., pp. 31-35 and Zudeieck, op.cit., pp.103-105, and Hannah Arendt's remarkable memoir, "Walter Benjamin" in Men in Dark Times (New York: Harcourt Brace, 1968).

change as opposed to mere contemplation. In this context Bloch now ventures his own formulation of the bid for praxis, an "orthopraxis" [37] that must also constitute his claim to Marxian orthodoxy. The messianic image of the new humanity, here identified with the heroic, reborn worker, is, as we shall later see, to co-exist in some discomfort with the image of the Faust-Prometheus, embodied in the aesthetic and intellectual genius who enacts the "becoming" of realised God-consciousness. This is but one of the many inner tensions in the relationship between Romanticism and Marxism that Bloch attempts to drive to the point of actual identity.

[37]The term "orthopraxis" as used in the "theology of liberation" needs to be understood in relation to Bloch's much-maligned (J.P. Stern) "theory-praxis" conception. See chs. 8 and 9 below.

CHAPTER VI

THEORY AND PLAUSIBLE PRAXIS: HOPE IN THE CONTEXT OF MARXISM

In the last chapter we engaged with the core of the first volume of *The Principle of Hope* which contains a "deduction" of the category of the "real Possible" and an explication of its constitutive elements. Bloch's subsequent attempt to re-integrate his position with that of the young Marx serves as the bridge that brings him back from extreme abstraction through an examination of the nature of practical enactment to the mundane human condition. This latter is even unreflectingly experienced, nevertheless sustained by the fragmented traces of the promise of the "real Possible" that persists in the cultural artifacts of the West. So, to conclude our account of the foundation of *The Principle of Hope* we now return with Bloch to the point of departure in a clearly discernible fulfilment of the method of mediation, that a work be material and visionary yet firmly embedded in the human condition as it is actually experienced. Such experience is scarcely normal in the accepted sense, we do well to recall that Bloch's heroic norms are Goethe and Hegel, and his attempted *tour de force* involves the enactment of this heroic humanity in the context and on the basis of Marx's teaching: it is a positive Prometheanism.

I. CHOOSING THE WORLD: RE-ENGAGEMENT WITH MARX

Although Bloch sets out carefully the historical context of Marx's eleven *Theses on Feuerbach*, the subsequent exposition which involves their re-ordering is not likely to prove easy material to a reader unfamiliar with the originals, which were written by Marx in 1845 for the purpose of self-clarification and not published until 1888 by Engels. There is little point in reproducing at length much of Bloch's fairly standard contextualisation, or, indeed, his analysis of the *Theses* except insofar as this might indicate how far his interpretation appears to diverge in a distinctive way from views that appear within the body of Marxism itself.

Bloch focuses upon the posthumously published *Theses on Feuerbach* in the context of Marx's development, that is just after the production of *The Holy Family* (1844) and before *The German Ideology* (1846). He indicates how, in negative reaction to Hegel and under the influence of Feuerbach (but aware of the latter's limitations), Marx provides in the *Theses*: "signposts out of mere anti-Hegelianism into reality that can be changed, out of materialism of the base behind the lines into that of the Front" (*PH* I,253). Bloch's account of Marx's development presents no particular difficulties to a reader acquainted with this through the standard textbooks.[1] Where, however, Bloch does innovate, his argument turns upon the interpretation he places upon the famous Eleventh Thesis:

> The philosophers have only *interpreted* the world, in various ways; the point, however, is to *change* it.

Given the historical circumstances of the writing of the *Theses* their ordering has been a matter of some discussion amongst commentators. Bloch groups them according to thematic content in the following way: epistemology expressed in perception and activity (Theses 5,1,3); anthropological-historical theses concerned with self-alienation and its real causes, and true materialism (Theses 4,6,7,9,10); uniting of theory and practice directed towards proof and probation (Theses 2,8); and, finally, the most important thesis, "the *password* that not only marks a final parting of the minds, (i.e. of the old and the new philosophers), but with those whose use they cease to be nothing but minds (Thesis 11)" (*PH* I, 254-5). Bloch recognises in Hegel's *Phenomenology of Mind* the first work to set the concept of work and action squarely in the epistemological context, albeit in abstract-idealist terms. The philosophers' concept of action derived from Hegel and Fichte, but most notably formulated by Cieszkowski,[2] lacked those features which in Marx make his thought of decisive, world-historical significance. Unlike both his antecedents and contemporaries, Marx produced a true "philosophy of action" which included a developed economic theory and a "timetable of dialectically comprehended tendency within it" (*PH* I,271). In reaching this conclusion Bloch appropriates and revises the critique of religious self-alienation that Marx took from Feuerbach and presupposed in his subsequent critique of the philosophy of law and of the state. According to Bloch, Feuerbach made a "kind of non-denom-

---

[1]Convenient contextualisations are provided by L. Kolakowski, Main Currents of Marxism (Oxford: Clarendon, 1978) vol.I, pp.141-6 and D. McLellan, *Karl Marx His Life and Thought* (London: Macmillan, 1973). The *Theses on Feuerbach* are reproduced in *K. Marx and F. Engels On Religion* (Moscow: Progress Publishers, 1957), pp.62-4.

[2]L. Kolakowski likewise accords considerable importance to his compatriot August Cieskowski, see *Main Currents of Marxism* vol.I, pp.85-88.

inational *pectoral theology*" out of a residual religious sensibility but "the whole apparatus of theology remains intact, it has just moved from its heavenly location to a certain abstract region, which reified virtues of the 'natural bias'" (*PH* I,267). Indeed, as we are to see later, Bloch regards the active "refunctioning" of religion, that is the alienated divine transcendence into explosive consciousness of the future kingdom as central and fundamental to his whole enterprise. Correspondingly, Bloch places Feuerbach on "that salvation line which leads from Hegel to Marx, just as the German disaster line leads from Schopenhauer and Nietzsche and the consequences" (*PH* I,274)[3]. Feuerbach's failure ultimately lies in his lack of class-consciousness, in an inflated (and impractical) universal tone, for:

> Without factions in love, with an equally concrete pole of hatred, there is no genuine love; without *partiality* of the revolutionary class standpoint there only remains idealism instead of forward practice. Without the primacy of the head to the very end there are only mysteries of resolution rather than the resolution of mysteries. (*PH* I,274)

We note in the foregoing passage the phrase "forward practice"; it is upon this qualification of the formal presentation of practice as effecting change in the world that Bloch expands on the basis of an interpretation of the eleventh and final Thesis. The statement: "Philosophers have only interpreted the world in various ways; but the point is to change it" is not to be understood as some variant of pragmatism (a doctrine Bloch associates with "American cultural barbarity") but in a sense distinctly Marx's own. "Pragmatic" is nevertheless an apt word, one readily applicable to Bloch's attempt to relate the utopian "categorical imperative" to the *Theses* of Marx. Bloch's relationship with Marx is scarcely innovative outside and beyond this rather narrow area of dependence. Not even Bloch's most fervent admirers could plausibly argue that his discussion of the Eleventh Thesis is particularly impressive and whilst he may be correct in asserting that in the Eleventh Thesis, "the future aspect is the nearest and most important" (*PH* I,274), his interpretation is not in itself capable of sustaining a complete identity between Marx's and Bloch's visions of that future. Polemic directed against American pragmatism, and then the

---

[3]This convenient scheme, common both to Bloch and to Lukács in his *The Destruction of Reason* (London: Merlin, 1980) obscures the former's significant, if somewhat obscure, relation to Nietzsche. Above all, it is in Nietzsche's notion of the reworking of the tradition in the light of a ruthlessly conceived modernity that both informs, and is subverted by Bloch's "*Unfunktionierung*". This is the equivalent of "transvaluation" (*Umwertung*).

simple reiteration of Lenin's dictum that "the whole genius of Marx consists in the fact that he gave answers to the questions which the progressive thinking of humanity had already posed" (cited *PHI*, p.277) is no substitute for the kind of careful argument which might justify the nature of Bloch's persisting concern with good theory (and "theory-practice") in the face of Marx's denigration of "contemplation" (*Anschauung*).

It is arguable that both Bloch's statement that "real practice cannot take a single stride without having consulted theory economically and philosophically, theory advancing with great strides" (*PH* I,277), and his assertion of the "theoretical-practical primacy of *true philosophy*" (*PH* I,280) in changing the world, actually run counter to the actual socio-historical consequences for intellectual reflection brought about by the *negation of philosophy* Marx originally demanded in the "Introduction to the Critique of Hegel's Philosophy of Right" of 1844. The dialectical juxtaposition of realization and negation has, as ever, painful consequences when enacted. Bloch's attempt to formulate a "subsequent philosophy" pushes Marx's statement, especially the second part: "the point, however, is to change it", from latency into potent actuality. So Bloch tempers the edge of Marx's sword: the real abolition of philosophy means death followed by a rebirth, the new birth of a system of thought to be identified with that of Bloch himself. Bloch stresses the apologetic motifs that can be drawn from Marx:

> The absolutely new aspect in Marxist philosophy consists in the radical changing of its basis, in proletarian revolutionary mission; but the absolutely new aspect does not consist in the idea that the only philosophy which is capable of changing and destined to change the world concretely is not - philosophy at all any more. (*PH* I,280)

The first part of this statement grounds Marxist philosophy in proletarian revolution, the second reasserts the primacy of philosophy, even if it is performed in a new key. Despite Bloch's efforts to harmonise his programme with that of Marx, there remains an incipient tension between the past-determined perspective of Marx (with its, fleeting, almost covert, glances towards the future) and the future determined outlook of Bloch (with its consistently directed interrogation of the past and present by the future). *In reality*, as regards the Marxian conception of the structure of reality and the alleged real hiatus of revolution, Marx and Bloch stand on different sides of a divide of history. The careful elision of this distinction by the casual parcelling together of the following elements within a single sentence is indicative:

> Philosophical change is thus a change according to the stipula-
> tion of the analysed situation, of dialectical tendency, of objec-
> tive laws, of real possibility. (*PH* I,281).

Bloch effectively makes a category mistake when dialectical tendency, objective laws and *real possibility* are included in the same conception as though they referred to readily commensurable items. Dialectics and objective laws belong essentially to the Marxian interpretation of reality as structured and driven from the standpoint of the
past by class conflict and thus by the evolution of the material relations of production. Bloch's "real Possibility" belongs by contrast to a
magisterial, even grandiose scheme which comes at us as it were from
the *future*. Bloch attempts to integrate his project with that of Marx
but does not succeed precisely because of a structural assymetry, which,
if not complete (Marx does give some hints about the future and its
"dreams") is at least so extensive and fundamental as to prevent any
ready assimilation.[4] To venture this critical comment is not, however,
to generate a critique of Bloch's own thought as such, but merely to indicate the incongruity of his attempt to present it as wholly consistent
with Marx's understanding of the nature of philosophy.

It is a highly problematic enterprise to attempt to read the whole
content of Marxism out of a postulated utopian "Eschaton" as Bloch attempts to do in his concluding remarks on Marx's eleventh *Thesis*. The
dialectical realisation of human reflection in identification with the
universality identified with the fate of a single class, in the terms
Marx asserts: "Philosophy cannot realise itself without the abolition
of the proletariat, the proletariat cannot abolish itself without the
realization of philosophy",[5] may enjoy a canonical status within
Marxism, but the simple equation of this with Bloch's "philosophical
'Eschaton'" of the renewal of philosophy and the "resurrection of nature" (*PH* I,281) presupposes the completion of the first stage of his
utopian journey, his ride into the blue. In consequence, this position cannot avoid the fundamental charge of being "utopian" in the sense condemned by Marx himself. Thus both as regards the evolution and structure of the Marxian critique (grounded in historical and philosophical
analysis) and the historical enactment of Marxism in socialist societies
Bloch runs into this danger. As Bloch's argument progresses it shows

---

[4]There is a certain obvious correctness about the criticisms of Bloch's thought made by
his orthodox Marxist-Leninist detractors in post-war Leipzig. Bloch's philosophy is poor
"orthodox" Marxism and gains importance in relation to criteria other than those given
axiomatic status by such consistent Marxists.

[5]*MEGA* I, 1/1, p.621.

signs of a gradual retreat from effective polemic into even more strident
rhetoric, sure signs that here there is real insecurity.

The tensions that underlie these efforts to prove an identity, between Bloch's statement of the "real Possibility" as the enactment of
philosophy as praxis, and the critique of contemplative philosophy
propounded by Marx in the *Theses on Feuerbach*, are deep-seated and
unconquered by Bloch's assertive rather than evidential approach.
This is a sensitive issue that surfaces in the subtitle to the concluding
section on "Changing the World or Marx's Eleven Theses on Feuerbach"
(*PH* I, 249-286) that we have examined in some detail. Bloch's subheading is indicative:

> The Archimedean point; knowledge related not only to what is
> past, but essentially to what is coming up. (*PH* I,282)

The reader must again test the plausibility of Bloch's handling of
the relation between past and future knowledge and establish if in fact
he has correctly applied this distinction to the "early Marx", the so-
called "humanistic" and "Romantic" Marx. These questions are present,
although differently formulated in the passage that concludes Bloch's
examination of the Theses. Thus already in the Fourth Thesis the
"Archimedean point has been discovered from which the old world
could thus be lifted off its hinges and the new ones cut to its hinges" in
the "worldly basis of today" (*PH* I,282). Consequently, Bloch asks,
"*what is it finally* that discovered the starting-point of the 'Eleven
Theses' i.e. the beginning *philosophy of revolution?*" It cannot be the
new proletarian mandate, nor any of the three traditional sources and
components of Marxism, that is German philosophy, British political
economy or French socialism. Bloch's proposal is daring, it "in fact has
hardly been fully considered by and in Marx himself" (*PH* I,282) and it
involves an addition to and expansion of Marx's designation of his temporal standpoint. Bloch cites the *Communist Manifesto*: "In bourgeois
society the past rules over the present, in communist societies the present rules over the past", which he creatively glosses as follows:

> And the present rules *together with the horizon within it,*
> which is the horizon of the future, and which gives to the flow
> of the present specific space, the space of new, feasibly better
> present. Thus the beginning philosophy of revolution, i.e. of
> changeability for the better, was ultimately revealed on and in
> the *horizon of the future;* with the science of the New and
> power to guide it. (*PH* I,283)

This is a set of statements which purports to restate Marx's position; but this is a Marx thoroughly impregnated with Bloch's category of "real Possibility", determined as it were by its presentation as "horizon". Such a reading is superficially commensurable with the immediate context but whether it in fact corresponds with the overall thrust of Marx's thought and its development is more doubtful. Thus, for example, in the *Grundrisse* and *Capital voll* Marx's work is predominantly directed at the articulation of the ontology of social reality dominant under capitalism, exposed through the demystification of its inner mechanism using the combined insights of Hegelian dialectics and political economy. Here we refer to the emergence of the "commodity dialectic" and the "fetishism of commodities" .

Any assertions about the nature and status of items with the Marxian corpus are liable to be contentious yet it is important to note the striking difference between the understanding of the relationship of the two areas of idealist philosophy and political economy in Marx and Bloch. For Marx the deductive-universal method of Hegel has to be synthesised with the inductive-generalised mode of political economy. For Bloch, political economy and its product in Marxian terms the "commodity dialectic" are used when required as part of the polemical apparatus of *Ideologiekritik*, but they are not *fundamental* to the creative impulse of his thought as in the case of Marx himself. Bloch argues that all previous knowledge was directed towards the past and to the object of contemplation (i.e. it is *betrachtbar*), and that this tendency was intensified by thinking in commodity form under capitalism. The polemical use of the commodity dialectic is explicit. It is evident that Bloch's point of departure, the deduction of the future-orientated categories and their relation to the Front, puts the analysis of the past as recovered through the critical history of material (i.e. economic) relations on a problematic footing. The contrast here is a difference of fundamental *episteme*. The contemplative way of thinking is alienated and bound to the past at the expense of an open relation with the future. Plato's anamnesis, Aristotle's (the "What-Was-Being") and even Hegel's dialectical occurrence-in-process seek in Bloch's words "to produce a correct consciousness via an existing Factum, whereas for real communists it is a question of overthrowing what exists" .[6] Once more Bloch captures Marx's present, infuses it with future reference and then identifies the *"seclusion of the preterite"* with a class standpoint. Marxism, so Bloch claims, even when it is historical in orientation in both "primitive communist history and as a history of class struggle" (*PH* I,284), does not distance and enclose the past or merely free the

---

[6]*Deutsche Ideologie, MEGA* I, 5, p.31.

present as an unbound point from which contemplation may be undertaken; far more creatively it implies a universal fructification of history. Consequently Marxist insight rightly understood permits Bloch to relate past, present and future. Bourgeois knowledge directed at the past finds the present embarrassing and it has no grasp on the formless future; over against these limitations Marx's conception is taken as a licence for Bloch's generous encomium, for:

> The dialectical-historical tendency science of Marxism is thus the mediated *future science of reality plus the objectively real possibility within it*; all this for the purpose of *action*. The difference from the anamnesis of the Become, together with all its variations, could not be more illuminating; this is true both of the enlightening Marxist method and of the enlightened, unenclosed matter within it. *Only the horizon of the future, which Marxism occupies, with that of the past as the ante-room, gives reality its real dimension. (PH I,285)*

Once having reinterpreted the Marxian management of study of the past from the standpoint of a present conceived as the embodiment of a potent future, Bloch then re-inserts his own, now legitimated, perspective into the broader philosophical tradition and then relates it into his universal concerns. Marx's conception of the ultimate destiny of mankind: "*human* society or socialized humanity" (Thesis 10) indicates that the world is changeable and "world-changing of this kind occurs solely in a world of *qualitative reversibility, changeability itself*, not in that of the mechanical Time and Time Again, of pure quantity, of the historical In-Vain" (*PH* I,286). Here there are the universal categories of the historical process, and, echoing Herder's "Genius of the Future", Bloch rises to near ecstatic Messianic utterance: "precisely the *hope of the knowledge of life'* became a real event in Marx, so that it might really be such knowledge" (*PH* I,286). For Bloch, Marx's "Eleven Theses" testify to: "socialized humanity, allied with a nature that is mediated with it, is the reconstruction of the world into homeland (*Heimat*)" (*PH* I,286).[7] This is a secular soteriology, nothing less than the convergence of *Heil* and *Heimat*, "salvation" and "homecoming" .

---

[7]The English word "homeland" scarcely does justice to the immensely rich resonance of the German "*Heimat*". The English, the first and most highly industrialised and the most deracinated people in Europe lost contact with the land and an ancestral sense of place very early; second, "homeland" has undergone ironic political perversion and it is virtually unusable as exploited by Bloch.

II. RECAPITULATION: INTIMATIONS OF THE ABSOLUTE

Informed opinions differ as to how successfully Bloch relates his position to that of Marx. Thus whereas Wayne Hudson regards Bloch primarily as a reformer of Marxism, by contrast we approach him more as a "refunctioner" of grandiose German cultural ambitions within the setting of Marxism. Bloch certainly lays hold of the Marxian understanding of the power to alter the course of history as the *sine qua non* of concrete utopia, but it is the universal, quasi-soteriological elements in the situation that fascinate and draw him forward. Bloch's uninhibited hypostatization of language and his articulation of the "reality" attained thereby is combined with a visionary conception of Marxism and its proposed fulfilment of history and the human condition. These tendencies constantly carry him into the realm of the universal, even, as we shall see, towards a *visionary*, rather than a revolutionary "concrete universal", that is the Absolute of the Novum.[8]

This sense that the latency of the Novum might overdetermine Bloch's thought is frequently sensed but it is closer to the surface on some occasions than others. Bloch's tendency to imply a self-transcending, yet personal and immanent life-force has been present from the outset and this once more becomes distinctly prominent in the Summary[9] that follows the exposition of the *Theses on Feuerbach*. Reverting to the literary mode of phenomenological self-description, Bloch writes:

> But who drives on within us? Someone who does not occupy himself, does not yet emerge. There is no more to be said now, this inner dimension sleeps. The blood runs, the heart beats without us being able to sense what has set the pulse in motion. In fact, if there is no disturbance, then nothing under our skins can be felt at all. That within us which makes us capable of being stimulated does not stimulate itself. Healthy life sleeps, dreaming within itself. It is completely immersed in the juice in which it is stewing.(*PH* I,287).

This organic, ontologised, interrogatory self-description exists in the lost Now which is experienced as constant grasping of the openness, the "still decidable real-Possible", is itself constituted and formalised by the "Unum Necessarium in the direction" (*PH* I,289), that is the call of the future Novum. Bloch stands between Augustine (and the tradi-

---

[8]This is a Hegelian term refunctioned by Bloch which indicates the strong affinity between them, despite the manifest differences.

[9]Entitled: "Summary Anticipatory Composition and its Poles: Dark Moment - Open Adequacy", *PH* I, pp.287-316. Bloch's stylistic change is remarkable and merits notice.

tion of theological and philosophical anthropology expressed through
the analysis of time extending down to Husserl and Heidegger) and
Hegel (who provides the archetypal and dominant synthesis of both
theological and philosophical traditions in terms of all-embracing
universality). The conjunction of the products of these two poles: on the
one hand the lost Now of the temporal dialectic and, on the other, the
Hegelian drive towards absolute universality, underlies what seems at
first sight a strange synthesis, in which Bloch juxtaposes the *"darkness
of the Now"* and the "outflow by the *openness of the object-based background*, towards which hope goes" (*PH* I,289). The utopian goal of this
projected, but as yet unachieved, resolution manifests itself in the following way:

> open adequacy does not make itself evident in the experiences
> of the *continuing* world-process, with experimented outflow, but
> in short, strange experience of an *anticipated keeping still*. The
> briefest *symbol-intentions of an Absolute.*(*PH* I,289).

Bloch's exploitation of proleptic signs, anticipations of the as yet
unachieved Absolute, refunctioned in terms of the Novum is activated
stylistically through a combination of extremely concrete, yet simultaneously hypostatised language, and suffused with wide-ranging literary allusions. The result is an indirectness that may often baffle the
reader. However, the existence of traces of the latent "symbol-intention", that is the "shape of the unconstruable question" (*PH* I,289,)
points to the unanswered and the ineffable dimension which has thus
far been located and explored as *possibility*. Now, in the recapitula-
tory Summary Bloch presents in continuity with *Geist der Utopie* an account of the hope for *reality* itself. So the recapitulation contains an
implicit *"Aufhebung"*, that is a shift from the analysis of mere possibility into the articulation of the to-be-hoped-for future real: the
"darkness of the Now" will become light. In terms which once again
combine concrete, quasi-phenomenological and hypostatising style
with literary allusion and consequent indirectness, Bloch asserts that:

> If the content of what is driving in the Now, what is touched in
> the Here, were extracted positively, a 'Stay awhile, you are so
> fair', then conceived hope, hoped-for world would have
> reached their goal. (*PH* I,290)

Bloch's use of Faust's words as a poetic indication of the nature of
ultimate fulfilment finally exposes his pervasive indebtedness to

Goethe, an influence that we have not yet fully acknowledged.[10] At this juncture Bloch continues his exposition of the nature of the New, anticipated in the real Possible of the future, through a renewed engagement with vitalism (Bergson) and empiricist psychology (William James, as influenced by Hume). Both schools of thought are found wanting in comparison with Husserl, who (paradoxically in the light of Bloch's previous assessment) reflects Plato, and from whom the "correct version" is learnable. It is worth reproducing Bloch's citation from Husserl because the latter's conception of the structure of time has had clearly a powerful influence upon Bloch's own account of the experience of time and futurity:

> As a movement is being perceived, moment by moment an As-Now-Comprehension is taking place in which the topical phase of the movement itself is constituted ... The flowing is not only flowing in general, but each phase is of one and the same form ... the form consists in a Now constituting itself through an impression, and a tail of retentions affiliating itself to this and a horizon of protention" (*Zur Phänomenologie des inneren Zeitbewusstseins*. 1928, pp.391,476).

On the basis of this quotation Bloch works towards a synthesis that represents a further nodal point in the structure of the whole work. What follows is the apogee of Bloch's argument, the pulsing synthesis that contains energy and momentum sufficient to carry the writer through two further volumes of *The Principle of Hope* consequent upon the position established in the first. Bloch expands upon the conception of time implied in structural terms by Husserl and traceable in the metaphysical tradition to Platonic origins in the *Parmenides*:[11]

---

[10]Bloch's use of this phrase, in fuller form,
> "*Werd ich zum Augenblicke sagen:*
> *Verweile doch! du Bist so schön*"
rendered in the translation by Philip Wayne
> If to the fleeting hour I say
> 'Remain, so fair thou art, remain!'"

Faust, Part One, (Penguin Books, Harmondsworth, 1949), is turned by Bloch into a philosophical principle by its identification with the hypostatised Latin dictum "*Carpe diem*" drawn from Horace, Ode XI. The idea of the active seizure of the present in the name of the future is central to Bloch's conception of time.

[11]The full citation is from *Parmenides* 156D-E: "For nothing crosses over out of rest as long as it is still at rest, nor out of movement while it is still moving, into rest; but the moment, this peculiar something lies between movement and rest, belonging to no time; and nothing within it, out of it, what is moved crosses over into it and what is resting into movement."

No flow can be thought of at all, let alone dialectically understood without that Now-Amidst in its time, which is not even
itself in time, but 'the peculiar Something', in Plato's words,
out of which the time (not only the conception of time) of the
real stream of movement arises and in which the movement is
united with restless rest itself (*PH* I,292).

Here, extraordinarily, Bloch the Marxist draws together Plato, Faust
and German mysticism:

And finally - as regards the flow as one towards outflow (rest) -
but the tenor of the Faust plan and the related tenor of mysticism has the moment as no abstraction within it. 'Stay awhile,
you are so fair': supposedly this can be said to the moment as
the highest moment, even to that perfectly fulfilled and so
steadfast and steadily lasting moment which is stressed in
Eckhart's mysticism as the trice (*das Nun*) (nunc stans) of perfection. (*PH* I,292)

It is this "real Now", over against the "stream of abstraction" of the
vitalists, that provides the structure in the Now and the Not-Having-
Itself of the "knot of the riddle of existence". With this assertion Bloch
reintroduces one of the ancestral metaphysical conceptions from the
German tradition, refunctioned under the guise of a Marxian dialectic,
which puts it there - but beyond - experience:

The Now of the existence, which drives everything and in
which everything drives, is the most inexperienced thing that
there is; it still drives continually under the world. It constitutes the realizing aspect which has least realized itself - an
active moment-darkness of itself. (*PH* I,293)

The Now of existence which comprehends the drive latent in reality itself is referred to by Bloch as the *Carpe diem* which forms the
epigrammatic centrepiece of his conception of meaning of history.[12] The
refunctioned phrase *Carpe diem*, a well-used derivation from Horace,
also represents the transience of the significant moment open to heroic
exploitation as by Lenin and Kierkegaard. Truly effective comprehension of the genuine *Carpe diem* comes with the extraordinary
men of action (Caesar), or with the equally exceptional historical in-

[12]There is a parallel between Bloch's designation of the Carpe diem and Tillich's notion of *kairos* or meaningful time as opposed to mere time, *chronos*. See, for example, *Systematic Theology* (London: Nisbet, 1968), vol.3, pp.393-396.

sight (Goethe seeing the Prussian army beaten at Valmy), or Marx and Engels (in their commentary on the "Eighteenth Brumaire"), but supremely with Lenin's "thoroughly thought-out Carpe diem" in the October Revolution. The *Carpe diem* is understood as the "fathomed presence of mind" that discerns the "transitory moment with the most fertile motif, of a meeting place of highly rarified mediation between past and future - in the midst of the unsighted Now (*PH* I,294). It is, to gloss Bloch, a dialectical penetration of the lost Now which refracts significance in despite of transience. In its turn the *Carpe diem* dictates the terms of Bloch's revisionary reading of the *Theses on Feuerbach*:

> All of this course already preoccupied a totally uncontempla-
> tive stance, manely apprehending-comprehending (*Begreifen-
> Ergreifen*) of the topical driving forces of occurrence itself. This
> cannot be achieved by the class society which necessarily over-
> looked the truly producing element in face of the product; but
> the correct path to achieve topicality likewise only began
> with situation-analysis. Its goal remains the illumination of
> that which both drives and remains hidden to itself in the fi-
> nal That-ground of occurrence. (*PH* I,294)

Bloch's imaging of this conjunction is profound and beautiful: "Not-there is the condition of the Now, and even the Here of this Not-there forms a *zone of silence in the very place where the music is being played*" (*PH* I,295). The fleeting present is thus grasped in anticipation of the future, rather than through an attempted recovery of the past (the traditional emphasis); it is understood as the experience of incognito in the forecourt of the future presence which is not yet conscious, which has not yet become. Bloch expounds this "lived darkness" indirectly through the full panoply of exploratory allusion: the "*Volksweisheiten*" (" No weaver knows what he weaves", or: "There is no light at the foot of the lighthouse, *PH* I,295); Oedipus' delayed self-knowledge; the structure of perspective in landscape; and even Marxism, are all sources of analogies for the attempted explication of the immanence of "now-time" [13] first presented in *Geist der Utopie*.

---

[13] The notion of "Now-time" (*Jetzt-zeit*) has to be understood in relation to the German mystical tradition and the re-working of temporal motifs in other areas of twentieth century thought. This is a difficult area, see for its excellent bibliography the article by Alois M. Haas "*Meister Eckharts Auffassung von Zeit und Ewigkeit*", *Freiburger Zeitschrift für Philosophie und Theologie*, Vol.27, 1980, pp.325-55. Whereas Bloch synthesises and identifies the *Jetzt-zeit* with the *Carpe diem* Eckhart effects a parallel identity between apparent opposites: "*So muss Eckhart vom nunc aeternitatis, dem 'Jetzt der Ewigkeit' sprechen — eine Redeweise, die Temporales mit seinem Gegensatz vereinigt —, allerdings indem er mit Zufügungen die Zeitlosigkeit dieses nunc betont: Das*

Bloch attempts to resolve his conception of the immanence and latency of the future in a reworking of the Young Hegelian critique of idealism and through this he reawakens the question of God as the only means by which the tensions in his position can be overcome:[14]

> The darkness is intensified as soon as not only we ourselves but also the other, turned side remains undecided, hence as soon as we turn to the *future dimension*, which itself, in so far as it is above all logically new, means nothing other than over *expanded darkness*, than our darkness in the bearing of its womb, in the expansion of its further history; and it is likewise intensified with regard to God as the problem of the radically New, who must not only become visible for us in order to be, so that the whole world-process is reduced elastically to a movement relationship between two 'separated' realities, but who contains *himself* only as *hope*, as Not-Being-For-Itself, like us in the shadowy dimension of what has not occurred, of what is still unreal. (*Geist der Utopie*, 1918, p.372)

If, for a moment, we reconsider our assessment of Bloch's thought on analogy with that of the thought-form characteristic of the major idealist thinkers then it becomes apparent that a fuller pattern of similarity has emerged. Thus, for example, the stages of Kant's thought: the transcendental aesthetic and formulation of transcendental argument then applied to the deduction and analysis of the condition and categories of reason, followed in turn by consideration of the traditional arguments for the existence of God and again later, almost as a heuristic afterthought, the practical utility of the residual idea of God, form a pattern still traceable in Bloch's *The Principle of Hope*. Correspondingly, after the initial "aesthetic" of anticipatory consciousness, the "deduction" of the categories of the New and their attempted re-integration into the Marxian vision of the renewal of philosophy, Bloch now considers the "mythological term God". This recapitulation, is crucial to Bloch's post-modern and qualified remythologisation of human life. Both *Geist der Utopie* and *The Principle of Hope* are kaleidoscopic inasmuch as although the decorative patterns change as the conceptual container is as it were turned in order to alter the perceived im-

---

'Jetzt der Ewigkeit' ist das *verum nunc, utpote impartibile, fixum, immobile, das presenti tempore befreit ist*", p.333.

[14]The translation of Bloch into a *theistic* framework by West German theologians has to come to terms with the specific atheism of the passage that follows which makes the *assimilation* of the God hypothesis the necessary condition of human realisation. See chs. 8 and 9 below. Marx maintained that the question of atheism was not even a nineteenth century concern but an issue settled in the eighteenth century.

age, yet the principles that effect the image remain constant, and even, given Bloch's explicit self-reference, unchanged. In Bloch's mature reiteration of a position first stated in *Geist der Utopie* he now gives a more precise indication as to how the secularizing process affects his understanding of God, time, the subject, and the driving force of history:

> the darkness of the lived moment therefore coincides in its total depth with the essential, but not-here-existing mode of existence of the goal-content itself, which was once intended by the mythological term God, and which, according to the passage quoted above, is in fact the goal-content, that does not yet exist here, has not yet been brought out, of existing itself. However, the Carpe diem or present of the absolute goal-content stands in the same ground in which the subject of existing stands, and from the same ground as the latter the goal-content as a Realized (*realisierter*) goal-content is still outstanding: from the ground of that unclarified hearth of existence which *is unmythologically termed agent and core of developing matter*. (PH I,298)

Here Bloch transposes and transforms the residuum of the theological inheritance (the mythological term God) into a dialectical categorical imperative (the unmythologically termed agent and core of developing matter) that now functions as the Front represented in the *Carpe diem* and the phenomenology of time-determined human existence. So Bloch closes the last possible bolthole of metaphysical transcendence, the future, by integrating it into his conceptual framework. Fulfilment of hope and its converse, the melancholy *Carpe diem*, the "not-seeing of the immediately entering Here and Now, also appears in every *realization*" (PH I,299) are inseparable. Here we are confronted with something irreducible, an unsurmountable infinite regress of expectation as each realization precipitates in its enactment something yet unrealized: "the wish, or ideal-content, precisely when it reaches its realization-goal, arrives at a point of darker reality than it possessed in the hovering, utopian, merely-existing real character" (PH I,299-300). The core of the utopian impulse is not the realization of the external elements alone (as in the Egyptian Helen) but also the internal: the subject; the Realizer must be Realized. Again this is where the Young Hegelian enterprise is itself refunctioned in the temporal dialectic:

> Realization, however much it cancels contemplative distance, never acts entirely as Realization, *because there is something in the subject-factor of Realization itself which has never real-*

ized itself. The subject-factor of tending existence is itself not yet here, it is not predicated, not objectified, not yet Realized; ultimately this is what is announced in the darkness of the lived moment. And this incognito still remains the basic impediment which accompanies every realization, when it is a full one. To remove it, to educate the educator himself, to create the creator himself, to Realize the Realizer himself, all humanistic wishful dreams are directed towards this; they are the most radical and the most practical. (*PH* I,300)

This passage confronts us with the coda to the insertion of the doctrine of the categories of the "Real Possible" into Marx's *Theses on Feuerbach*. It is, in effect, the basis of a refunctioning of Feuerbach's programme for the reintegration of the alienated, infinite-tending self lost in a projected transcendence.[15] Bloch's focus upon the *"growing self-mediation of the producers of history"* (*PH* I,300) contains both the realization of the concrete and the elimination of the human fiasco, the constantly attendant melancholy, that haunts all realization within the object.

III. THE FIRST EMERGENCE OF THE MOMENT

As Bloch now edges his argument forward we become aware that the landscape is familiar - yet different. As it undergoes "Realization" the unrealized factor in the subject is now recast in terms of the original psychological currency of *The Principle of Hope*; thus anxiety is related back beyond its neurotic sources stemming from unusable libido back to the "metaphysical horror" of which hell was a mythological epiphenomenon. The onset of epilepsy, paranoia, anxiety in the face of nothingness, and the *"unbearable moment "(der unerträgliche Augenblick)* (*PH* I,301) all bespeak the melancholia arising out of the "strangulating, starving nothingness in the Real-Possible" (*PH* I,301). Bloch's illustrations drawn fron Dürer, Büchner, and Tolstoy all serve to intensify his vision of the healing of this unstaunched, ever-opened wound in human experience:

And here too the location is always the Now, yet not as a bloody gash in the darkness of the Now and what is to be found within it, but hope begins to blossom, with positive symbol-intention breaking into this darkness, hope mysteriously con-

---

[15]It is interesting to compare Bloch with Karl Barth with regard to their mutual responses to Feuerbach. Both "realize the realizer": Barth posits this in the God-man Jesus Christ, Bloch in the anticipatory subject.

firmed in the inconspicuous. The element of this positive aston-
ishment is the *reposeful moment*, the moment where an otherwise quite insignificant perception or an image felicitously
shatters and catches the existing-intensive. (*PH* I,302)

So it is in the words of *Geist der Utopie* (1923) that "the element of
the final state, embedded everywhere, emerges in the world and no
longer leaves it" .[16] Here Bloch "heightens" his exposition once more
climbing from the psychological into the concrete phenomenological
style which then takes on the implications of a form of "theological"
ultimacy. On the one hand the process orientated upon the "Stay
awhile, you are so fair" is directed at both the external and the internal realization of utopia and focussed in the "only archetype which
has nothing archaic about it", that is "the *purely utopian archetype,
which lives in the evidence of nearness, to that of the still unknown,
all-surpassing summum bonum* (*PH* I,305). Yet this is simultaneously
clad in the language of ultimacy, it is the "*summum bonum*". Here the
apparent paradox of the non-archaic clad in the mantle of ultimacy is
underlaid by the reconstructive impulse of Bloch's thought which implies the reappropriation of a whole cultural tradition, including, in
suitably re-functioned form, the ancestral mythological and metaphysical structures of transcendence. The "heightening" is also applied on
the supra-historical plane as Bloch reiterates his rejection of the
inescapable archaism of Platonic *anamnesis* judged in the light of the
new supreme archetype:

> The archetype: highest good is the invariance - content of the
> most felicitous astonishment, its possession would be that
> which transforms in the moment and in fact as this movement,
> into its completely resolved That. The archetype of the high-
> est good is therefore not archaic, not even historical, because
> there has never been a single appearance which could have
> even begun to fulfil its image. Even less does it return, with
> Plato's anamnesis, to the immemorial dimension of a perfection
> in order to fill its Optimum with it. The place to which this
> archetype of unconstruable happiness returns in solely the it-
> self still completely unappeared origin at which it stops off
> and which, through its Omega, it brings to its Alpha, to the
> appearing genesis of Alpha and Omega at the same time. All
> the forms of the unconstruable absolute question, in their
> bright-part, hence circle or surround the Optimum of this

---

[16]Bloch cites *Geist der Utopie*(1923), p.248 at *PH* I, p.304.

breaking into the successful achievement of the Omega, in which the middle-Alpha of the That or world-impulse emerges as solved. (*PH* I,305)

In consequence, Bloch maintains without irony that the "Summum bonum would be perfectly successful appearance of the Successful"; this is the "All", the utopian Totum towards which the inconspicuous (even hidden) symbol-intentions work and in relation to which every appearance passes into the "matter itself" (*in die Sache selbst*). The climax is sustained, the "All" attained; yet at such a moment its converse, its point of resistance and counterpoise cannot be ignored except at the cost of courting illusion, hence the penultimate subheading in Bloch's summary: "The Not in origin, the Not-Yet in history, the Nothing or conversely the All at the end" (*PH* I,306). So here, in reworked, re-contextualised and transferred form, the ancestral German dialectical-mystical juxtaposition of All and Nothing re-emerges. This is, in effect, the secularised residuum of the theological problem of evil now subsumed into a theodicy-relic[17] of a peculiarly Germanic form.

Bloch restates the negative dialectic of the "Not that drives, need, and above all the hunger protests against "Nothing". Out of this a correlation of basic emotions and ontological concepts can be developed that may, in turn, take on cosmic dimensions, "every lived movement would therefore, if it had eyes, be a witness of the beginning of the world which begins in it time and time again, *every moment, unless it has not emerged, is in the year zero of the beginning of the world*" (*P H* I,308). The Not seeks its All through a Goethian "Die and become" (*Sterbe und werde*) of existence.[18] "Not" and "Not-Yet" relate to the All as to a god; but their relation to Nothing is mere "use". Thus Bloch contrasts cycle with process (and thus progression), for:

> There is no dialectic of the determined mightiness, determined pre-appearance of this kind of Nothing, i.e. no progressive negation of the negation: annihiliation like the Peloponnesian Wars, the Thirty Years War, are merely misfortunes, not dialectical change (*sind bloss Unglück, nicht dialektische Wendung*); the mortification of Nero, Hitler, all these appar-

---

[17]Again Bloch's strategy is thrown once more into relief when we compare it with Barth's, thus Bloch's *"das Nichts"* and Barth's *"die Nichtigkeit"* see *Church Dogmatics* III/3, pp.289-368, and K. Luthi, *Gott und das Böse* loc.cit. These are both responses to the German mystical tradition which merit careful mutual exploration.

[18]Words drawn from Goethe's *"selige Sehnsucht"* in the *West-Östlicher Divan* and thoroughly representative of the German cultural tradition.

ently satanic outbursts belong to the dragon of the final abyss, not to the furthering of history. (*PH* I,310)

This subsumption of historical "misfortune" into distinction of "goal" and "use" is embedded in one of the most alien, obscure and tendentious passages of *The Principle of Hope*; its Anglo-Saxon reception is problematic in the extreme. The dialectical juxtaposition of alternative possibilities, "the open alternative between absolute Nothing and absolute All" (*PH* I,312) is tied back into Bloch's militant optimism: there must be no softening of the demand for self-determination imposed upon human-kind; indeed self-annihilation is not ruled out by any form of *a priori*. Final reality is:

> the changeable alternative between absolute Nothing and absolute All: the absolute Nothing is the sealed frustration of utopia; the absolute All - in the pre-appearance of the realm of freedom - is the sealed fulfilment of utopia of Being as utopia. The ultimate triumph of Nothing has been conceived mythologically as hell, ultimate triumph of the All as heaven: in reality *the All is itself nothing but identity of man who has come to himself with his world successfully achieved for him.* (*P H* I,312-3)

So, finally, we reach an outermost ellipse in Bloch's complex, convoluted structure, within which German dialectic, Marx's natural man, and consistent materialism lie together in a synthesis stylistically informed by Goethe's *Faust*, Part II. In terms still perhaps cryptic to the uninitiate we may now understand the "three sources and components" of the Bloch's utopian humanism:[19]

> The That-proposition: In the beginning was the deed, the All-proposition: The insufficient, here it is done - both unidealistic propositions define the tendency-arc of matter which is qualifying itself: Our intention - variant with it remain: naturalization of man, humanization of nature - of the world totally mediated with man. (*PH* I,313).

___

[19]See Faust I, 1237, "Am Anfang war die Tat", in effect an early "*Umfunktionierung*" of John I,1: "In the beginning was the Word"; see in addition the Chorus Mysticus in Faust II, 12106-9:

> The insufficient
> Here becomes an event.
> The indescribable
> Here it is done.

It is this vision of the human as containing *all* potentialities (artistic and musical included) realized with unparalleled vigour by the genius of Goethe which affords us grounds for the hypothesis that the integrative image, the potential fulfilled by the massive and diverse matter of *The Principle of Hope* is neither philosophical nor merely negatively theological (i.e. simply a definition of the human *against* the Christian tradition, following aspects of the Young Hegelian critique), but, more positively, the image of the perfectly fulfilled man, the *successful* man, whose latencies have been actualised as fully as possible. Through the inner mastery of the anxiety that springs from the dialectical engagement with Nothing *he* achieves the peace, the *Carpe diem* given in the anticipation of Utopia. Such a reading of Bloch indicates on the one hand the nature of his rich achievement (and the grasp upon cultural inheritance as a conscious goal), and on the other it highlights the alien character of such thought to the Anglo-Saxon mind with its predilection for linear clarity and resistance to theory.

The severely repressed, and almost inacessible character of the ancestral struggle to retain the reality of the present "Now" is then explored with regard to the Romantic poet Jean Paul. It is mainly with the inbreaking of the revolutionary impulse (manifesting itself for example in such moments as the dialectical realization/abolition of the proletariat) that the pre-appearance of the utopian present, the paradigmatic *Carpe diem*, draws nigh and the real possibility of an unalienated world impinges upon consciousness. In such moments of "concrete revolutionary work" temporal extension and intentionality tend to implode into dialectics:

> There is definitely utopian present in this, precisely in the sense of begun *abolition of the distance of subject and object,* therefore also of self-abolishing utopian distance itself. *The magnetic needle of intention then begins to sink, because the pole is near;* the distance between subject and object diminishes, as the point of unity dawns pre-consciously, where the two poles of utopian consciousness: dark moment, open adequacy (for the That-intention) reach the point, coincide. Accordingly utopia cannot go any further here, it goes instead into the content of this presence, i.e. into the presence of the That-content, together with its no longer alienated, no longer alien world. (*PH* I,315)

Finally, in consummation of a synthesis that posits the utopian Real Possible as the critique and the appropriation of the idealist tradition itself, Bloch crowns his edifice: "The All in the identifying sense is the Absolute (*das Oberhaupt*) of that which people basically want" (*PH* I,316). It is this identity that "lies in the dark ground of all waking dreams, hopes, utopias themselves and is also the gold ground onto which the concrete utopias are applied" (*PH* I,316). This is the culmination of Bloch's theoretical argument, the utopian recovery, in suitably purged, refunctioned form, of the German dialectical tradition and its philosophy of identity. Thus after scaling many false summits and breaking through much cultural undergrowth we now attain the lookout point from which the landscape of utopia can be surveyed and conquered in all its aspects.

IV. INITIAL POSTLUDE: THE UTOPIAN GENRE

It is our contention that the theoretical cruxes of Bloch's argument in *The Principle of Hope* have now been adequately represented. Congruent, however, with the principle of cyclic development (borrowed primarily from Goethe) we are now plunged once again into a turbulent exposition of the dream and yet, by virtue of the extended synthetic and dialectical argument now interposed, into a distinct and developed realm. Bloch drives back into the cultural tradition heaping up images, the traces of which are pursued from pre-Christian antecedents through their Christian equivalents into their Enlightenment reworkings; the idea of love, most particularly, lies at the centre of Bloch's attention. Out of the Pandora's box of the unfinished world springs the concrete anticipation taut with the polarity between enlightenment (and the destruction of illusion) and genuine mystery (the That-riddle, the utopian Totum) to which Marxism with its open world informed by dialectical materialism is the unlikely natural inheritor. The breadth of Bloch's synthesis and its consequences are breathtaking; his vision that of an all-comprehensive dynamic materialism:

> The substance-formation of the world - right down to the unleashing of the most intensive force of production, of the true atomic nucleus: existence, quodditas - are full of the tendency of the Not-Yet towards the All, of the alienated towards identity of the surrounding world towards mediated homeland. Even after and precisely after the building of the classless society whose substance-problems (tasks) of salvage, humanization continues to work. The hope of the goal, however, is necessarily at odds with false satisfaction, necessarily at one with revolutionary thoroughness; - crooked seeks to be straight, half to be full. (*PH* I,336)

With these words Bloch concludes the second and major part of Volume I of *The Principle of Hope* and with it the theoretical thrust of the whole work. The third part, "Wishful Images in the Mirror (Display, Fairytale, Travel, Film, Theatre)", with the qualification in parenthesis "Transition", reverts as we have indicated to the eclectic excavation of the images of the wish, and of wishful thinking, which draw all sorts and conditions of humanity to their good future, should they so wish. We do not need to linger over these passages of rich invective and luxuriant cultural allusion. From the marketability of the commodity ego, right through to abject conformity to the requirements of the ruling class, the cultural artifacts of the bourgeois West erect deceitful signposts: "to the dancing wild-animal, to the travelling man-in-chains, to the perfect marriage of the castrated husband" (*PH* I,341). Bloch's loathing of the "American Dream"[20] is here given unrestrained expression in denunciations of the commodity culture of capitalism, the repressed cruelty of the Christian middle class and the fascistic tendencies of the petty bourgeoisie (the masters of repression in child-murder, lynching, the Klu Klux Klan and Nazism). The fantasy of false hopes, and the presentation of wealth as grace characterise a society in which:

> In general, nothing happens in the mirrors of the scribbled kitsch-dream except coincidence, and the blessing which it brings the lucky devils multiplies, in all its Atlantic magic, the cheap Don Quixote of meaningless hope. (*PH* I,352)

Bloch is the master gatherer of cultural artifacts; his method is eclectic and cumulative but his fundamental standpoint that of an intellectual patrician[21] who can afford to rip open the underbelly of a manipulated popular culture and mock its higher pretensions from the Rococo period through to the "age of machine-made goods and formalistic Bauhaus-impotence" (*PH* I,386). With a distaste all too typical of the German Jewish Marxist intellectual exile, Bloch's feelings explode when he considers the dance as brought low by the "American filth" embodied in jazz, as opposed to the new schools of dance developed by

---

[20]Bloch's passion is no doubt partly a product of the close proximity of his own "dream" and conceptions of success to what he undoubtedly experienced in personal terms as an American nightmare.

[21]Bloch's prescient comments on the early stages of the organised tourist industry are characteristic of the all-pervasive tension in his thought between the recapitulation of the ideal of a heroic culture and the cult of the genius on the one hand and the collective mass democratisation demanded by socialism on the other, see *PH* I, pp.341-5.

Isadora Duncan[22] and the residual traditions (and intrinsic democracy) of the folk-dance. More ambiguous perhaps was the Dionysian Expressionist dance of Mary Wigman (inconceivable without Nietzsche) which, through its execution and proximity to ecstasy leads Bloch into a discussion of religious dance in antiquity. Repressed by Christianity, the sexual and the religious dance was projected heavenwards only to be rediscovered in the "true new art of dance" in the "most substantial joy" that "arises with the storming of the Bastille and its consequences" (*PH*, I,402).

Brief consideration of the cinema releases in Bloch a further flood of minutely detailed comments upon the enhancement of representational sensitivity that film affords through its " micrological world of sensory perception and of expression" (*PH* I,408), and upon its exaltation in the Soviet Union (under Lenin's benign guidance) and degradation in America (where film is the most desecrated form of art). Out of the poisonous dream-factory of Hollywood comes "escapist utopia" and "White God propaganda" (*PH* I,410), whereas,

> A *good* dream-factory, a camera of dreams which are critically inspiring, overhauling according to a humanistic plan, would have had, had and undoubtedly has other possibilities - and this within reality itself. (*PH* I,410)

The subsequent discussion of the theatre as a paradigmatic institution is dominated not surprisingly by Brecht. Through allusions to Goethe, Schiller, Shakespeare, Stanislavsky and Wagner, Bloch opens up the question (although sometimes in a highly oblique manner) as "In what and to what end does the stage really remove us" (*PH* I,422). Not surprisingly, Bloch's answer reflects once more his fundamental concern in *The Principle of Hope* with the transformation of the human condition:

---

[22]It is perhaps yet again ironic that faced with what was arguably a truly popular musical form emanating from an oppressed class that Bloch could write of jazz:

"Where everything is disintegrating though, the body also contents itself effortlessly along with it. Nothing coarser, nastier, more stupid has ever been seen than the jazz dances since 1930. Jitterbug, Boogie-woogie, this is imbecility gone wild, with a corresponding howling which provides the so to speak musical accompaniment. American movement of this kind is rocking the Western countries, not as dance, but as vomiting. Man is to be soiled and his brain emptied; he has even less idea amongst his exploiters where he stands, for whom he is grafting, what he is being sent off to die for" (*PH*, I, p.394).

However else Bloch and Adorno may have disagreed they were at one in their hostility to jazz.

> There is a social process (between individual and community,
> between contrasting forms of community themselves) which ex-
> tends from the Greek beginnings of the drama into the future,
> right into the society of no longer antagonistic, but naturally not
> vanished contradictions. (*PH* I,428).

The less than satisfactory discussion that follows comes closer than
anything else in Bloch's masterpiece to sheer absurdity with the dubious idea of "optimistic tragedy" (*PH* I,428).[23] More plausibly, some
great dramas have a lasting resounding power and topicality assimilable into Bloch's "daybreak". The discussion gradually dissolves into a
mass of fragments; we find ourselves once more in the world in which we
began, weary, chastened, purged, yet somehow prepared to grapple
with the startling conjunction of the mundane and the exalted in all
their complexity. This is the context of the drive towards a good future,
which capitalism resists. The greatest enemy is not merely "great capital, but equally the load of indifference, hopelessness" (*PH* I,446). Capitalism presents a false dilemma: a false happy end or its own
(genuine) nihilism; by contrast, Bloch posits "as expropriating and as
liberating truth ... a humanity which is finally socially possible" (*PH*
I,446). Against illusion:

> The work against this, with which history continues, indeed
> has been continuing for a long time, leads to the matter (*Sache*)
> which could be good, not as abyss (*Abgrund*), but as mountain
> into the future. Mankind and the world carry enough good fu-
> ture; no plan is itself good without this fundamental belief
> within it. (*PH* I,447)

So ends volume one of *"The Principle of Hope"*. Now having scaled
the mighty first pillar of Bloch's massive bridge-like structure we are
in a position to survey the middle span, a review of utopias. After this
interlude we shall then once more re-engage with the recapitulation of
the hope-principle in relation to religion, death and human consummation.

---

[23] Bloch's occasional lapses into the actual self-caricature of forms of socialist pretension are instructive to all those who might venture into the remythologisation of cultural
identity. This is an aspect of the pattern implicit in all attempts at consistent ideology,
religious and non-religious, which attempt to bridge the unbridgeable in human experience.

CHAPTER VII

THE REVIEW OF UTOPIAS: THE CENTRAL SPAN

In volume I of *The Principle of Hope* Ernst Bloch sets out in an interlocking dialectical pattern the basic terms of his reappropriation of the utopian principle, which we have expanded at length on lines suggested by the work of other German thinkers, who, although contrasting as regards both intention and content, nevertheless share certain similarities of structure and of method. The latter consist first in the isolation of a distinct dimension of experience through its quasi-empirical location; second, the establishment of that dimension's transcendental status and then, third, a further "deduction" of its fundamental "categories", that is its constituent elements. Following this pattern of "critique" it is now possible to proceed with the analysis of examples of the Front, the utopian drive towards Noch-Nicht-Sein using the previously established theoretical schemata. So it is that Bloch, having once worked out the fundamental basis of his experience now subjects utopia ideas, "outlines of a better world" in "medicine, social systems, technology, architecture, geography in art and wisdom" (*PH* II, 459) to protracted and detailed examination. The theoretical aspects of volume II of *The Principle of Hope* are far less prominent now the formulation and "deduction" of the principle itself lies behind us; the review is nevertheless a considerable challenge and represents a remarkable tour de force of eclectic learning. Bloch adopts the stance of the polymath, inviting criticism both as regards the legitimacy of such comprehensive ambition in an age of exploding growth and fragmentation in knowledge, and as directed at the detail he presents of the many specific areas of learning, each of which has its own relevant expertise, and experts. In an era of pervasive pluralism and cultural fragmentation it is our view that any serious attempt at synthesis deserves critical attention.

The relatively untheoretical nature of volume II of Bloch's text is such as to allow for the far more economical rehearsal of its contents; at the same time the copious quantity of illustrative material is such as to require a careful statement of critical intention. Our aim is, therefore, to represent primarily the theoretical structure of *The Principle of Hope* inasmuch as this is detectable, and thus to compress the illustrative content correspondingly. Argument about quality of the individual contributions in each area within the overall synthesis may, given an adequate Anglo-Saxon reception, continue for some little time as scholars confront Bloch's intrusions into their intellectual spheres of interest. There is a thorough and consistent dependence of volume II upon volume I and a continuing line of analysis which allows us to review Bloch's survey of paths into utopia within a single chapter.

I.THE FIRST UTOPIA: THE BODY AND ITS OWN[1]

Characteristically Bloch begins his panoramic[2] review of life under the utopian motif with the body, thereby confirms his consistent dialectical materialist standpoint and a creditable appreciation of the simple conditions of human happiness: How are we to stay healthy and feed ourselves well and cheaply? Bloch's realism is characteristic: "A fortnight off, that is already a great deal for most people, then back to a life that nobody wants" (PH II,451); but, beginning with body means also a concern with spirit. Here Bloch is genuinely prophetic in that, whatever sociological interpretation may be put upon it, sport has become an ever increasingly important factor in national and international social life. Bloch traces the history of modern sport seeing in it a form of exploitation: "in backward bourgeois conditions sport often stultified the mind, and for this very reason is promoted from above" (PH II,452); and emancipation for the "body should not be concealed at all but rather shed the distortion and disfigurements which an alienating society based on the division of labour has inflicted on it too" (PH II,453). Underlying the preoccupation with sport is a deeper concern for health, a conception open to a variety of definitions but again explored at far greater length in a section on medical utopias (PH II, pp.459ff), which are traced from Plato's Republic through More's Utopia, Bacon's Atlantis, the lesser known Swesen's Limanova, The Island of Progress into Nazi eugenics. Bloch's remarks have been overtaken by medical realities but he shows a distinct sympathy for eugenic principles em-

---

[1]The title of this subsection is a playful inversion of the title of Max Stirner's Das Ich und sein Eigentum, The Ego and its Own (1844), a radical subjectivist position upon which Marx subjected to devastating hostile criticism in The Holy Family (1844).

[2]Bloch's use of the word "panorama" is significant: it indicates both the desire to represent totality in the "panoramas" constructed in the nineteenth century in order to represent historical events as public spectacle, and stylistic intention, that is the ability to "pan" the whole and then to draw into close up detail without, as it were, any break in continuity. Opinions are divided on the success of Bloch's stylistic experimentation. "Panorama" implies both a historical reference and a cinematographic technique translated into literary style.

ployed in the right social context; so given that brilliant births take place, sometimes out of unfavourable circumstances, it is nevertheless plausible to argue that:

> Efficient breeding would have a social field here to keep it busy for a long time, before entering or being able to enter the still largely opaque field of controlled insemination. The control of the individual biological disposition and the abolition of the element of 'fate' about it are certainly a goal, but first this planning will pull down the real slums before it approaches the slum of the human body. There is everything to be said for reducing the aggressive drives and promoting the social ones even by means of organic breeding; just as the nutritional value of cereals and the sweetness of cherries has been improved. But the breeding society must first be bred itself, in order that the new human institutional value is not determined by the demands of the cannibals. (*PH* II,460)

Consistent with his Marxist position Bloch asserts the priority of the social dimension and advocates "social hygiene" as a first principle. Old age and death are, Bloch claims, best tackled under socialism (as in Russia) where "the fight for a healthy vigorous old age becomes the same as the fight for the preservation of valuable cadres in all areas of the great programme of construction" (*PH* II,462); indeed, beyond this, "A future is indicated here in which a significantly possible ageing has replaced the pathological kind, and even physiological decline is no longer acknowledged to be inevitable" (*PH* II,462). Bloch recognises the contextual definition of health and the social imperative:

> Health is a social concept, exactly like the organic existence in general of human beings, as human beings. Thus it can only be meaningfully increased at all if the life in which it stands is not itself overcrowded with anxiety, deprivation and death. (*PH* II,467)

It was within the context of the historical denial of this principle within capitalism that Malthus's theory of population arose. This exploited the conflict between rate of human propagation and the limited ("diminishing return" law) increase in the means of nourishment. The repressive Malthus, Marx's true *bête noire*, is characterised as a "mere mechanistic first-aid client, without primacy of the social milieu and without plans to change it, without Pavlov and knowledge of the whole human being as a creature who is cerebrally and socially controlled"; it is this, Bloch asserts, that "prevents the co-operation of doctor and red flag, with the latter leading the way" (*PH* II,469). There is, on the contrary, room on earth for everyone if it were "run by the power of satisfying people's needs instead of by satisfying the needs of power" (*PH* II,469). At all quarters Bloch calls for the clinical treatment first of a society intensely dirty and diseased, and then, in complete congruity with his adoption of the nature-reforming "early Marx" and assimilation of the Eleventh Thesis, that the world is to be changed, he asserts that:

> The Marxist approach is consciously to make history and no longer to suffer it passively. And the Marxist approach is also consciously to intervene even in the *reconditioning* from which human beings emerge and in which they physically live before they surface historically at all. (*PH* II,470)

In terms of Bloch's recurrent image, people cannot walk upright in a crooked society.[3] Thus he diverts his attention away from the body and from health as the broader content of the bodily function to society to "Freedom and Order", in a survey of social utopias. (*PH* II, 471-624) Here Bloch re-ascends to some degree to the level of magisterial comment characteristic of volume I but with less exalted abstraction.

II.FREEDOM AND ORDER: THE POLARITIES OF THE SOCIAL FUTURE

Bloch concludes the first subsection of volume II of *The Principle of Hope* with the words "*As if newborn: this is what the outlines of a better world suggest as far as the body is concerned*" and places this firmly in the social context: "But people cannot walk upright if social life itself still lies crooked" (*PH* II,471) Bloch begins his review of social utopias with the extravagant and the improbable, the Cockaigne (*Sklaraffenland*) of the imagination and the lunatic delusions of Fourier, Saint-Simon and Comte.[4] This extremity is allowed for inasmuch as,

[3]Thus: "In capitalist society health is the capacity to earn, among the Greeks it was the capacity to enjoy, and in the Middle Ages the capability to believe" (*PH* II,p.465). Bloch's depiction of sport and the body as the prime locus of utopian fulfilment exhibits a certain self-consciousness; it is an ethos tied to the social goals of the post-war "socialist" regimes of Eastern Europe, in particular the identity of the DDR which was long denied international recognition.

[4]See Krishnan Kumar, *Utopia and Anti-Utopia in the Modern World* (Oxford : Blackwell, 1987).

Lunacy, as a loosening up for an invasion of the unconscious, for possession by the unconscious, also occurs in what is Not-Yet-Conscious. The paranoic is often a project-maker, and there is occasionally also a mutual connection between the two. So that a utopian talent slips off the rails in a paranoid way, indeed almost voluntarily succumbs to a delusion. (*PH* II,473)

The bizarre Church of Intelligence in Saint-Simon's utopian vision is an unapologised aspect of the contrast between light and darkness drawn rarely enough in the history of war and exploration. By reference to such utopians More, Campanella, Owen, Fourier, Saint-Simon, Bacon, and the "coolest utopia", that of Plato, and last and most significant, Augustine's *City of God*, Bloch illustrates the richness and the diversity of their presuppositions. The utopian visions in the *Republic* and *The City of God* are regarded as reactionary and pessimistic, respectively, and have not affected in a profound way the properly understood utopian vision. The apparent dismissal of a thinker or school of thought, whilst simultaneously effecting an appropriation through the technique of refunctioning is a ploy once again used by Bloch. The treatment meted out to Plato and Augustine is one of the less successful examples of *Umfunktionierung*. It is possible to argue, against Bloch, that it is precisely these two utopian visions which have had the most powerful historical and social impact and influence upon social theory, however weak or indirect their effect upon the utopian imagination might be said to be. Bloch's general objection to the utopian visions is that such conceptions of the ideal state:

> very often saw all contradictions resolved by their prescription, health had become paralysed in them as it were. No fresh questions, no different countries appear in the margin any more, the island, although a future one itself, is largely insulated against the future ... utopia was confined to the best constitution, to an abstraction of constitution, instead of being perceived and cultivated in the concrete totality of being. (*PH* II,478)

The utopian vision divorced from Bloch's conception of the utopian imagination is rigid, closed and predetermined. Bloch's response takes the form of an improbable totalism. It is the dependence of utopian organisation and social utopias upon their conception in a "Totum" which indicates that without comprehensive treatment the utopian imagination remains, in effect, a figment. Paradoxically we may infer from this that Bloch himself intends such a totalistic presentation in the form of a general theory of utopia.

At the outset Bloch recognises that utopian conceptions are socially conditioned[5] although not so explicitly as "bourgeois Natural Rights"; all are, as it were, tied to a historical timetable and their anticipations thus relate to their individual contexts.[6] It is not altogether surprising given their utopian dream origin that Bloch emphasises the individual character of the utopias. In consequence the problem of their translation to social reality is severe:

> utopias are taken even less from the drawers of *a priori* possibilities for instance, independently of history, than they are from the depths of sheer *private* feeling. Even the Novum of an abolition of private property (which is anticipated by most social utopias, in that no longer topical section which transcends to the final level), even this Novum is not a priori unalterable. (*PH* II,480)

Accordingly, the abolition of private property looks very different in the works of Plato, More and Owen. The toleration of individual utopian diversity and Bloch's demand for an appreciation of the concrete conditions that given the realization of utopia comes to explicit expression illustrating once more Bloch's desire to remain "orthodox" (in the light of Marx's harsh critique of utopian socialism) and to retain flexibility in outlook:

> Until the designing of the future is concretely corrected in the work of Marx and brought into the truly comprehended timetable of a due tendency, so that it does not stop but only now vigorously begins. Without the growing wealth of anticipations, of still abstract plans and programmes, which are now to be recalled, the final social dream would not have come either. (*PH* II,481)

---

[5]Thus, for example, "Augustine's work is influenced by the incipient feudal economy, that of More by free trading capital, that of Campanella by the absolutist period of manufacture, and that of Saint-Simon by the new industry", (*PH* II,p.479), These kinds of correlation would require detailed justification of a kind they do not receive from Bloch.

[6]Again, for example, "More's utopia of freedom thus corresponds in its non-communist sections to the coming parliamentary form of English democratic politics, as does Campanella's utopia to the absolutist one on the continent" (*PH* II,p479). Such "anticipatory" correlations are even more difficult to justify in more than the most general terms.

The demands of practice imply the work of Marx; openness, theoretical formality - even perfection cannot survive without toleration of the social dream. Only such a dream permits intellectual protest against the imminent foreclosure of the socialist vision (a tendency ironically all too evident in Marxism-Leninism and its enactment, despite the simplistic apologia for the Soviet Union which Bloch persistently rehearses in *The Principle of Hope*). Bloch strives to hold together in a new context the tension between the unfixed, open dream characterising utopian anticipatory consciousness finally crystallised in the Front and the necessary condition of transformation of reality in the directions indicated by and embodied within Marxism.

III.THE NEW STOICISM: UTOPIA REFUNCTIONED

In the context of this general presentation Bloch embarks upon an extended historical exposition of "social Wishful Images of the Past" beginning with Solon, progressing via Diogenes the Cynic and Aristippus the Hedonist to Plato and the *Republic*, a work "as well thought-out as it is reactionary" (*PH* II,484). Bloch sees in Plato the reversal of the popular dream of the ideal state and he creates, in the image of Sparta, a principled class society. Bloch stresses the ambiguous reception of the *Republic*, it appeals both to the proponents of an ordered class society and such radicals as Thomas Münzer, the theologian of the German peasants' revolution and of course the subject of one of Bloch's key early works. Münzer's citation of Plato's utopia is to be understood as a "productive misunderstanding" (*PH* II,488) which transmitted the conception of the Golden Age as a classless commune into primitive communism.

In contrast with the Platonic utopia, which remained humble in proportions never outgrowing the Greek city-state, Bloch develops a refunctioned Stoic conception of the international world-state which, despite its Greek, Hellenistic and Roman variants, had a universal quality inspired by the example of Alexander the Great's short-lived empire. Despite the idealizing weakness of the Stoic model (attributed by Bloch to the Stoic indifference towards external circumstances), its real historical significance lay in "the programme of world citizenship, which here means *the unity of the human race*" (*PH* II,493). The vision of Zeno and Poseideinos contains not only these ideals, but more importantly for Bloch, a far-reaching supersession of the merely contingent factors that divide the body of humankind. In the Stoic conception the basis for a fundamental re-constitution of the basis of human social life can be found, in relation to which Bloch's preoccupation with the search for a contemporary analogate to natural law may be pursued;[7] thus:

> The cosmos in the state now levels all social distinctions, even that of the sexes, man and woman, Greek and barbarian, freeman and slave, all distinctions due to limitation vanish in the intellectually and quantitatively unlimited realm. Even blood and family, the ties from the age of agriculture and the polis, do not hold the new human beings together, instead equality of moral inclinations determines the bonds in megalopolis … This is the new natural state, that in which physis stands against the statute (thesis) but coincides with the right law (nomos). A far-reaching equation; it had less of an influence on the later social utopias, but a decisive one as Natural Right. (*PH* II,494)

In Stoicism Bloch finds the original example of a social model that combines the ideal of classlessness and a levelling of social distinctions with a reconciliatory conception of nature, as mediated in natural law, that permeates all aspects of social life. The early Stoic conception lacked the economic basis for its realization, and although it was fundamentally optimistic in outlook its orientation towards the goal mythologically represented in the Golden Age was not revolutionary, but more a process of "pantheistic accclimatization to approved fate" which was succeeded, so Bloch asserts, by the mitigation of life circumstances (in slavery or marriage, for example). The utopia of the Stoics pressed towards completion and a harmony with the "existing God-nature that is the world" (*PH* II,495).[8] In a manner characteristic of Bloch's whole enterprise he purports to advance concretely realizable ideals *compatible* (at the very least) with Marxism. How far the result is to be seen as a reinforcement of the latter, or, alternatively, its subversion, was a question of particular importance in Bloch's East European reception. Quite clearly so far as Bloch is concerned the realization of the vision in prospect, here that of Stoicism, ostensibly awaits

---

[7]Once more rhapsodic generalisations incorporated into "panoramic" overview are underpinned elsewhere, in this instance in *Naturrecht und menschliche Würde, G.A.6,* where Bloch gives further substance to his rehabilitation within the Marxist tradition of a refunctioned conception of "natural law" as the basis of the defence of human integrity within any society.   This is certainly one of Bloch's most significant contributions to socialist thought as it implies (however concealed under the rhetoric of conformity) a recognition of the manifest deficiencies of a political tradition originating in Marx's *Critique* of Hegel's *Philosophy of Right* and the subsequent practical denigration of human rights as "bourgeois rights".

[8]The discussion of "Stoicism" is an important strand in early nineteenth century social and political reflection traceable, as regards its German antecedents, to Hegel's treatment of it in the *Phenomenology of Mind.*   Again see *Naturrecht, GA 6,* pp. 140-150.

the necessary condition of its enactment as provided by Marxism. Here, as elsewhere, Bloch has an emancipated approach to the gathering of cumulative data unbridled by any class-bound *a priori* principles of selection.

The freedom implicit in Bloch's method of recovery again becomes apparent in an inspired discussion of the early Western social order which had at is very heart the Augustinian assimilation of the Stoic utopian ideal. This leads Bloch into his first extensive engagement with the religious aspects of the cultural inheritance which, albeit in transformed, refunctioned form, is a dimension socialism cannot afford to neglect. St. Paul's idea of world-citizenship was informed by Stoic influences[9] over against the Jewish-centredness of Peter.The intra-Christian debate in the early Church is of no great intrinsic interest for Bloch, what he focuses upon is the Christian reworking of the relation of utopia to nature. The following passages bring to the surface issues fundamental to Bloch's life-long engagement with both religion (here particularly with Christianity) and Marxism as mutual, even if conflicting, features of the transformation of culture and society. Bloch assimilates the teaching of Paul into his account of the Stoic ideological domination of the era:

> But in early Christianity, possibly even in St. Paul, the explosive element was clearer than the element of reformatory completeness which is part of Stoicism, even where it converts to Christianity. This is the end of the resemblance, to which St. Paul had alluded, of the Stoics, the Freemasons of antiquity, to early Christianity; the Stoic utopia seeks transfiguration through correspondence to nature, the Christian utopia so through the critique and crisis of nature. (*PH* II,496)

Bloch as a Marxist, an atheist and, in a very distinctive sense a materialist, certainly wants a utopian transfiguration through correspondence with nature over against the Christian critique and crisis of nature. But on what conditions may this be attained? What are the consequences of choosing the former when the latter has in reality exercised such a sway over the history of the West? We shall return to these questions in an expanded form in the following chapter. At this juncture

[9]Bloch is referring to Acts 17, 28. Recent work on the New Testament both amongst those using sociological method and the more explicitly political approach of the theology of liberation has produced an image of the synoptic Jesus bearing strong similarities to that of Bloch, see ch. 8 below where we examine in some detail Bloch's use of religious conceptions.

Bloch provides an account of Christian origins, some aspects of which may perhaps be novel to readers unfamiliar with recent developments in New Testament studies.

IV. THE INDISPENSABILITY OF EXODUS

Bloch begins his own distinctive interpretation of Christian origins with an outline of the Exile of Israel and a depiction of the power of the religious creativity of Moses who, after his murder of an overseer and subsequent flight from Egypt, imagines a God who is "no master's God, but one of free Bedouins" whom he encountered in Sinai thus: "Yahweh begins as a threat to the Pharaoh: the volcanic God of Sinai becomes Moses' god of liberation, of flight from slavery" (PH II,496). The Exodus experience endowed the Bible with the indelible memory of "nomadic, and thus still half primitive communist institution" (PH II,496), that is a community without a division of labour or private property. Thus Bloch interprets the early history of Israel in Marxist terms regarding it as a period of economic innocence corrupted by contact with the Canaanites, whose class distinctions and ostentatious wealth provided the basis for the exploitation denounced by the prophets who at the same time proclaimed judgment and the earliest conception of a social utopia. Through the Nazirites and Rechabites, and from Samson, Samuel and Elijah down to John the Baptist there runs, so Bloch argues, a line of protest from the half-primitive communism down to the agapeistic communion of early Christianity. Singling out the prophet Amos, Bloch sees in him the prototype of a succession that culminates in Joachim of Fiore, a founder figure in medieval chiliasm. In Micah and supremely in Isaiah there is envisioned a time of uncorrupt happiness, one of "socialist wealth": "Ho, everyone that trusteth, come ye to the waters, and he that hath no mercy; come ye, buy, and eat; yea, come, buy wine and milk without money and without price".[10] As swords are beaten into ploughshares and spears into pruning hooks[11] so universal peace complements the abolition of the cash nexus and commodity-dominated existence. This is, Bloch maintains, "the original model of the pacified international which forms the core of the Stoic utopia: with real influence, the passage from Isaiah formed the basis of all Christian utopias" (PH II,498). Bloch handles gently the problematic character of the correspondence between this prophetic vision (and its concept of time and thus of the future) and what actually took place

[10]Isaiah, 55,1.
[11]Isaiah, 2,4; Micah 4,3f.

after Augustine.[12] It is only in the modern (i.e. post-Marxian) era that the transition from latent and potential to explicit and actual utopia is now capable of realisation:

> The experience of time has certainly undergone many changes, the Futurum above all has only recently been augmented by the Novum and become charged with it. But the content of the biblically intended future has remained intelligible to all social utopias: Israel became poverty as such, Zion became utopia. (*PH* II,499)

It is not surprising that this persisting utopian consciousness of the Promised Land, extending from the Old Testament to the nineteenth century proletarian socialist Wilhelm Weitling[13], provides the context in which the life and teaching of Jesus is to be understood. Rich collaborators were protected by Roman occupiers against "desperate peasants, patriotic resistance fighters" and "prophets, who would quite unreservedly be called agitators now" (*PH* II,499). The social revolutionary message of the Matthean John the Baptist speaks of purging and the burning of chaff in unquenchable fire;[14] this is (to use a term Bloch does not here use, but the implication is plain) class-warfare directed towards social and national revolution. In the light of the Matthean synoptic teaching the messages of Jesus and Paul are in a state of contradiction:

> the coming of Jesus himself was by no means as inward and other-wordly as a reinterpretation since St. Paul, which always suited the ruling class, would have us believe. His message to those that labour and are heavy laden was not the cross; they had that in any case, and in the terrible cry: "My God, why has Thou forsaken me? Jesus experienced the crucifixion as a catastrophe and not in a Pauline way. (*PH* II,499)

[12]Here is ground common with the development of twentieth century theology, that is the re-discovery of the eschatalogical dimensions of Christian thought.   This is reviewed in G. Sauter, *Zukunft und Verheissung Das Problem der Zukunft in der gegenwärtigen theologischen und philosophischen Diskussion* (Zurich, 1965), and ch. 8 below.

[13]Bloch's allusion to Weitling indicates that his sympathies diverge markedly from those of Marx. See D. McLellan *Karl Marx His Life and Thought* pp.155ff. for an account of Marx's brutal dismissal of Weitling, a real proletarian (and Christian and humane) socialist.

[14]Bloch refers to Matthew 3, 10-12.

Leading post-war New Testament historians and theologians have recently produced markedly similar accounts of the life and death of Jesus. For example, J. Moltmann's two texts, *The Crucified God* and the earlier *The Theology of Hope* closely reflect elements drawn from the structure of Bloch's position.[15] Whether this assimilation does justice to the global intentions of *Bloch's* work is quite another matter, for, as we shall see in the ensuing chapter, the refunctioning of *religion* involves the integration of theology into a theory radically at variance with traditional Christian theistic self-understanding. Bloch goes on to outline an account of Jesus' conception of the Kingdom of God as alive in the chosen community of the Pharisees. The eschatalogical juxtaposition of "this world" and "the other world", that is of present and future aeons, is to be strictly understood as a chronological succession of events in the same location. This "other world" is a utopian earth corresponding with the vision of Isaiah's new hearers and a new earth:

> The aspiration is not another world after death, where the angels are singing, but the equally terrestrial and supra-terrestrial kingdom of love, of which the early Christian community was already supposed to represent an enclave. The kingdom of the other world was interpreted as other-wordly only after the catastrophe of the Cross, and above all after the Pilates and especially the Neros had become Christian themselves; since for the ruling class everything depended upon defusing the communism of love and rendering it as spiritual as possible. (*PH* II,500)

There is some correspondence between this conception of Jesus' teaching and some form of "liberation theology" but of course the latter is complicated by Christological and ecclesiological factors to which we shall return. Bloch does not attempt to identify Jesus with this context to the extent of attributing to him the role of armed freedom-fighter. In Jesus' self-understanding as an "apocalyptic thinker" Bloch rightly recognises the eschatological suspension of the ethical that conditions Jesus' teaching: "the eschatological sermon has precedence for Jesus over the moral one and determines it"(*PH* II,500). The catas-

---

[15]We return to this theme in detailed terms in ch.10 where we note that the Moltmannian appropriation of Bloch is tempered by a very different theological "refunctioning" of Hegel and Luther as regards the "death of God". Again the work of Jean Paul, Heine, and Nietzsche is influential. See also E. Jüngel, *Gott als Geheimnis der Welt* (Tübingen: J.C.B. Mohr, 1977) and R.H. Roberts, "Nietzsche and the Cultural Renaissance of the 'Death of God'" in *From Hegel to Heidegger: Explorations in the Afterlife of Religion* (The Bristol Press, forthcoming).

trophic intervention envisaged in Mark 13 relativises all concerns with military or economic power. This is an unsparing vision which demands unambiguous loyalty in a community of the New Age; that is in the "social utopia intended by the early Christian in its communism of love and in the International of whatever bears a human face, however poor" (*PH* II,501). So the Stoic beliefs were supplemented by a social mission from below inspired by a mythological power figure. Again, with remarkable sympathy towards Christianity, Bloch sees retained in the tradition that followed a resistance to the power of the existing world and its dehumanising content remained, despite the partial loss of its sense of social mission. There is, however, no specific social utopia in the Bible, nor, indeed, is Christianity merely an outcry against deprivation but also "an outcry against death and the void" into which the Son of Man is "inserted" (*setzt...ein*) (*PH* II,502). The Bible both relentlessly directs attention to the themes of the Exodus and the kingdom but it also resists its instantiation as a "baptized Babel" or its embodiment in a Church as in Augustine, whom Bloch regards as the chief architect of the religion of the West with its vestigial utopian consciousness.

In the highly competitive religious economy of the Graeco-Roman world Pauline Christianity initially triumphed, and in doing so it significantly changed the original utopian consciousness of the Jesus of the gospels: the fresh leap onto a new earth was supplanted by a leap out of this world into inwardness and the other world. In consequence: "inward transcendence and empty promises" were expressed within the Church that came itself (in the face of the disintegration of the Roman Empire) to embody Stoic principles as a higher state within the state. However, precisely because of the nature of the Stoic utopia (it consisted in adaptation to a world already complete in itself) there was a tension between the explosive latency of the teaching of Jesus and the Stoic conception of the world resolved in Augustine's utopia, the *De civitate Dei*, in which the new earth appeared as an other world incorporated in the Church itself. The interpretation of the precise character of Augustine's epochal vision of the two cities is a considerable and continuing intellectual task[16] and Bloch's representation is but one of many. Suffice it to say that here, as ever, Bloch demonstrates his acquaintance with primary texts with energy and commitment.

At the heart of Augustine's compromise between Church and the Roman Empire is the assimilation of the institutions of the latter into a

---

[16]Once more U. Duchrow, op.cit., pp.15-180 provides an indispensable commentary upon the background to Bloch's appropriation of Augustine and biblical material.

complex, social synthesis fraught with its own inner tensions and unresolved states of development; here for Bloch the key conception is that
of a process: "political utopia appears for the first time as history, indeed generates it, history emerges as *salvation history towards the
kingdom*, as an unbroken, uniform process, harnessed between Adam and
Jesus, on the basis of the Stoic unity of the human race and the Christian salvation it is to attain" (*PH* II,504). Out of this arose a critique of
the state and of its violence which combines, from Bloch's standpoint,
political acumen with mythologically intensified dualism. In the final
analysis, Bloch conceives of Augustine's *De civitate Dei* as caught between two possible resolutions: on the one hand the City of God appears
to be the future utopian goal of history, on the other it often seems to exist already as a great power or anti-power over against the antagonis-
tic City of the Devil. The actual resolution is achieved through a doctrine of grace but the powerful utopian dream of the future in the millenium is "sacrificed to the Church, in which it is supposed already to be
fulfilled" (*PH* II,507). It is this displacement that Bloch seeks to re-
verse, through a reworking of the dynamics that inform religious reality itself: the central experience of the Judaeo-Christian tradition,
that of God, has itself to be refunctioned so as to re-energize the pervasive feature of the anticipatory (and eschatological) horizon of Western culture and its socio-economic matrix. The attraction of Bloch to the
theologically or religiously-minded reader is his forcible re-opening of
the question of God and the nature of religion as an irreducible aspect of
human nature. His conclusion, the abolition of God in and through the
fulfilment of religion is problematic, yet it has not, paradoxically
enough, deterred theologians from an extensive appropriation of
Bloch's ideas, as will become apparent in the third volume of *The
Principle of Hope* to which we now turn.

CHAPTER VIII

RELIGION AND CONSUMMATION: TRANSCENDING WITHOUT TRANSCENDENCE

The Principle of Hope is best seen in terms of the image of two great pillars supporting the central span of a bridge: the first pillar consisted in the argument of the first volume which asserts and explicates the priority of the future, "Not-Yet-Being", as the horizon of liberated human existence; the middle span is a largely historical survey of utopias subjected to consistent critique from Bloch's distinctive standpoint; the second pillar is constituted by the third and last volume of the *Principle* which contains a powerful restatement of Bloch's position through the paradigm of the new Promethean humanity prefigured by the young Goethe's *Faust*, Hegel's *Phenomenology*, and Cervantes' *Don Quixote*. These paradigms are employed in a refunctioning of the meaning of religion and, less plausibly, death. Characteristically, Bloch is prolix, as ever his fertile cultivation of images often overburdens the structure of the multi-layered position which it is our concern to articulate. In volume three we encounter the new "identity" of the Humanum in which the reader is taken beyond a mere "aesthetic" or "analytic" of the future into the realm of the new "dialectic", a transcendental fusion of refunctioned ultimates presented, however problematically, as the real fruit of Marxism. Religion, in a suitably refunctioned form, is central to this vision. It is as ever our aim to let Bloch speak for himself and to relate his account to areas of influence and discussion worthy of further exploration.

Volume three of *The Principle of Hope* consists in three broad divisions: the first presents us with the new Prometheus explored under the images of Faust and Don Quixote as types of humanity: the second confronts the "strongest non-utopia: death"; and the third moves into the religious sphere: into the "refunctioning" of God as the locus of human realization, that is at the point at which the earth itself is represented as real extra-territoriality.

I. The Pursuit of the Greater Happiness

Bloch begins the final volume of *The Principle of Hope* with the sense of frustration and confusion born of self-ignorance: we do not know who we are, and nobody is what he would like to be, or could be. A desire for the new is intrinsic to human personality but it is soon suppressed (as were the dreams of youth in the first volume) by social class and the educational programme of the technical school and the *Gymnasium*. In order to walk upright we require "guiding images" that enable us to become like proper human beings (*PH* III,930). Again, pursuing the analogy between Bloch and the ancestral methods of German idealism most notably seen in its Kantian form, what Bloch proposes are in effect "regulative ideas" drawn not from the bloodless residuum of rationalism and Deism (e.g. the ideas of God, freedom and immortality) but a comprehensive vision of what it is, or rather what it *can be*, to be human in the fullest sense. There has to be an superior image, an identity that informs human endeavour, for it is "precisely because human beings as such are still undefined that they need a cross between a mirror and a painted picture when they look inside" (*PH* III,931). As opposed to the Americanized guiding image, the employee, Bloch posits "socialist liberation ... a freedom not merely from but chiefly for, ... (which) still remains open to defining moral work" (*PH* III,931). What takes place in the concluding volume of *The Principle of Hope* is the moral informing of the new humanity given in socialism; it is also a highly ambitious attempt to relaunch in a benign, universalised form the German cultural mission to educate humankind. Given the failure of idealistic attempts to dispel the contradictions and ambiguities of class society through conceptual means, it is only in terms of the open future and the "guiding panels" set on the paths to that future that the time line to a proper state of humanity can be drawn.

Here Bloch is venturing onto dangerous territory in a century marked by the world-historical adventure of Germany and he thus first confronts somewhat equivocally the Nietzschian exhortation to live dangerously.[1] As in the dialectic of freedom and order in the social utopia, so here Bloch recognises the contemporary tension between the "danger" of innovative, forward-orientated genius and the "safety" of mediocrity:

---

[1] *"Gefährlich leben!"*, K. Schlechta (ed.) *Friedrich Nietzsche Werke* (Munich: Hanser, 1966), vol.II, p.166.   The passage from the *Die frohliche Wissenschaft* is rendered by W. Kaufmann "For believe me: the secret for harvesting from existence the greatest fruitfulness and the greatest enjoyment is - to live dangerously!", *The Gay Science* (New York: Random House, 1974), p.228.

The Babbitt walks only well-trodden paths, and when the world is changing he thinks of his Sunday trousers. No writer sounded a more dubious call to the soldierly life-will than Nietzsche, barbarically and decadently heralding in early imperialism, yet at the same time no one warned more compellingly against the dubious aspect of "small-scale happiness". *(PH* III,936)

Bloch seeks to differentiate between the brutal inheritance of Nietzsche perverted and the "anti-bourgeois-conformist" who "indisputably belongs elsewhere" (*PH* III,936). The "genuine insight of soldierly becoming was, after all", Bloch informs us, "never wholly unrelated to the revolutionary one" (*PH* III,936). The pursuit of great happiness is alien to the "tick-tock of small-scale happiness": the dangerous life of the revolutionary is no mere end in itself but directed to the end represented by the great happiness. Unfortunately, French happiness is devoted to Cupid and Epicurus; English happiness corrupted by the "sweet lemonade" of the Labour party living under the sign of Fabius the hesitator; and Italian happiness is corrupted by its fascistic sources of inspiration in Machiavelli, Sorel and Gentile: thus the problem has characteristically to be resolved by a refunctioning of the totality of the tradition and by a return to pre-Socratic Hellenism.

Here, as ever, Bloch does not build alone and he must simultaneously to come to terms with earlier such recoveries, notably those enacted by Nietzsche and by the poet Hölderlin. Thus Bloch, reflecting the search within German Romanticism for a new image of the human does not immediately accord priority to the ancestral Christian imagery but pre-empts this with a reworking of Nietzsche's antithesis of Dionysius-Apollo, that is the juxtaposition of vitalistic ecstasy over against form and order. Nietzsche gave new utopian life the "tension between sensual pleasure and peace of soul, which had become philistine and common place" (*PH* III,949), but his grasp of this antithesis and that of its cultural reception are "far from being grasped in sufficiently processual, processual-utopian terms" (*PH* III,951). They are in effect reified and thus static; the refunctioning of the antithesis is to be achieved by a third term: the "still only approaching third element, that of undistorted Being-With-Ourselves" (*PH* III,952). In a characteristically Hegel-like pattern of the supercession of antitheses Bloch posits the futurity of the Novum as the resolution-to-come. Similar triadic developments are detectable in the subsequent discussions of the *vita activa* and *vita contemplativa* (*PH* III,953-957), and solitude and friendship (*PH* III,965-973). All these antitheses enjoy a dialectical life "as counterparts, not as crossroads" in classless society. This is, it need scarcely be said, not the mode of resolution of class-contradictions apparently envisaged by Marx or Lenin, for Bloch makes no attempt to fix or to foreclose the question as to the nature of the human in terms of the triumph and apotheosis of a particular class.[2] The revisionist-visionary interpretation is expressed thus:

> In the classless synthesis the sought-for Totum is at work, that which according to Marx liberated both the totally developed individual and real generality. And ultimately it is a Totum because it is a Totum of the goal-content, of the human content which is still circulating but has not yet been fixed. Within it resounds or claims the general, that which concerns every human being and constitutes the hope of final content: identity of the We with its self and its world, instead of alienation. (PH III,973)

The greater part of the concluding volume of *The Principle of Hope* is directed precisely at clarification of an answer to the question as to the "goal-content", the general, unfixed human content or "identity" alluded to in Bloch's statement above, which is referred to parenthetically in the title of the fifth section of the whole text: "Wishful Images of the Fulfilled Moment", that in effect constitutes the whole third volume. Here Bloch presents a magisterial exposition of the human Novum proleptically consummated in the image of Goethe and his self-reflected creation in the character of Faust. Bloch expounds the sufferings of the young Werther in the context of *Sturm und Drang* and excavates the German origin of Promethean titanism, and traces it through the development of Goethe from *Tasso* to *Faust* and into the prolix maturity of *Wilhelm Meister*. Bloch rejoices in the tremendous Humanum revealed in Goethe's appreciation of the Gothic aesthetic impulse paradigmatically realised in Strasbourg Cathedral; in this vision he conceives the *"world itself"* as productivity working "towards its full content or a *material Faust" PH* III,985). Into his cultural cauldron Bloch tosses Shakespeare's Ariel and Prospero, the "dark radiance" of Don Juan, the historical figures of Frederick II, Peter the Great, Napoleon, Byron and Mirabeau and this culminates in an invocation of the demonic in poetry from which Goethe, Beethoven and Dante all

---

[2]Here as often Bloch produces what amounts to a tendentious interpretation of Marx for purposes of legitimation rather than representation. Bloch's ambitions for the refunctioning of religion are incompatible with Marx's declared intention and (in debased form) his chief political interpreter, Lenin. See for a concise presentation, D.B. McKown, "Lenin's Critique of Religion", ch.3 of *The Classical Marxist Critiques of Religion: Marx, Engels, Lenin, Kautsky* (The Hague: Nijhoff, 1975).

drew their power. These figures are on-the-way; beyond them hovers, unfixed, the Eternal-Female (*das Ewige-Weibliche*).

The foregoing remarks give a renewed impression of the extraordinarily effusive character of Bloch's depiction of the guiding images of the human, which, like jungle growth in an over-heated conservatory, proliferate to the point of near impenetrability. Bloch's hymn to the undiminished potency and the products of Goethe's creativity, constantly reborn through his " recurrent puberties" (*PH* III,998), reaches its fullest crystallisation in an exposition of the "fulfilled moment". Here again the use of the moment characterised under the often used Latin tag *Carpe diem* "seize or grasp the day" can be seen to constitute one of the unifying threads running right through *The Principle of Hope* as was noted earlier. This "moment of full Being-There and its Intentional-Absolute" is, as Bloch understands it, the key to the humanity (such as it is) of Faust and is expounded in one of the finest passages in the whole of *The Principle of Hope*. Indeed the third volume of Bloch's work can be seen as a gigantic, ecstatic literary gloss upon the developments of the period 1807 to 1845, that is between Hegel's *Phenomenology of Mind* to the *Theses on Feuerbach*.

II. FAUST AND THE PHENOMENOLOGY: TRANSFIGURATION

Bloch is prepared to cast the role of Faust, and thus the whole direction and reflexive structure of Goethe's masterpiece, in terms of a "dialectical journey in which every pleasure attained is deleted by a separate new desire which awakens within it", but "every attained arousal, is refuted by a new movement opposing it; for something is missing, the fair moment is yet to come" (*PH* III,1014). It is precisely here that Bloch makes a highly illuminating connection important for his total interpretation of the human condition in the modern, Western world: "Faust's dialectical world-tour, with its continual corrections, has only one parallel: Hegel's 'Phenomenology of Mind'" (*PH* III,1015). Recognition of this parallel is crucial to the effective decipherment of *The Principle of Hope* and it amounts to the culmination of a development (begun in the great *Critique of Pure Reason*) in which Kant's categorial analysis of the limits of reason and human knowledge are broken and transcended in Hegel's re-historicisation of the way of man from mere sentience to full self-consciousness. This development comprises the ambiguous assimilation of God (the Absolute Mind) into a scheme which was then demystified by Feuerbach, and finally inverted in material terms by Marx. Bloch provides what amounts to a cultural "aggregation" of this series of related steps allowing pre-modern tradition (with its multiplex literary, visual, plastic and musical aspects) is

to be recovered and refunctioned in the framework of a historical, future-orientated modernist consciousness grounded in the consistent dialectical materialism of Marx. The distinction drawn between Goethe's
Faust and Hegel's *Phenomenology* is of crucial importance in that it
indicates upon what level Bloch is prepared to "recover" the mystical
and eschatological tradition in order to consummate his post-modern
synthesis:

> Goethe's Faust *certainly does not*, as is finally the case in
> Hegel's Phenomenology, sense and touch the Being-For-Itself of
> the fulfilled moment, *as loss of objectivity itself*, as resolution
> of all *objectiveness*, therefore not only of alienated objective-
> ness, into the subject, one which has finally become worldless.
> On the contrary, precisely Faust's contact with the fulfilled
> moment is such because at the same time it has around it the
> sphere, no longer alienated from this moment, of an at last *ade-
> quately contacted object-basedness* (reclamation of land, eternal
> realms) ... Faust is one of the extremest guiding figures of ven-
> turing beyond the limits intends purely in the human moment
> and its world against the status of mere situationalities to-
> wards the cry: and. Stay awhile, spoken to the moment, thus
> becomes a symbol of true, utterly immanent homecoming, of the
> real Ithaca. Only a symbol; because the poem and the philoso-
> phy succeed only in shaping as existent the utopian *intention*,
> not the utopian *content*. (PH III,1022)

Once penetrated the meaning of this passage is clear: the Hegelian
struggle for objectivity must not be resolved; Faust takes up the striving
towards the immanent homeland which subsists permanently in intention. There is no final achieved bed of ease, for the "Faustian heaven
knows only movement and as yet no finite rest-symbol of landing" (*PH*
III,1022). The further exposition of this perpetual activity of
"venturing beyond", illlustrated through allusion to Hamlet, then the
development of a contrast between the figures of Faust and Don Quixote
in literature (*PH* III,1027-1057), and finally in music (*PH* III,1057-1103)
generates powerful resonance. The culmination of the volume follows
directly upon this: utopian futurity in continual movement confronts and
thereby comes into conflict with the finality of death:

> What does even the highest moment mean, the 'Stay awhile,
> you are so fair' intended in the most central utopia, when
> death, without itself being affected, cancels from the capacity

for experience with the greatest command of existence its - existence? (*PH* III,1107)

Standing squarely in the tradition of Marx and Feuerbach, Bloch rejects the "obscurantist interest of the ruling classes and their spouting clergy in transcendental fraud" (*PH* III,1107) -yet somehow not all "overreaching ... into the post mortal sphere" is opium for the people. Here Bloch advances claims, the terms of which indicate the nature of his recovery and transformation of the tradition:

> Everything particular and fixed among the death-defying wishes and rituals, the Greek, Egyptian and Christian death-hopes, is sheer fantasy, but the sphere of this specific hope itself, which is recalled in the following section, is more than legitimate; for not man yet knows whether the life process does not contain or admit of transformation, however obscure. (*PH* III,1108-9)

In short, Bloch wishes to demythologise the symbolic objectifications surrounding the death-barred future and yet retain the dimension of intentionality that has structured his whole argument. The affinity of this with Rudolf Bultmann's demythologising programme within Christian theology is apparent.[3] Repeating the pattern seen throughout the whole work Bloch once more embarks upon a detour into extended illustrative commentary upon conceptions of the after-life in Greece, Egypt, the Bible, Islam and Buddhism, and then in Romanticism and nihilism (*PH* III,1103-1182). It is only in Marxist socialism (introduced characteristically as an addendum) that there is a "disappearance of lethal nothingness in socialist consciousness" (*PH* III,1172). The "red hero", uncomforted by thoughts of personal immortality, is exemplary in his death strengthened only by consciousness of the communist cosmology of consistent naturalism. The seemingly irreversible descent into the annihiliation of death is (in "an astonishing turn-about") prevented by what amounts to a dialectical sleight of hand of some obscurity:

> Death, which both as individual death and as the distance possibility of cosmic entropy confronts future-oriented thinking

---

[3]Bloch, like Bultmann is attempting a hermeneutic of the origins of the Judaeo-Christian tradition which distinguishes between existential analysis and mythological or metaphysical accretion. As Heidegger provided the required existential analytic for Bultmann, so Bloch, for a later generation provides the anticipatory categories utilised by Karl Rahner, Moltmann and J.B. Metz.

as absolute negation of purpose, this same death, along with its possible future-content, now enters the final conditionality, the core conditionality which is illuminated by still unguaranteed joy and the lights of latency of the authentic. Death is thus no longer the negation of utopia and its ranks of purposes but the opposite, the negation of that which does not belong to utopia in the world; it strikes it away, as it strikes itself away before the *non omnis confundar* of the main issue: in the content of death itself there is then no longer any death but the revelation of gained life-content, core-content. (*PH* III,1180)

It is apparent that for Bloch the dynamism necessary to maintain hope in the face of death (regardless of whatever linguistic strategy may be employed to defuse its threat) can only be sustained by religious mystery. In consequence, the last sub-section (*PH* III,1183-1353) of *The Principle of Hope* is, apart from a brief Marxist post-script (*P H* III,1354-1376), permeated by an extended survey of religion.

III. THE REFUNCTIONING OF RELIGION

The "explosive religion" capable of generating the "leap" learnt from miracle is a "fundamental archetype of religious and above all of Christian-advental imagination" (*PH* III,1308). At the core of this religion, the Faustian wager is resolved in terms that even St. Paul (in a suitably refunctioned form), may endorse: "Behold, I shew you a mystery; we shall not all sleep, but we shall all be changed, in a moment, in the twinkling of an eye" (I.Cor. 15,51ff).

In justification of our contention that religion refunctioned is the consummation of *The Principle of Hope*, we now examine in greater detail a presentation in which Bloch is, following Marx, to pluck the "living flower" of human life that is revealed once the "imaginary flowers" have been disposed of by the critique of religion. Characteristically, Bloch's approach is indirect, it begins with an account of the "growing human construct to religious mystery, to astral myth, Exodus, Kingdom; atheism and the utopia of the Kingdom" (*PH* III,1183), and continues with a wide-ranging survey of the messianic appearances and the occult to which is appended a review of founder-figures in ancient religions. By contrast with ancient Egyptian religion, Bloch represents Buddhism and the Orphic cult, Moses and Jesus as figures capable of contemporary refunctioning, they can be "believed in as saviours, not just mythical teachers, not just as pointers towards salvation (*P H* III,1191). More specifically: "Moses ... forces his god to go with him, makes him into the exodus-light of his people; Jesus pervades the transcendent as a human tribune, utopianises it into the Kingdom" (*PH* III,1191). However plausible or inadequate we might regard Bloch's broad categorisation of types of religion it is only those religions with binary aspects which have fundamental significance for him. At the foundation of this hermeneutic of the religious dimension of human life there is a mutual recognition and a discrimination made of considerable import for what follows:

> But whether distinctive or not, whether pervading nature and transcendence or not: words of salvation are always spoken by human beings. And men in the hypostases of gods spoke nothing but *longed-for future*, one which in these illusory hypostases was of course itself only illusorily graspable. This illusion, in some invocations to the gods, indeed to the kingdom of god to come at last, could be one which, instead of reconciling people to given reality and its ideology, regarded it as a delusion and allowed no peace to be made with it. But for such protest, summarising, utopian-radical and humane, prophets are needed, not formulations of a ritual, even though the prophets only replaced the old God-illusion with a new one. With Moses and Jesus this new illusion also contained unreality, but apart from simply mythical unreality it sometimes also contained a quite different unreality, one of what could be or at least what ought to be, which could thus be understood as a pointer towards utopian reality. There is therefore a functional connection between *growing self-commitment of founders to religious mystery* on the one hand and the actual proclamations, the miraculous abyss became human on the other side, that of glad tidings. (*PH* III,1191-2)

Bloch is proposing an implicit theory of the maturation of religion; religious founders represent a mythologically disguised possibility of becoming human, which is defined (given the whole preceding argument) as follows:

> This specific venturing beyond, the more mature religions become, proves to be that of the most powerful hope of all, namely that of the *Totum of a hope which puts the whole world into rapport with a total perfection.* (*PH* III,1192)

There are, however, two possible patterns of emergence: the first is the astral-mythic type of belief which originates in and tends to re-ally itself with despotism and the ideology of domination; the second occurs

where "venturing beyond" is allied with plebeian movements and provoked by prophetic, contrastive founders.Such religion becomes con-
formist only through ecclesiastical compromise and a process of accom-
modatory interpretation. In the framework of Bloch's hermeneutic of
religious assertions Christianity is accorded an extrordinarily high
status on condition that it be true to its inner nature:

> And if the maxim that where hope is, religion is, is true, then
> Christianity, with its powerful starting point and its rich his-
> tory of heresy, operates as if an essential nature of religion had
> finally come forth here. Namely that of being *not static,*
> *apologetic myth, but humane eschatological, explosively*
> *posited messianism.* It is only here - stripped of illusion, god-
> hypostases, taboo of the masters - that the *only inherited sub-*
> *stratum capable of significance in religion lives: that of being*
> *hope in totality, explosive hope. (PH III,1193)*

The presentation of religion in these terms has negative and positive consequences for acts of appropriation directed at the tradition and
in relation to contemporary religious experience. Thus both Rudolf
Otto's category of the numinous and Karl Barth's *deus absconditus* over
against the despotic God of theistic heteronomy are given qualified
approval. Barth's theology preserves, paradoxically, a reverence for
man, for only "in the deus absconditus is the *problem* maintained of
what the legitimate mystery of the *homo absconditus* is about, of what
the community contains of kingdom in its ultimately commensurate
sphere, one not psychologised, not secularized" (*PH* III,1194-5). Drawing besides Barth upon Otto, Spinoza and Münzer, Bloch argues that:

> the *Utterly Different (das Ganz Andere) also holds good for*
> *the ultimate humane projections from religion.* It is only the Ut-
> terly Different which gives to everything that has been longed
> for in the deification of man the appropriate dimension of
> depth. The Utterly Different gives to the hubris of Prometheus
> that true heaven-storming quality which distinguishes the
> Promethean from the flatness of mere individuality and from
> the feeble humanization of the taboo. (*PH* III,1195)

For Bloch historic Christianity contains within itself a prefigurement of the contemporary refunctioning of religion which was first apparent in early efforts to come to terms with the disjunction between an
inherited belief in God and the Kingdom proclaimed by Jesus. Bloch's

own treatment of this relation involves a partial transposition and re-application of the left-wing Hegelian critique:

> God becomes the kingdom of God, and the Kingdom of God no longer contains a god: i.e. this religious heteronomy and its reified hypostasis are completely dissolved in the theology of the community but in one which has itself *stepped beyond the threshold of the previously known creature, of its anthropology and sociology.* This is why precisely the religion which proclaimed the Kingdom of God, in the midst of men (cf. Luke, 17,21) has preserved the Utterly Different most resolutely against the Old Adam and the old becomeness: here as rebirth, there as new heaven and new earth, as transfiguration of nature. (*PH* III,1196)

This passage contains the kernel of Bloch's understanding of the nature of the end of both traditional metaphysically-conceived religion and mythicised cosmic religions, and the subsequent reinstatement of religion as the realisation of the mystery of the human condition, that is as unforeclosedness and openness to the "last leap and the utopian Totum". The latter is the recovery for which Bloch argues on the assumption that it is the only means sufficient to impede and subvert heteronomy and alien hegemonies. Without it, mankind is reduced to utter banality. Thus:

> The wishful content of religion remains that of feeling at home in the *mystery* of existence, a mystery mediated with man and well-disposed to his deepest wish, even to the repose of wishes. *And the further the subject with his founder of religion penetrates into the object-mysterium of a God conceived as the supreme Outside or the supreme Above and overpowers it, the more powerfully man in his earth-heaven or heaven-earth is charged with reverence for depth and infinity.* (*PH* III,1196)

The restatement of religion in these terms recalls the notion of religion as heuristic fiction in the later parts of the *Critique of Pure Reason*[4], and indeed of Hans Vaihinger's Neo-Kantian systematic presentation of the philosophy of "as if"[5]. Bloch owes a great deal to Otto

---

[4]Despite Bloch's disclaimer of the rigidities in Kant's retention of the "ideas" in their heuristic employment as the contents of the dialectic of pure reason his position is not dissimilar.

[5]Vaihinger's *The Philosophy of "As If"* remains a classic of Neo-Kantian thought and its structural affinity with Bloch's position is apparent.

(but rather less to Barth), when he regards the basic features of religion as: "Numen, numinosum, mysterium, even No to the existing world owe never anything but the *secret humanum* itself" (*PH* III,1198). These aspects of "mystery", that is the "numinous" in Otto's *Idea of the Holy* are of value only when constantly interlinked with the religious key concept of the kingdom which justifies the refunctioning itself:

> For even grace, even if it is supposed to be far from the power of the human will and not to come from the merit of works, its concept comes after all from the hope of a leap and of the recognition of being able to be prepared for the most perfect. Hence precisely that unmistakable non-passivity even in the thickest god-forms of religion, hence the superadditum of most tremendous insatiability of every religious shudder, even when it seems to waft down from above. Hence the ultimate transformation, convertibility of the astral-mythic alien mysterium into the mysterium of a citoyen of the kingdom and of its paradoxical relationship to becomeness. Hence finally above all the most powerful paradox in the religious sphere so rich in paradoxes: *the elimination of God himself* in order that precisely religious mindfulness, with hope in totality, should have open space before it and no ghostly throne of hypostasis. All of which means nothing less than just this paradox: the religious kingdom-intention as such *involves atheism, at last properly understood atheism.* (*PH* III,1199)

Such a project is recognisable as a refunctioning of the left-wing Hegelian critique of religion and reduction of the God-projection into its human correlate. What is remarkable about Bloch's argument is his making the elimination of the God-hypothesis, that is atheism, the condition of a *renewal* of religion which is conceived the guarantee and continued recognition of the freedom only granted through openness to the future. Understood in the context of the early twentieth century struggle with nihilism (itself a particularly marked feature of German culture of the Weimar period) the remaining pages of Bloch's treatment of the numinous (*PH* III,1199-1203) merit careful appraisal. Bloch's postulation of atheism at the heart of the rehabilitation of religion is the basis of his much repeated aphorism that is presented at the beginning of *Atheismus in Christentum Zur Religion des Exodus und des Reichs*:[6]

[6]G.A. 14, p.15.

*Nur ein Atheist ein guter Christ sein, nur ein Christ kann ein
guter Atheist sein*

The philosophical brinkmanship involved in playing-off atheism
against nihilism continues as Bloch struggles to sustain a consistent materialism adequate to his vision of the human.The "leap" in the dialectic demands the religious residuum without which his position
would lapse into nihilism:

> The place that has been occupied in individual religions by
> what is conceived as God, that has ostensibly been filled by
> that which is hypostatised as God, has not itself ceased after
> it has ceased to be ostensibly filled. For it is at all events pre-
> served as a place of projection at the head of utopian-radical
> intention; and the metaphysical correlate of this projection re-
> mains the hidden, the still undefined-undefinitive, the real
> Possible in the sense of mystery. The place allocated to the
> former God is thus not in itself a void; it would only be this if
> atheism were nihilism, and furthermore not merely a nihilism
> of theoretical hopelessness but of the universal-material anni-
> hilation of every possible goal and perfection-content. Materi-
> alism as the explanation of the world in its own terms has only
> in its mechanical form failed to touch even marginally on the
> place of the earlier god-hypothesis; but it has also failed to in-
> clude life, consciousness, process, the switch from quantity to
> quality, Novum and dialectics as a whole. (*PH* III,1199)

Bloch's reconstruction of the notion of projection in utopian terms is
presented as a correction of materialism and as a counter to the threat
of nihilism, it therefore encapsulates his most fundamental intentions
and is the position in relation to which the subsequent re-theologisa-
tions of the philosophy of hope in German theology have to be judged.
The Anglo-Saxon neglect and ignorance of Bloch is remarkable, his
work is, perhaps, the single most important confluence of Jewish, Christian and Marxist thought in the twentieth century. Bloch juxtaposes
the benefits of religion critically refunctioned with the rehabilitation
of a constrictive materialism and presents this as a protest against the
all-pervasive abyss represented by nihilism. Bloch's positive critique
of Feuerbach avoids some of the potential difficulties of direct confrontation; but the implications are clear: religion and materialism
rightly understood stand in acute mutual need of each other. Materialism should take up and develop Feuerbach's critique of religion and
thus cancel out the transcendence and reality of every god-hypostasis,

but it should do this, so Bloch maintains, without removing what is really intended by the *ens perfectissimum* from the goal of utopia towards which human freedom is directed. This rejection of divine hypostasis together with the retention of futurity implies the disappearance of the *ens realissimum*, a most real being understood as a given, in favour of the future perfect and that which will become. The kingdom, albeit now in partially secularised form, remains the utopian totality, a "messianic Front-space" distinct from theism but capable of accommodating an astonishing diversity of anticipatory motifs, from Prometheus to the Messiah. Any concept of God a world-ruler thwarts human freedom, and, so furthermore:

> The utopia of the kingdom destroys the fiction of a creator-god and the hypostasis of a heavenly god, but not the end-space in which the ens perfectissimum contains the unfathomed depth of its still un-thwarted latency. The existence of God, indeed God at all as a special being is superstition; belief is solely that in a messianic kingdom of God-without-God. Atheism is therefore so far from being the enemy of religious utopia that it constitutes its precondition: *without atheism Messianism has no place.* (PH III,1200)

Against Hegel and the German idealist assimilation of Christian theology into identity philosophy, Bloch argues that the "history of man's consciousness of God is certainly not the history of God's consciousness of himself - but of the highest possible Front-content in each case of an existence open in its Forwards, in its Above, in its depth" (PH III,1200). Bloch is obliged (like Schleiermacher before him) to distinguish "higher" from "lower" religions; thus religions that have posited the hypostasis of God are characterised by the "Front-intensity of radical longing" whereas Taoism and Buddhism lacking such a hypostasis are strictly speaking fairly useless judged by the criteria of "transformation". In Judaism and in Christianity (certainly Bloch's preferred religious tradition) existing is understood as a *transcendere*, a "transformed existing, one of an attempted rebirth towards the new man, through the founder and his god" (PH III,1201). The benefits of the Judaeo-Christian tradition lie primarily in this capacity to effect transformation; Bloch has decisively repudiated the Marxian dismissal of religion in favour of a qualified reinstatement:

> Nature itself is transformed in the Christian apocalypse and, unlike every ideal landscape of aesthetic pre-appearance, it passes first through destination to its transfiguration. *Trans-*

formation, therefore, in the atheism of religion, above it, constitutes the last criterion of its sphere, a criterion which equally flows from religious penetration into the Above, that which is intended as God. Judaism, Christianity, as the highest religions, show the entire intended seriousness of this transformation; and of course only a concept of knowledge which has enriched itself with religious conscience can do justice to this. And the end of religion is thus, in this knowledge, as comprehended hope in totality, not simply religion but - in the convolutions of Marxism - the inheriting of it, meta-religious knowledge-conscience of the final Where To, What For problem: ens perfectissimum. (*PH* III,1201)

Bloch maintains that "god-making" is, in Lenin's words "necrophilia",[7] but the translation of the god-hypostasis into "unconditional hope-content" provides the basis of a new anthropology and the appropriation of religious eschatology. In a manner that somewhat strains the previous argument Bloch throws a whole series of real and mystical religious teachers (Cadmus, Orpheus, Homer's gods of Olympus, the Egyptian sun of the dead, Babylonian astral myth, the Chinese Tao, Moses or the exodus and the "emphatic god-men Zoroaster, Buddha and Jesus") into a single, all-comprehending framework; in the highest forms all:

describe precisely the *growing commitment of the founder to the experimental glad tidings of an ens perfectissimum*; and the social mandate for this penetration and the human substance of its perfectum always correspond with each other. In the astral myth the founder disappears, his god is the complete outwardness of starlight, in Christianity the founder becomes the glad tidings itself, and his God finally disappears in one single humane All Saints Day. (*PH* III,1203)

IV. THE DIALECTICS OF BIBLICAL MESSIANISM

Bloch has laid down his hypothesis, the translation of the hypostasis of God into the Front of the future, the utopian goal of *ens perfectissimum.* This is then used as an interpretative principle applied in

[7]In terms of the polemics of the "orthodox" Marxist-Leninist tradition Bloch might appear to fall into the category of the "god-builders" such as Gorky, Lunacharsky and Bogdanov against whom Lenin polemicised. The context in terms of Marxist discussion lies in Lenin's attack on Mach and Avenarius in *Materialism and Empirio-Criticism* (1908).

a detailed review of primitive, Greek, Roman, Egyptian and Chinese
religion, each of which is evaluated in terms of its latent Novum. The
range of Bloch's knowledge is remarkable, but the compatibility of his
hypothesis with the Judaeo-Christian matrix is all too obvious, and
the connection between Moses and Jesus though the medium of messianic
religions far more persuasive, than the looser, more eclectic treatments
of other major religious traditions. Bloch's high regard for the basic
historicity of the biblical narratives is again remarkable. Moses represents a leap in religious consciousness which prepared the way for a religion of opposition expressed supremely in the exodus from Egypt
which provides the "exodus archetype" (PH III,1232) comprising both
suffering and rebellion. The God of exodus is correspondingly interpreted as *Deus Spes*, the God of hope who calls into existence the Messiah, the "hoped-for higher Moses" (PH III,1238). This God was later
transformed by Philo into the Logos-centred "second God", a so-called
man-god. Messianic religion assumes a dominant status:

> Every founder of a religion appeared in an aura *which belongs
> to the Messiah*, and every foundation of a religion has, as glad
> tidings, *the new heaven, the new earth on the horizon*, even
> when both perfectednesses have been abused by the masters'
> churches for the idealization, i.e. the apologetics of an existing
> order (PH III,1241).

The subsequent disquisitions on Zoroaster and the Buddha add little of substance and indeed create further difficulties in what are perhaps somewhat implausible attempts at assimilation. Far more convincing is Bloch's account of Jesus who is represented as the central and
decisive embodiment and fulfilment of the Messianic religion effectively invented by Moses. Bloch begins this section with a characteristic citation of Thomas Münzer, in which he stressed the transformatory
role of faith: "We men of flesh and earth are to become gods through
Christ's becoming man and with him are God's pupils, indeed by him
are taught and made gods, indeed for more, we are completely changed
into him, in order that earthly life may swing into heaven."
(Philipp.3) (PH III,1256). With an earthy grasp of the commonsensi-
cal, Bloch regards the basic facts in Jesus' life as "taken from historical
stuff, not the golden stuff beloved of legend" (PH III,1256). Jesus' life is
to be seen in the setting of Jewish expectations and Hellenistic mystery
religion. Contrary to attempts to dissolve the historical Jesus into le-
gendary invention compatible with Roman and Greek religious conceptions, above all the dying saviour-god, Bloch argues that:

On the contrary, the *life and gospel of Christ* contrast especially sharply and concretely with the generality of the
framework of expectations and even with the later *cult image*
gospel *about Christ*. Christianity was thus prevented from becoming such a pneumatic and theosophical religion as the neo-
Docetism of the so-called Christ myth makes it into a mythol-
ogist's religion. And finally, even more than the birth in a
stable and the death on the cross, Christ's *influence as a person*
on his disciples proves his reality. If Jesus were invented, if his
person had only been interpolated later into the myth, then the
earlier gospels would be imaginative-speculative and only the
later ones historicist; yet the precise opposite is the case. (*PH*
III,1258-9)

Bloch then proceeds (*PH* III,1259-74) with one of the most gripping
and invigorating portrayals of the immediacy of the historical Jesus to
be found anywhere in the twentieth-century literature. As we saw in
the first chapter of this book, Bloch's understanding of religion is pervasively influenced by his study of Münzer and it is in terms of the parallel between the latter and the historical Jesus that this remarkable
passage is to be understood. Jesus' resistance to the transformation of his
persona from preacher to Messiah, and his temptations and desponden-
cies are uninventible: "they say Ecce homo, not Attis Adonis" (*PH*
III,1259), indeed his *"last, fearful supper, his despair in Gethsemane,
his abandonment on the cross and his exclamations*: they do not accord
with any legend of the Messiah-King, nor even with that of the suffering Messiah" (*PH* III,1259) and, subsequently, it is the historical resistance of the original narratives which prevented the complete success
of the Gnostic-Docetic dissolution of Christ: "a vegetation god would
not have put up this resistance" (*PH* III,1259).

Bloch's view of Jesus owes much in negative terms to the now
relatively little known book by Arthur Drewes, *Der Christus Mythos*,
besides the works of Reitzenstein and Bousset.[8] Curiously Bloch plays
down the "expectation" in the Jewish contemporary context and we
have little evidence of the influence of the consistent echatology thesis
of Weiss and Schweitzer upon him. Bloch's discussion of biblical
material is extremely dated as it focussed upon controversy that took
place in the first two decades of the present century. In the light of this
it is all the more remarkable that his presentation of the historical

---

[8]See Ansgar Koschel, *Dialog um Jesus mit Ernst Bloch und Milan Machovec* (Frankfurt
am Main, Peter Lang, 1982) and, as regards a general survey: Hermann Deuser and Peter
Steinacker (eds.) *Ernst Blochs Vermittlungen zur Theologie* (Munich: Kaiser, 1983).   The
latter contains an indispensable introduction to the relevant bibliography.

Jesus has gained rather than lost plausibility. This is because of an increasing recognition of the Jewishness of Jesus which corresponds with Bloch's own Messianic concerns.

By contrast with radical mid-twentieth century tendencies in New Testament scholarship Bloch propounds a straightforward historical realism, complemented with a "Christology" of some sophistication not surprisingly congruent with his broader conception of the nature of religion. In positive terms:

> Thus *Christian faith more than any other lives from the historical reality of its founder*, it is essentially the imitation of a life on earth, not of a cult-image and its gnosis. This real memory acted over the centuries: the imitation of Christ, however great the internalization and spiritualization, was primarily a historical and only as such a metaphysical experience. (*PH* III,1259)

This conception of the active memory of Jesus and the imitation of Christ is one that deflated both cult and heavenly images: identification with and the companionship of Jesus was of decisive importance. As regards an explanation of the significance of Jesus, Bloch argues in the following way in what amounts to a Christology. The general transformation in religion, the move from "general-mythic towards into the religious-philosophical Novum" is given particular concrete form: "if Christianity is not a baptized natural or astral heaven, it is equally not heaven as the throne-room of Jahweh" (*PH* III,1260). Like Hegel, but with a different integrative content, Bloch is proposing a transition from religion as mythic enactment to religion as philosophical and human consummation. In Jesus, who "put himself as the Son of Man into this Above", is "more precisely present in this superhumanization of his God than Zoroaster or Buddha" (*PH* III,1260). Jesus did not simply project "existing man" into this "Above" but the "utopia of something humanly possible whose core and eschatological fraternity he exemplified in his life" (*PH* III,1260). In consequence of this:

> God, who was a mystical periphery, became the humanly commensurate, humanly ideal central point, *the central point at every place in the congregation which gathers in his name.* This required a founder who was convincing, a founder in whom the word became flesh, tangible flesh, crucifixis sub Pontio Pilatio. This required the uncounterfeitable delicacy of a hubris which presents itself with much calm assurance that it was not and is not even perceived as such. (*PH* III,1260)

To what extent this may be counted as legitimate representation of Jesus' messianic consciousness as refracted through the experience and interests of the early church and reflected in the New Testament texts is disputable, and it takes the reader into a critical discussion without an obvious outcome. Bloch's views (and positions analogous thereunto, even if not derived therefrom) are more widely held than is immediately apparent. The Czech philosopher Milan Machovec and the West German theologian Dorothee Sölle[9] propose analogous resolutions of the God hypostasis in combination with the impulse towards liberation, the enactment of the kingdom. Bloch restates in secularised form the "work" of his conception of the Christ who in his "person" represents the resolution of God into humanity, "the word became flesh, tangible flesh"; thus:

> A man appeared here as simply good, this had never happened before. With a characteristic *downward attraction*, towards the poor and the despised, yet not at all condescending. With *upward rebellion against-above*, unmistakeable are the lashes of the whip against the money-changers and all 'who afflict my people'. (*PH* III,1260)

What Bloch provides is a "theology of liberation" in the sense that what Christology serves to explain is the revolutionary *end* of a traditional theology grounded in *theism*. Bloch shares with Hegel the sense that we are at a terminus on the religious track of human history and it is upon this that the West German theologian Jürgen Moltmann bases his diverse (and not easily integrated) "theologies" of the "end" of theism and the beginning of a specifically Christian understanding of "God" .[10] Bloch's own account is distinctive inasmuch as he resists all efforts to re-invest the Jesus of the synoptic narratives with triumphalist motifs or to permit a docetic *décollage* into mythological super-humanity. The test case is Jesus' attitude to poverty and Bloch here makes some sound discriminations in his understanding of the "option for the poor":

> Poverty is closest to salvation, wealth prevents it, inwardly and outwardly. But poverty for Jesus is certainly not already a

[9]D. Sölle, 'Stellvertretung Ein Kapital Theologie nach dem "Tode Gottes" (Stuttgart: Kreuz, 1965).

[10]The failure of systematic integration between the various "theologies" of Moltmann is ably indicated by Jozef Niewiadowski in *Die Zweideutigkeit von Gott und Welt in J. Moltmanns Theologien* (Innsbruck: Tyrolia Verlag, 1982). This contains a full bibliography as does R.J. Bauckham's *Moltmann Messianic Theology in the Making* (London: Marshall Pickering, 1987).

component of salvation so that it does not need to be eliminated. Nowhere is poverty, ordinary, inflicted, wretched poverty, defended; only voluntary poverty is recommended, and this advice is given only to the wealthy, to the rich young man (Matt. 19,21). (*PH* III,1260)

Bloch regards the attitude to poverty as central and crucial: it is not an end in itself but the means to an end and it must be understood in the framework of the "interim ethic" of the kingdom. It is apparent that Bloch's reading of Franciscan and mystical tradition has strongly influenced his conception of the role of poverty in the promotion of the brotherly community, which "built on principles of love-communism, wants to have no rich members, but also no poor members in the forced, deprived sense" (*PH* III,1260). The community of Acts regarded as an extension of Jesus' original teaching belongs to the brief period of time ceded to the old earth before its dissolution; however, Bloch does not propose the continuation of the primitive community as such, or its naive re-enactment. What he is prepared to countenance (and here it would seem he really parts company with Marx) is the rehabilitation of inwardness as the consequence and fruit of the teaching of the synoptic Jesus and the subsequent tradition where it remains true to itself:

> The talent which must be turned to good account is only goodness or the inner treasure. This treasure is recovered by the *imitation of a love* which no longer wanted anything for itself, which is prepared to give its life for its brother. Classical love was eros towards the beautiful, the brilliant, Christian love thus instead not merely to the oppressed and the lost but to the inconspicuous among them. (*PH* III,1261).

Christian love "contains the pathos and the mystery of smallness" (*PH* II,1261), this is the love imported in the unexpectedness of finding the redeemer as a helpless child in humble circumstances. It is, however, the precise character of the stumbling block represented by Christian love in the context of the hierarchies of the power of rulers which must be determined with the highest precision:

> Against the power of rulers Jesus is precisely the sign that contradicts, and precisely this sign was contradicted by the world with the gallows: the cross is the world's answer to Christian love ... To justify itself, this same world using its pagan myths, later turned the death on the cross into a voluntary sacrifice, as if this had been Christ's intention and not its own. As if this

death had itself arisen from love and was, as Paul put it, the price which Jesus paid God to redeem men from sin. Jesus is not the Messiah although he died on the cross but because he died on the cross: thus Paul, who had not known Jesus, dialecticized the white terror. (*PH* III,1262)

In a remarkable act of empathy, Bloch, an atheist Jewish thinker unearths a Messianic Jesus who stands well apart from the religion of Paul. The latter was responsible for the view that it was Yahweh who "also wanted Golgotha, he is not like Satan but like a creditor, only more dreadfully loving than any before him: he gives his own son to wipe out a debt which otherwise - given the commercial code of heaven - could not have been remitted" (*PH* III,1262). Contrary to this Bloch sets the "real Jesus" who died as a rebel and martyr fearing his coming death in Gethsemane. It is at this juncture that Moltmann's highly influential representation of the "crucified God" [11] runs counter to the eschatalogical triumphalism of the "theology of hope". Bloch maintains that:

Subjectively and objectively the death on the cross came from without, not from within, from Christian love; it is the reward for the rebel of love and his catastrophe. It is the catastrophe for a Jesus who preached not an other world for the dead but a new heaven, a new earth for the living. (*PH* III,1262)

V. ESCHATOLOGY AND TRANSCENDENCE

Jesus is for Bloch an eschatological figure, he really spoke the words of Mark 13 and foretold the destruction of Jerusalem and the disappearance of the old aeon, yet, at the same time, he subverted the triumphal messianic expectation, hence the High Priest Caiaphas' insistence upon Jesus' death, against the will of the Roman Procurator. It was Caiaphas who understood Jesus correctly as an eschatological figure directing his teaching against restoration: "Jesus is in fact *eschatology through and through*: and like his love his morality can only be grasped in relation to his kingdom" (*PH* III,1263). The reversal of

---

[11]Moltmann's re-Hegelianisation of his theological version of Bloch's futurist philosophy as focussed exclusively in the "crucified God" places immense strain upon his remaining affinities with the latter. Moltmann's critique of "theism" is insufficiently distinguished from Bloch's standpoint by his neo-Hegelian exhumation of the "death of God". See further to this P. Steinacker, *"Der Verkleinerte Held - Gott in höchster Menschennahe. Überlegungen zur Wirkung Blochs auf die Christologie"*, in H. Deuser, P. Steinacker (eds.), op.cit., pp.186-210.

world-orders that Christ proclaimed is given ultimacy in a brief re-working of the Christology of Chalcedon in which Bloch recapitulates in pregnant and uncompromising terms the main thrust of his argument:

> The glad tidings operated theologically as the abolition of ab-solute God-transcendence through Christ's homousia, i.e. *equal-ity to God*. It operated democratically and mystically as the *perfection of the exodus god into the god of kingdom, the disso-lution of Jahweh in this glory*. The creator, indeed the Pharaoh in Yahweh falls away completely; he remains only as a goal, and the last Christ called only the community to be its building material and city. (*PHIII,1265*)

It is not surprising that Bloch's presentation of a consistent opposi-tion between Jesus and Yahweh leads to a re-evaluation of the motif of sacrifice and a rehabilitation of Marcion. As regards sacrifice, Jesus, as God's mediator, supplants and through his death depotentiates Jah-weh. It is a mortal *man* who expresses (unlike the Yahweh of Moses and the prophets) "devotion to the end" (*PH* III,1265) and not a god en-snared, as it were, in the problematics of his own impossibility. The doctrine of sacrifice as it developed in the tradition belongs accordingly to theodicy, not, Bloch maintains, to Christianity when it interprets Christ's death as a "real payment in terms of the Roman commercial code, it belongs to demonic jurisprudence, not religion" (*PH* III,1266). Je-sus does that of which Yahweh is incapable, despite all later trinitar-ian rationalisation of the self-offering of the cross. The revision of the doctrine of God embodied in Jesus involves a total transvaluation:

> A new god comes into being, one hitherto unheard of, who gives his blood for his children, who, as word became flesh, is ca-pable of suffering the fate of death in a completely earthly way, not merely in the ritual of the Attis legend. Here a man, through the hubris of complete devotion, overhauled every idea of God to date; Jesus becomes a love of God such as has never been conceived in any god. (*PH* III,1266)

Bloch's appeal to the theology of J.S. Bach's *St. Matthew Passion* in support of this view is an indication of his readiness to integrate both traditional and New Testament materials into his perspective. The eschatology contained in passages of Paul[12] and the Epistle to the

---

[12]For example, Romans, 8,38f.

Hebrews[13] is cited at length. The imagery of the serpent in the wilderness lifted up by Moses and applied to Christ (John 3, 14ff.) is the occasion of an extended excursus on the serpent-cult as a universal representation of the struggle between Yahweh and humanity. In this way Christ *becomes* Prometheus, for when Bloch asserts that: *"The serpent of paradise above all is Jesus,* indeed he is its last, highest incarnation; and again its head is crushed by Yahweh" (*PH* III,1268), he comes very close to an identification of Yahweh with the demiurge against which a titanic, Promethean struggle must take place. It is with Bloch that the identification of Christ and Prometheus discussed within the ill-fated Christian-Marxist dialogue of the late 1960s and early 1970s originates.[14] For Bloch, it is Marcion who brings forward with particular clarity the "anti-Yahweh, in favour of Christ as the total Novum or paradox in Yahweh's world" (*PH* III,1270). Bloch's strange "serpent Christology" is centred upon militant struggle for the "new God, who was absolutely strange" (*PH* III,1270) and his transvaluation of the origin of Christianity would call for fundamental revision of subsequent doctrinal developments. Bloch's interpretation of the consequences of Jesus' proclamation of the kingdom is striking:

> The humble were to be raised up, the cross was to be *smashed,* not to be carried on to become the thing itself. Jesus' shyness, indisputable and self-obstructing, disappeared after the experience of the transfiguration, which was also hallucinated by his apostles, and only they were sorely afraid (Matt. 17,2-6). From this point on, external obscurity, his instructions to the apostles in Caesarea Philippi that the were to tell no one he was the Christ, no longer applied (Matt. 16,20). The deepest Humanum-commitment into heaven was proclaimed, the subjective factor of Christ-likeness inherited the transcendental factor, the glory of God became the apocalyptical glory of Christ and his followers. And this utterly new religious matter was created - not for the sacrifice on the cross, which is and remains a theodicy of the world-creator, world-ruler, but for the *triumphant image of the tribune behind the death on the Cross.* (*PH* III,1271)

---

[13]Hebrews 2,17; 4,15. Bloch provides a lively but somewhat resuscitation of the Ophite sect as justification of his interpretation of the "serpent" dubious Christology in the context of early Christian origins.

[14]A discussion famously summarised in J.M. Lochman's *Christus oder Prometheus? Die Vorfrage den christlich-marxistischen Dialogs und die Christologie* (Hamburg: Furche, 1972).

The consequent translation of the "glory of God" into the "apocalyptical glory of Christ and his followers" is a step entirely congruent with the basic structure and consistent direction of Bloch's thought. There is, however, a "second eschatology" in which the "wishful mysteries of resurrection, ascension and return" (*PH* III,1271) come to play a dominant, even if from Bloch's standpoint, problematic, role. Precisely why this "second eschatology" arises in its particular form is somewhat obscure; even odder is Bloch's recourse to the Fourth Gospel on the vehicle of motifs compatible with the transition from ontological theism into kingdom eschatology. There is, in sum, a profound implausibility in Bloch's postulation of the "triumphant image of the tribune behind the death on the cross" (*PH* III,1271). Bloch's Jesus is startlingly real[15] and he downgrades Paul in favour of the historical Jesus understood as a Jewish figure. Yet, and this is crucial, Bloch wants to substantiate the continuing importance of a utopian eschatology which is conveyed in its most dynamic form in the Christian tradition, which for very good reasons takes as its energising source the resurrected, ascended Lord who is to return in glory. In short, Bloch wants driven anticipation and the yearning for the kingdom, but how could this ever be generated and sustained by the "fore-gleam" of a failed Messiah rather than by what is here designated as the "afterglow" of the downgraded "second eschatology".

Bloch is caught in a dilemma: his whole exercise involves the systematic unearthing of the repressed eschatology of Western religion and culture and includes a generous rehabilitation of the historical Jesus, yet his designation of that Jesus as rejected crucified Messiah as the exclusive origin (that is in terms of Christianity) of this hidden history places an impossible burden upon the historical figure itself. This is recognised inasmuch as Bloch does not exclude from his scheme the "wishful mysteries of resurrection, ascension and return" (*PH* III,1271) for these are essential to the articulation of the eschatological afterglow which is, as he has implicitly recognised, essential to the continued dynamism of the tradition: "The real-memory of Jesus after his death necessarily established dimensions of hope unlike those of any previous founder" (*PH* III,1271). The watershed is reached at the point where the continuation of the presence of Christ is justified as mere wishful thinking:

> Abide with us, for it is toward evening" (Luke 24,29): Thus for
> the apostles the presence of Christ had not ended even on the
> way to Emmaus, thus the *wishful mysteries of resurrection, as-*

---

[15]For example, G. Vermes, *Jesus the Jew* (London: Collins, 1973).

cension and return came into being. Consequently this *second eschatology.* the Christianity of this after-gleam started out only from the empty tomb, only with the ascension did the Son of Man fulfil eternity, only with the return was the advent-consciousness of the first followers stretched to that of all later followers. (*PH* III,1271).

The presentation of this extension of consciousness, the growth of the expectation that Jesus had to return "to fulfil the *kingdom of man*" (*PH* III,1271) is congruent in *content* with Bloch's total project but corresponds in *form* with an orthodox depiction of Christian origins. The question is, however, this: could the *content* of Bloch's position, that is the extinction of Yahweh in favour of the kingdom of *man* (even supposing that it were correct) have ever aroused and sustained the eschatological consciousness (later repressed) that has to be recovered and refunctioned? Bloch's commitment to the latencies and indispensable imperatives of eschatology and the category of hope is so great that it carries him yet further into an examination of the continuation of Jesus' representation in the *paraclete,* the mysterious helper, comforter and adviser. The reader is thus confronted with an astonishing endorsement of the Fourth Gospel in terms of a parallel with the Saoshyant, the Zoroastrian counterpart of the "comforter". Here an alternative reading of the Christian tradition is postulated that conflicts with that of Paul as it is concentrated in the interpretation of the sacrificial death on the cross. In the Johannine structure of continued witness there takes place a reduplication. The promise of Christ: "And I will pray to the Father, and he shall give you another Comforter, that he may abide with you for ever" (John 14,16) signals for Bloch a retrospective interpretation of Jesus'self-understanding which re-asserts Messianism upon a level superior to that of the sacrificial death on the cross, for, he maintains, "the belief in the Messiah who had appeared in turn contained that in the one who had not yet appeared" (*PH* III,1272). It is now the Holy Spirit which in effect becomes the true advent of the Son. In these alternative strands of the Christian tradition associated with the names of Tertullian and of Joachim of Fiore and his teaching of the Third Kingdom is of central importance. The historical Jesus slips into the background as the *paraclete* ceases to be tied to the condition of the former's appearance and a change of emphasis is evident, one which conforms fully with Bloch's rehabilitation of the utopian motif:

The paraclete no longer speaks of himself, he posits the reality in which inwardness has become spiritual outwardness. The paraclete thus becomes the utopia of the Son of Man, who is no longer utopia, because the kingdom is present. Now all of this does not break out of homesickness for Christ, on the contrary, precisely the *essence of Christ* is repeated in heightened form in the comforter who has become the Holy Ghost. (*PH* III,1273)

Into this interpretative scheme Bloch fits the apocalyptic images of Daniel 7,13f.; it is the Son of Man who "takes part in the leap into the Novum" (*PH* III,1273) and he concludes with a far-reaching panegyric based upon the integration of the resurrection into his distinctive account of Christian origins and the later (primarily mystical) tradition:

> Christ's resurrection from the dead has no analogy in the history of religion, but the apocalyptic transformation of the world into something as yet completely inexistent is not even hinted at outside the Bible. And by virtue of the exclusive relation of this absolute Novum or omega to human content, the mysticism of heaven and of its place. In Christian mysticism, above all in Eckhart, precisely this was therefore thought of as nothing then than the fulfilled moment of us all, as its - Nunc stans to the kingdom. This is religious protestation, no longer relating to the self as to something unrevealed and no longer relating to sursum corda as to a hypostatized Above in which man is not found: Eritis sicut Deus is the glad tidings of Christian salvation. (*PH* III,1274)

This passage contains the kernel of Bloch's interpretation: the contents of the Bible as interpreted through its apocalyptic dimension, the German mystical tradition, and the later Young Hegelian reduction of religion in Feuerbach are combined in what amounts to the formulation of a total theory of religion. Following a brief interlude in which Bloch attempts to assimilate Islam into his account we then return to the expansion of this intense personal vision as represented in the "Core of the Earth as Real Extra-territoriality" (*PH* III,1278-1311). "Extra-territoriality" in a post-theistic yet somehow legitimate conception of transcendence, essential to the maintenance of goals adequate to the dignity of humankind; it is the true dimension of realisation.

VI. THE EMERGENCE OF EXTRA-TERRITORIALITY

It is our contention that the refunctioned religious dimension of human life is of determinative importance in Bloch's masterpiece, and that this implies more widely the seemingly indispensable role of religion in the defence of human values which are to be resistant to pre-determination or reduction in any given social system. The defence of dynamic teleology in Bloch's conception of "extra-territoriality" begins with the triumphant assertion that "the drive upwards at last becomes a drive forwards" (*PH* III,1278). Thus *any* society (not merely the capitalist, but also the socialist) must be relativised by Bloch's principle; all social norms are penultimate and in need of the dimension that transcends all immanent pretensions:

> Men can want to be brothers even without believing in the father, but they cannot become brothers without believing in the utterly unbanal contents and dimensions which in religious terms were conceived through the kingdom. With a faith which, in its knowledge, or this knowledge, has now destroyed all the illusions of mythical religion. But even the most clearly visible goal in the un-resting, moving context of a society which is beginning to become classless cannot be attained unless the subject overshoots the goal. (*PH* III,1279).

Ideas of prophecy and human freedom drawn from the biblical heritage are the antithesis of Greek *Moria*, fate: morality and individual resolve confront the fixities of determinism frozen in astral myth. Change and the counter-move of freedom are the distinctive biblical contributions that challenge all resignation in the face of fate. In a brief theological postlude Bloch restates the concept of God as the "utopian hypostatized idea of the unknown man" (*PH* III,1283) and relates this to the *ens perfectissimum* (the refunctioned successor of the *ens realissimum*) and to the late Enlightenment's fulfilment of the Christian conception of man (more precisely the "son of men") as representative mystery. Feuerbach is thus, according to Bloch, the enactor of the inner truth of Christianity: "God as the creator of the world disappears completely, but a gigantic creative region in man is gained, into which - with fantastic illusion, with fantastic richness at the same time - the divine as a hypostatized order is incorporated" (*PH* III,1284-5). Feuerbach assumes heroic proportions in Bloch's account, as he represents the turning-point in the philosophy of religion, "from him onwards the final history of Christianity begins" (*PH* III,1286). More questionable is Bloch's claim that Feuerbach knew "that a residue remains in the affinities, however demystified, which essentially gave rise to Christmas, Strasbourg Cathedral, the St. Matthew Passion" (*PH* III,1286) which has now to be wrested out of the hands of clerics by means of the fuller enlightenment. In a (from the orthodox standpoint) ironic interpretation of the words of Anselm, *Cur Deus homo*, Bloch

finds the religious key to the dynamic of culture itself: that is in the
demythologisation and *retention* in disabused form of that to which
the term "God" has (when rightly understood) witnessed. It is this
"inheritance" that is to be recovered and refunctioned for the benefit of
humanity:

> But *religion as inheritance* (meta-religion) becomes conscience
> of the final utopian function in toto: this is human venturing
> beyond self, is the art of transcending in league with the
> dialectically transcending tendency of history made by man, is
> *the act of transcending without any heavenly transcendence but
> with an understanding of it as a hypostatical anticipation of
> being-for-itself.* (PH III,1288).

The notion of transcending without heavenly transcendence con-
tributes a criterion by which the putting of the Humanum into God and
the resultant ambiguity of the names of God can be construed and interpreted: "Thus all appellations and nominations of God have been huge
configurations of and attempts to interpret the human mystery, intending the hidden human figure through all religious ideologies and despite these ideologies" (*PH* III,1288). The critical return of religion to
its genesis in the human wish can escape the false dilemmas of hell
(the prevention) and apotheosis (the non-privation) of the mythological hypostatisation of the displaced "wish". God appears "as the hypostatised ideal of the human essence which has not yet become in reality" (*PH* III,1289). Redefinitions of this "god" merely displace a
fixed postulate and Kant is the supreme exemplar in this regard. For
Bloch it is only Feuerbach who detects and decodes correctly the motif
of the *Cur Deus homo* in the unmasking of the anthropological significance of God:

> The idea of God, *the transcendent unreality of which in past
> and in future is taken seriously* is fulfilled as an ideal solely by
> its anthropological dissolution, yet by a different, completely
> different dissolution than into human existence as it has been
> brought out so far, in human prehistory. Barth, or theistic
> heteronomy, calls the great religious manifestations 'bomb
> craters' which show that a revelation has taken place. Feuer-
> bach, or atheistic autonomy, interprets these manifestations,
> especially the biblical ones, the other way round, the only
> right way, as protuberances which show that a total wishful
> extension of the Humanum has taken place and an equally total
> attempt on the meaning of the world. Indeed instead of many

separate *hopes*, in the great religions of the world *hope itself* was attempted, which was meant to embrace and to concentrate the many separate hopes. But absolutely nothing but ens realissimum, and that with subservient man's reflection of proskunesis and throne. The truth of the ideal of God is solely the utopia of the kingdom, and for this the precondition is precisely that no God should remain on high, because none is, or ever has been, there anyway. (*PH* III,1290).

In this chapter we have outlined Bloch's positive, but radically atheistic refunctioning of religion and have shown it to be the ultimate *locus* of resolution in *The Principle of Hope*. It is upon this foundation that Bloch then immediately proceeds to develop an existential mode, a way of being human, concomitant with the analytic of religion. Furthermore, the argument in *The Principle of Hope* forms the basis of the latter, better known account of religion in *Atheismus im Christentum*. Of all the Marxist revisionists (the prematurely deceased Benjamin being the sole comparable figure), Bloch is the only one to free the religious dimension from its class-determined framework and propound a demythologised, de-ontologised account of its continuing and *fundamental* role in human experience. By these means Bloch relocates extensive common ground between Marxism and great tracts of the history of western thought upon which he elsewhere offers consistently illuminating commentary. In more particular terms Bloch provided an intellectual basis for dialogue between Christianity and Marxism, and also material, however problematic, used for reconstruction within contemporary Christian theology.

CHAPTER IX

EXTRA-TERRITORIALITY AND THE MATERIAL ESCHATON

In the last chapter it became apparent that religion in its re-appropriated refunctioned form is neither marginal nor secondary but *fundamental* to the culmination of Bloch's intellectual and aesthetic vision. In seeking to reintegrate religion into a complete account of the education of humankind Bloch is taking up and reworking a number of characteristic German concerns, evident in the tradition since G.E. Lessing's *Education of the Human Race* (1780), that here appear as an attempt to unite the interests of heroic European (and supremely German) *Bildung* or cultural formation with those of Marxism. It is a recognition of this tension between end and means that underlies our examination of the concluding passages of *The Principle of Hope* and then our final more comprehensive assessment of the value of Bloch's grandiose, yet deeply flawed venture.

I. ATHEISM AND UTOPIAN SPACE

The residual "space" occupied by the imagined and refunctioned God is that towards which Bloch now directs his search for the inspirational power for a renewal of the human condition. The skilled management of atheism is therefore required in order to permit the reappearance in benign form of what was devalued or transferred into belief in God. The actual history of atheism is a history of loss (rather than gain) that Bloch is obliged to reduce and minimize because it has produced the nihilism which haunts the modern era, and even *The Principle of Hope* itself:

But no atheism which delivered from fear brought deliverance from the wishful contents and treasures of hope of religion, except in its most meagre and totally negative form, in the vulgar materialism of the nineteenth century, which preserved itself only by its educational embourgeoisement from the complete loss of the hope contents, i.e. from nihilism. On the contrary, atheism brought these transcendental treasures into immanence; and in Feuerbach it brought them quite reflectedly into man. (*PH* III, 1292)

Bloch's optimistic attitude to the history of the cultural integration of atheism is of course integral to his refunctioning of the "most powerful religious positivism" (*PH* III, 1292), that is the utopian function that both negates regression and renders usable the core of the religious impulse. The Deus Optimus Maximus, the God of the greatest hope, is rendered in terms of dialectical atheism:

> Hence this utopian element is and remains irreligious, because it is strikingly meta-religious, i.e. it belongs precisely to *atheism* which has arrived and is *finally comprehended in its depths dimension*; but the concept of atheism, according to its last positivum, is the realm of freedom. (*PH* III, 1293)

The baseline of the human condition, that is freedom itself, is only preserved by the "kingdom", the refunctioned translation of regressive, alienated transcendence into the open future. Atheism, so Bloch claims:

> Keeps the world open at the front and forwards; for this it has cleared away Jupiter and the throne and the world-creating, world-encircling ghost of an existent ens realissimum. What was formerly designated as God designates no fact whatever, certainly no throning existence, but an utterly different problem, and the possible solution of this problem is not God but Kingdom. (*PH* III, 1293)

This "hollow space" requires careful designation and placement; here Bloch redefines his relationship with Marxism through a gloss upon Leibniz's statement of the axiom: *"Nihil est in intellectu, quod non fuerit in sensu"* with the rider: *"excipe: nisi ipse intellectus"*.[1] Nothing is in the mind or intellect which is not in the senses, except the mind or intellect itself. In other words the constitution of the intellect is prior to its employment and thus the Kantian priority of the transcendental status of the conditions of mental and perceptual acts is reasserted. This defence of the *a priori* integrity of the intellect is the paradigm for the integrity of both "superstructure" and religious projection. In short, Bloch distinguishes the constitution of reality itself from its interpretation, and thereby he resists the reductive potential of Marxism or any other analytical schema:

---

[1]Leibniz *Nouveaux Essais*, II, I, par.2.

the senses may therefore have provided the intellect with absolutely everything and without them it may be a completely
empty page, but the senses have not provided the intellect itself; to which by analogy may be added, in connection with
economism: nothing can be in the superstructure that was not in
the economic substructure - except the superstructure itself. And
the same applies to the superstructure in the superstructure, to
the religious deification of the wishful images, even of the obscure powers of nature and history: a field, a hollow space, a
specific topos must be methodologically presupposed and objectively pre-ordered if religious wishful images, even images of
ignorance, and especially the images of a genuine mystery-rela-
tion, around the incognito, are to be projectible in the way in
which they have actually been projected in the history of religion. With this analogy to the Leibnizian rider it therefore
emerges that the problem of the religious *projection space in
and for itself is not an illusory problem*, and this space,
although certainly no reality in the sense of factual existence,
is *no chimera* either. (*PH* III, 1295)

Here is the real nub of Bloch's contextualisation of the limits of
Marxism. The ancestral German and idealist pattern of transcendental
analysis involves a "deduction", but not a *reduction* of the categories.
Bloch may be understood as reinterpreting the reductive implications of
Marx's (as opposed to Feuerbach's) critique of religion and idealist pattern of thought. The autonomy of the intellect, the superstructure
(*Überbau*) and the utopian, future-oriented sphere of freedom is sustained against any interrelation of those spheres which might subject
that autonomy to materialist determinism. Thus Bloch struggles to
preserve the transcendental status of these three dimensions whilst simultaneously asserting the "material unity of the world" (*PH* III,
1295). His first step is the setting of restraints upon the reductive potential of "narrow" Marxism, and the second is confrontation with Nietzsche, the unnamed author of a further threat. It is inconceivable
that Nietzsche is not the target of the following remarks:

And nothing could be more wrong - insofar as atheism is taken
seriously in object-based, not just in anthropological terms -
nothing could be more wrong than the consequence-making of a
belief in hollow space in which no kind of Being whatever is to
be found, not even the correlates of a utopian Being instead of
that of God, of a Not-Yet-Being which is Kingdom. Pure belief
in hollow space can either despair nihilistically or it may be

hectically delighted because for it meaning and God have both disappeared at the same time; and then of course humanity, surrounded by nihilistic night, merely phosphoresces, or, surrounded by a vacuum, fluoresces as in a Geissler tube. (*PH* III, 1295)

Against reductive Marxist determination and outright Nietzschian nihilism Bloch posits the *"fermentation, open sphere of influence* for the human subject" (*PH* III, 1295); this is the "second determination" that succeeds the "first determination" of the emptiness of the "hollow space cleared by continuity of Being" (*PH* III, 1295). Along lines suggested by the late *Theogony* of Feuerbach, Bloch wants a reworked "natural religion" which may inhabit the "open Topos of the In-Front-Of-Us" (*PH* III, 1296). Bloch then repeats his juxtaposition of the "latency of Nothing" with the "latency of All" (*PH* III, 1296) in a characteristic refunctioning of the dialectic of "Nothing and All, chaos and kingdom" (*PH* III, 1297) which persists in the field of religious hypostases even after the demise of those hypostases themselves: a hell of Nothing is juxtaposed with the All of fulfilment. Only by the refunctioning of these ancestral conceptions can Bloch characterise the extra-territorial incognito, that dimension of existence essential to human freedom. Indeed, moreover, it is only religion and specifically Christian mysticism put through the Kingdom transposition (and not philosophy as such) which can indicate where it is that the human subject may blossom or die:

Precisely the extra-territoriality of the incognito again and again presupposes for the clearing of the incognito that the hollow space itself into which the divine hypostasis has collapsed has not also collapsed; the extra-territoriality of the incognito would otherwise be based neither on the new heaven nor on the new earth to which it points. (*PH* III, 1298)

The story of the life of Jesus here offers the self-extinction of God as the first stage on the way to the recovery of the *homo absconditus*. The practical penetration of the sphere to be retained in a form purged of its mythical chimeras is exemplified historically by the "narrow path" of Christian mysticism, and this is focused most intensely in the exquisite heightening of the mystic's awareness of time itself and its ontological culmination in the unity of the instant. This identification of the basis of the true discovery of the human in the conjunction of the materialist transformation of the "space" inherited from religion with Christian mysticism (primarily of the German tradition) makes the problematic nature of Bloch's return to the pragmatics of realisation in alliance with Marx unambiguously clear. In textuality composed of brilliant yet at times obscure rhetoric Bloch recapitulates *in nuce* his categories in the context of what is for him the highest, most quintessential form of religion.

II. MYSTICISM AND THE HOMO ABSCONDITUS

In a brief space (*PH* III, 1298-1303) we find the final point of convergence in *The Principle of Hope*. The subtitle of the passage "Stay awhile in the religious layer: the unity of the instant in mysticism" is an accurate indication of the contents, a synthesis between the successive layers of aesthetic and religious experience summarised under the Faustian motif of "Stay awhile, you are so fair" and suffused with the pantheistic ambiguity of German mysticism. Moreover, the universality of this synthesis is enhanced by the quasi-Hegelian conceptuality brought into play: "The Here and Now therefore returns at this *highest place,* has to say its Being-For-Itself" (*PH* III, 1298). We are confronted with the "fermenting All" which springs up in the "darkness of the lived moment" (*PH* III, 1298). In specific terms Bloch asserts an identity: "'Stay awhile you are so fair': the fulfilment of this hope . . . becomes the *same as mysticism* or more precisely as the instant or nunc aeternum in mysticism" (*PH* III, 1298-9).[2] Mysticism is "immersion" (*Versenkung*) as opposed to the "orgiasm" (*Orgiasmus*) of primitive religion and as such the experience that lends itself supremely to Bloch's refunctioning of transcendence into striving immanence:

> Christian mysticism above all is *immersion* without any frothing Being-Beside-Oneself, . . . precisely the kind of immersion which should correspond to the deepest emotion of nearness in the shape of a pouring-forth-faith of subject-into God, of a pouring-forth of God into subject. (*PH* III, 1299)

Bloch's references to Plotinus, Daniel Czepko, Richard of St. Victor, Eckhart and St. Teresa are all intended to justify his claim that in mysticism the heteronomous "Being-Beside-Oneself" capitulates to an autonomous "Becoming-For-Oneself" (*PH* III, 1299), which may be understood as a transition from multiplicity into primal unity through purification, illumination and union. Entry is gained to the "castle" of the soul (*Inburgheit*) in which dualism disappears and the ego and non-

---

[2]See Gerhard Marcel Martin, *"Erbe der Mystik im Werk von Ernst Bloch"* in H. Deuser, P. Steinacker, op.cit., pp.114-127.

ego fuse into one. So the mystical path reappears in refunctioned form in a synthesis that implies the creative appropriation of Feuerbach, yet is also somehow to be compatible with Marx. The enslavement to dualism:

> disappears in mystical union, because it causes the sharpest dualism to disappear: the castle no longer has any dividing walls between ego and non-ego, subject and object, subject and substance; it is itself built without otherness. No more otherness (*Anderheit*), this ultimately has been the hugely anticipatory illusion of all mystics, yet a phantasma utopicissime fundatum. The axe which splits the world into subject and object is pulled out mentally by the mystic; then all that is held back seems to cancel itself out. Thus an entering into the immediacy of the moment takes place, one which is both undivided and completely esoteric; an entering takes place into a moment which for mystical experience is no longer located in time. Time and moment were never so close, indeed so fused, as eternity and this moment. Its name therefore becomes *nunc stans* or *nunc aeternum*, a name in which the ostensibly most tense antitheses: moment and eternity, interchange, in perfect dialectical unity. The God of mysticism was the *God of this nunc aeternum, therefore the God of this highest moment*; in it Now is Always, Here is Everywhere. So that the antitheses of God and not-God is also cancelled out, it also belongs to objectivities outside the castle. God dies by being born in the nunc aeternum; hence for Eckhart God is sheer Nothing, i.e. the All which has become predicateless. (*PH* III, 1300-1)

Thus Bloch brings his account of the extinction of the hypostatised God as the basis of a refunctioned religion and the source of utopian structured space open to experience together with the mystical identity experienced in the *nunc stans*, the moment which both includes and abrogates mere time. This is the culmination of Bloch's representation of the destiny of humanity: its extinction *in*, yet distance in utopian consciousness *from* the material unity of reality, the All. This has to be construed in positive, rather than self-abnegatory or passive terms which would be incompatible with the revolutionary impulse of Marxism. The connection between mysticism and revolutionary action is justified with reference to individuals who have embodied this tension. First amongst these is Thomas Münzer, the "revolutionary among mystics . . . (who) read in the unity of non-scriptural illumination the unity of an Internationale across all separations." (*PH* III, 1301) It is Münzer's conception of a Christian faith "which is the same in form in all the hearts of the elect on earth" is not learnt from the Bible but "through the right teaching of the spirit".[3] The rendering of this "unity in the people" into a movement of history as such was achieved by a second great figure, Joachim of Fiore, who taught the coming of a Third Kingdom,[4] is a collective tendency enhanced and united with mystical individualism in the Brethren of the Free Spirit. In consequence, an ecumenical and catholic task awaits humanity:

> All mankind now completes the movement into mystical Christ-likeness as into the Third Kingdom - to the salvation of the pure, to the destruction of the impure; mankind goes beyond the Kingdom of the laws and of grace, it attains plenitudo intellectus. (PH III, 1302)

"Knowledge" is therefore suffused with the movement of cosmogenesis, as then Eckhart, so now Bloch calls on his own terms for a return to the primal ground (Urgrund) of the entire world process: mystical function has to become a spring of world-change itself. This connection has more the status of passionate assertion than rational argument but it is certainly consistent with the earlier stages of the evolving structure of The Principle of Hope. In reality, however, Bloch cannot do more than restate an identity of goals in the new humanism informed by refunctioned religion. An all-comprehending theory of religion cannot in itself be a world-transforming theory without some considerable supplementation:

> Undoubtedly the unions of mysticism will never return in the old form, and the lightning in which the indescribable is close will no longer open up a heaven from which figurative haloes plunge down. But in the depth of this enthusiasm there always lay the intended breakthrough of a touching of self, a touching of ground, into a kingdom that was to contain no mysteries other than the human ones and no other order than that of a corpus Christi, with vine and shoots. The Kingdom of Christian mysticism was built in the dimensions of the Son of Man, with the suddenly opened moment as his crib. This nunc stans, which itself steps forth on the Here and Now, is so far from being other-

---

[3]Münzer, Expressed exposure of false truth (1524), cited PH III, p.1301.

[4]For a historically well-documented but theoretically unilluminating study of the revival of interest in Joachim see Marjorie Reeves and Warwick Gould, Joachim of Fiore and the Myth of the External Evangel in the Nineteenth Century (Oxford : Oxford University Press, 1987).

world as to be the closest this-world of all: *thus the nunc stans of the mystics in the literal and in the central sense means the same as the 'Stay awhile, you are so fair'*; only in the problem of the nunc stans does this Faust-goal here form and context of the *identity staked out in it.* (PH III, 1303)

The immanent resolution of religion entails a movement back "into the core of man as well as into the problem-subject of nature" (*PH* III, 1303). With a distinctly personal reworking of the accepted usage of the term *nunc stans,* Bloch presents this not as the expression of the transcendence of the temporal order but as the "precision formula for the next immanent immanence, i.e. for the temporally so distant and still absolutely undetermined world without any possible alienation." (*PH* III, 1303). "Religion" is exhaustively translated into the Romantic grasping of the ungraspable in experience and the self-immolation of Germanic mysticism. This is a new, recontextualised version of the "alienation of alienation" a conception as attractive as it is dangerous.

III. MIRACLE AND THE KINGDOM

Bloch's first step in translating his ambitious synthesis into the sphere of praxis is through a consideration of "miracle", which is interpreted by means of a distinction drawn between mere miracle as sorcery, and miracle as an eschatological sign of the coming kingdom, the messianic Novum of the apocalypse. The Matthean and Markan miracles are messianic in these terms, and it is they, rather than Bloch's exposé of the mystery of religion as such, which are capable of translation into a critique of reality. So in terms of messianic liberation: "Miracle is the blasting apart of the accustomed status quo thus attains its most radical expression in Jesus" (*PH* III, 1306). Referring back to the dualisms of the then contemporary religious context of the New Testament (which Bloch identifies with Mandean-Persian dualism) miracle is interpreted as protest: *"it was only against this world and its irredeemable connections* that the miracle, as interruption, occurred" (*PH* III, 1307). By these means Bloch is able to assimilate the later rationalisation of miracle in Thomas Aquinas'statement that "A miracle is a sensory effect which happens through divine agency, contrary to the order of the whole of nature"[5] to his own reinterpretation of miracle as the concept "of the leap, which stems from explosive religion" (*PH* III, 1307). Given the redefinition of the core content of religion, the shift from transcendence into forward-orientatedness and the kingdom,

---

[5]*Summa contra Gentiles*, 3. c.101.

then religion in its refunctioned form is open to yet further transformation on the path towards positivity. The "leap" of explosive religion corresponds (precisely *how* is not clear) with the Hegelian and the materialist dialectical transition from the category of quantity to that of quality. Bloch puts it more obliquely:

> Precisely the concept of the leap has been learnt from the miracle; in a purely mechanical causal world, a world contrasting in every form with miracles, the concept of the leap thus had no place, but it did in one no longer conceived as static and no longer conceived as finite. (*PH* III, 1307)

The "leap" that "established the pattern of the new world"[6] is derived from the religious antecedent, that is "the formerly miraculous-sudden element, a fundamental archetype of religion and above all of Christian-adventual imagination" (*PH* III, 1308). Bloch recognises and promotes the displacement of superstition but seeks further to rehabilitate and enhance the real residuum with a notion of miracle conceived as the necessary condition of emancipatory change, that is the as *qualitative* transformation. Again in Bloch's more involved words:

> But if even the miracle has a relative, converted truth at least in the fact that the world moves in (historically) mediated leaps and makes breakthroughs possible (without any alliance with transcendence, without transcendental interactions themselves): then the miraculous in these leaps and possible breakthroughs contains a partial pre-appearance and possible complete re-appearance of its content as long as the opposite of the miraculous, namely the In Vain or Nothing, has not yet totally and really occurred. The faith of hope, with the miraculous as content which is still undetermined in terms of content but unmistakeable, is therefore superstitiously in mechanical empiricism or, which amounts to the same thing, in abstract utopia, but certainly not in concrete utopia and in its still open, dialectical-processive world. (*PH* III, 1309).

Bloch's isolation of the non-superstitious, demythologised core of religion, that is the qualitative leap together with the self-commitment of man into transcendence is not to be hypostasised into a false other world but found in its real dwelling place, that is in the

---

[6]This dialectical discontinuity here related to Hegel *Werke* II, p.10 is of pervasive importance in Bloch and for the difficulties of the Marxist tradition as he experienced them.

"incognito of every lived moment" (*PH* III, 1310). The only language capable of representing this is to be found in the religious *unio*, the union of moment and eternity that underlies the "real Faust problem" and music itself. A quasi-Pauline awakening: "Behold, I show you a mystery: we shall not all sleep, but we shall all be changed, In a moment, in a twinkling of an eye"[7] is what best characterises the drive towards Being, towards the "homeland" that it as yet "no Present in any place" (*PH* III, 1311). The universal correlate of this as yet ungrasped futurity to be found at the root of religious experience requires the coincidence and identity of the two themes fundamental to Bloch's masterpiece: the forward-orientated drive of Faust and the *Phenomenology of Mind*, together with the best-formed most persistent access to this consciousness provided in religion and, above all Christian (and especially German) mysticism. Drive and grasp are fused with the goal of identity:

> The miraculous is the Stay Awhile of the most central kind; only here does it have its local sign. The miraculous is the flash of light of the subject and of the object, beside which nothing alienated exists any more and in which subject and object have simultaneously ceased to be separate. The subject has ceased with its truest attribute: the desiderium; the object has ceased with its untruest attribute; alienation. This arriving is victory, and the goddess of victory, like the ancient Nike, stands on a point: as concentration of Being, brought out and gathered in and to the Humanum. (*PH* III, 1311).

We may conclude that it is of the essence of religion that it acts as a proleptic, ciphered, mystically experienced point of access to the alternatives of Nothing and the All. The identity towards which man strives, the "unmanifested core" that is the material goal of humankind is subject to a symbolic integration: "Ciphers of nature and the highest good are the final evidences in which the core of man reveals itself as identical with the core of the earth" (*PH* III, 1311). The identification of the goal-and future-orientatedness with the quest for Being itself is a striking example of synthesis, but the further step of identifying "identity" with the material, the "core of the earth", is problematic inasmuch as it arbitrarily postulates the end of "alienation" (*Entfremdung*) understood as "objectification" (*Verdinglichung*) as the point of ultimate fulfilment. As a re-Hegelianisation of Marxism, Bloch's scheme proposes an identity

---

[7]Once more Bloch cites 1 Cor. 15, 5ff.

achieved in the material rather than the ideal, but even after huge exploration and recapitulation of the cultural and religious inheritance the question as to the original *purpose* of mediation remains unclear. Why does humanity need to engage with transcendence in order to de-mythologise and identify with the material goal? What is the purpose of such complex diversions away from the merely material, if the goal of humanity is the extinction of such mediations understood as the pre-condition of the realisation of the Humanum? Bloch treads a narrow tightrope between materialism conceived as total fulfilment and materialism lapsing into monistic reduction:

> The goal of all higher religion was a land in which milk and honey flow as really as they do symbolically; the goal of the content-based atheism which remains over after religions is exactly the same-without God, but with the uncovered face of an absconditum and of the salvation-latency in the difficult earth. (*PH* III, 1311)

Bloch's account of religion is followed by a brief rendering of the "practical", that is the moral implications of his analytic of existence, in which the "good" is understood teleologically and as threatened by death, in "The Last Wishful Content and the Highest Good" (*PH* III, 1312-1353), the penultimate subsection of *The Principle of Hope*. Bloch begins with the Socratic dilemma: "Nothing is good in itself if it is not desired. But nothing is desired when it represents itself as good" (*PH* III, 1312) and interprets this in the light of Marx's stress upon use value: "Everything good is rightly utility value, which is enjoyed, and not exchange value or commodity, by which money can be earned" (*PH* III, 1312). What is it, however, to wish the best? Bloch disposes of the dialectics of the simple wish which turns out to be nugatory (he attempts to show in illustrations drawn from German folk tales) and relates this discussion back to the "categorical imperative" of the "Anticipatory Consciousness" in the "Foundation" of the first volume of *The Principle of Hope*. We have come as it were full circle. Here we have moved beyond the pragmatic location and organisation of the genuine guiding images towards their teleological presentation as "what is final, humanly final" (*PH* III, 1317). The human models that were set forth in the eighteenth and early nineteenth centuries were split by the antithesis between the bourgeois as the "real private individual of free competition" and the citoyen as the "abstract, unegotistical generic individual of an equally abstract polis" (*PH* III, 1318). What had been a division and conflict recognised in the great idealistic writers of the period (Bloch cites Schiller, Hölderlin and

Shelley) is given concrete analytical status by Marx. The problem of
the ideal as such persisted only in Kant who continued to live on
ancient ground, that is the "pre-bourgeois predominance of the summum
bonum question" (*PH* III, 1319). It is precisely because the bourgeois and
post-bourgeois world is fraught with division that Bloch reverts to a
previous era. The move is at once crucial and characteristic in his "refunctioning" programme and corresponds with his reworking of the
concept of natural law pursued at length in *Naturrecht und menschliche
Würde*.

> It is precisely the relative uniformity of pre-capitalist, espe-
> cially of medieval society, which makes it receptive to a cen-
> tral goal-question and its content. Particularly when a society
> such as the medieval is already living in final relation to sal-
> vation, with the universal ideology of terrestrial-celestial
> gradation. *Permanence, unity, final purpose*: these are the
> three formal definitions elaborated here of the highest good as
> the highest ideal; this is precisely why this problem was
> closer to the heart of a relatively undivided society than of a
> disunited bourgeois society. Hence therefore the prevalence of
> the One, Necessary, over the brilliant-partial ideal images of
> more recent sentimental poetry and of its immediate revolu-
> tionary interest. (*PH* III, 1319).

Bloch seeks the reinstatement of the ideal conceived as
"permanence, unity and final purpose", derivable (albeit in a form to be
transformed) from a social system prior to that of capitalism. As became apparent in our review of the utopian visions in volume II of *The
Principle of Hope*, it is Stoicism which provides the basic insights
Bloch promotes; in the words of Cicero: "Ultimate good which does not
add itself to any other things, but to which all things will be drawn".[8]
This is a conception taken in turn from Plato of "a being in which the
good always wholly and in every respect inheres until the end, never
needs any other but is perfectly self-sufficient."[9] The unity of reason
and the highest good in which goodness and truth coinhere survived in
Augustine, but broke down in scholasticism in the conflict over the primacy of will or intellect, goodness or truth in the divine being. It is
Kant who for Bloch retranslated the theologically transmitted and
conditioned unity of the highest good and the most powerful happiness
back into the human universe and provided a new cipher for the

---

[8]*De finibus bonorum et malorum* I, 42.
[9] Phileb. 60c.

"Kingdom of God on earth". Crucial to Bloch's scheme as a whole is Kant's definition of the "highest good as the hope content of a world in which virtue and bliss are united" (*PH* III, 1320) and his equation of *summum bonum* and *suprema spes*, the highest good and the supreme hope, a "this worldly hope-content, though with a chiliastic gleam" (*PH* III, 1320). Kant's highest good is disconnected and remote, allied to the formal "citoyen" aspect of the bourgeois and divorced form his real, empirical aspect; in other words, to use a term Bloch does not employ at this juncture, he is morally "alienated" and abstracted from the material basis of life in capitalist, industrialised society.

Bloch's resolution of this outstanding problem, the necessity of, yet the alienated distance of the ideal from the material basis is conducted at several levels: first, in terms of refunctioned mysticism; second, through the theory of value; third, through religion and art in more general terms; and, fourth, through Marx and Marxism. The diverse elements in this approach make strategic sense when they are grasped against the background outlined in the preceding chapters. In a resonant evocation of the "That" which indicates the core of things Bloch anchors this fundament in its "basis-manifestation in hunger, in need, in the universally interest-based substructure of history" (*PH* III 1321) and reverts to the *Carpe diem*, now recapitulated in the context of the ethical goal, the new "practical reason" of striving:

> Tendency and latency of the Stay Awhile, related to the highest good, live precisely by virtue of this on the frontier concept of the unum, rerum, bonum which mysticism guarded for so long. Guarded together with the relation to the moment, as has been shown: the nunc stans of mysticism is co-existence, indeed opened identity of all moment-worlds in the making present of the highest good. And as nunc stans provided the state of the Stay Awhile with its most radical formula, so permanence, unity, final purpose add to this formula precisely the fundamental definition of the highest good. (*PH* III, 1323)

The identity of world-drive and striving with moral formation and final purpose bestows upon the whole process a unified universality that in turn appears to invest everything with the immanent attributes of theism without God in a synthesis that heads towards the All and purports to exclude nihilism: "the What of the That, the content of the all-pressing dynamic-material world-core becomes one of the fulfilling All and not one of the preventing Nothing" (*PH* III, 1323). Paradoxically and mistakenly, religious mythology identified this final world-purpose as the hypostasis of a "completed being-here (*Da-Sein*) in a

heaven posited as ens realissimum" (PH III, 1323), the very opposite of
what it in fact is; mysticism must be relocated as "event at the height
of the world process" and not "as event within an Olympus, i.e. a
finished eternity from the beginning, indeed without beginning and
end" (PH III, 1324). Bloch continues to tread a narrow line, a knife edge,
when he repeats the transposition of God to the Front. So transposed,
the highest good thought of as God functions in the "real form of the
absolute question working in the core and on the Front of the world
process" (PH III, 1324). Thus the concept of God, conditioned by the
categories of permanence, unity, and final purpose functions along lines
indicated by Neo-Kantianism, that is, as was recalled earlier, as
"heuristic fictions". In Bloch's words these attributes provide the
"processive guiding image only with its antitheses to the fleeting, to
the multiplicity of chaos, to the In Vain or to nihilism, but they do not
yet give any decidedness of positive content whatsoever." (PH III,
1324). Organised, teleologically coherent reality confronts and over-
comes nihilism but without, so Bloch argues, the hypostatised God of
theology. The retention of permanence, unity and final purpose indicate
the "invariance of direction" of the historical process as it heads towards a "being-here" which has displaced and supplanted yet fulfilled the point of identity in the most essential being, an identity
without "otherness" (Anderheit) and "alienation".

The gradual movement towards complete immanent identity and
resolution in the refunctioned concept of identity leads to a curious,
half-acknowledged logical impasse. On the one hand the purpose and
teleological structure of the human and cosmic order is preserved
through a refunctioned Stoicism shorn of its theistic hypostasis; on the
other, however, it is only by virtue of the constant, dynamic transformation of the energy base of theism into future oriented anticipation of
the Kingdom that the synthesis retains its energy and thus its capacity
to represent direction and teleology as anything other than wholly
empty assertions. There are here signs of forced synthesis; plausibility
is retained only by virtue of a refual to press to the limit the conflict-
ually related components:

> But the real problem of this being-here lives only within the
> process which pursues this being-here, indeed: *there would be
> no process at all if this real process did not exist, and this real
> problem would not exist if there were no process.* The That
> which in man but also in the problematic subject of nature seeks
> to attain absolute satisfaction of needs, i.e. the highest good,
> first posits, by virtue of this objective guiding real problem, the
> future into which the unfulfilled momentary world drifts even

further, with intended final goal. And likewise it first posits the past into which the momentary world again and again sinks because as yet nothing manifested, resolved into manifestation, corresponds to the intended final goal or to the highest good. The highest good is itself this goal which is not yet formed, which in the tendency of the process is ultimately signified, which is the latency of the process is ultimately real-possible. Thus a utopian-cosmic perspective appears in the midst of the subjective-and intensive-existential perspective when it can be established that: that which is meant by the highest good, formerly called God, then the kingdom of God, and which is finally the realm of freedom, constitutes not only the purpose-deal of human history but also the metaphysical latency problem of nature. (*PH* III, 1324)

The final sentence of this passage reveals the direction of Bloch's thought in a three stage demystification of the utopian dynamic: God, Kingdom of God, and then the Kantian realm of freedom all come together to unite the purposiveness of human history with the "metaphysical latency problem of nature". This is the viewpoint that has somehow to be reconciled with the Marxian and Marxist tendency so to stress the universality of causally determined history and nature as to demolish the Kantian realm of freedom (a time-honoured conceptual stately home now finally vacated by its last divine Inhabitant staying on in reduced circumstances). The relative absence of references to Kant (as opposed to Hegel) in the Marxian and Marxist corpus, and the identification of individual freedom and rights with merely and solely *bourgeois* freedom and rights is pervasive and indeed pernicious in its consequences. Bloch's extraordinary, *quasi-theological*, rather than political reinstatement of the realm of freedom is an indication of the scale of the exclusion which he has to overcome.

Bloch's colossal mediation concludes with an end result so close to the Neo-Kantian retention of the secularised shadows of theism on the level of heuristic, practical (i.e. moral) principles that the overall stability of his whole venture is called into question. The history of the God hypothesis and its central role in the growth and later decline of Western culture can, when presented in Bloch's cumulative and monumentally well-informed terms, act as a kind of shock absorber between inflated human pretension and the prosaic causalities of evolutionary or Marxist materialism. Whether when examined in the course of a relentless pursuit of truth Bloch's "open system" is more than elaborate ornamentation of a hideous building it is our unfortunate destiny to enter, unadorned, is another matter. The presentation of the God hypothesis in terms of its "use value" (congruent with the dictates of his understanding of the Marxian ethical imperative), whilst at the same time systematically subverting its "truth value" through a three stage demythologisation, places (at the very least) a huge burden upon the receptive capacity and sympathy of the reader. Only a reader well-versed in the theological aspects of the tradition and conversant with a high bourgeois culture can hope fully to understand Bloch; yet this same reader must also accept the consistent transvaluation of this dimension as the condition of accepting Bloch's conclusions. That Bloch's thought has appealed above all to German theologians well-schooled in the litanies of contemporary atheism should therefore come as no surprise, for they constitute a substantial proportion of that limited readership equipped with the cultural pre-understanding essential to an intelligent reception of Bloch's *Principle of Hope*.

IV. MARX AND THE ANTICIPATORY IMPERATIVE

Bloch's remaining steps in the practical dimension may be reviewed very briefly. The first was as we have seen the restatement of the question of teleology conceived in the form of the concepts of permanence, unity and final purpose and then by the mystical perception of human existence as conditioned by the transposition of hypostatised ontological transcendence into the latency of future immanence. Second, as regards the issue of "value" Bloch approaches it from the standpoint of the ancestral relativist critique, ultimately stemming from Socrates, but restated definitively, so far as Bloch is concerned, by Kant. After allusion to Scheler, Aquinas, Adam Smith, Ricardo, and Marx, Bloch unsurprisingly stresses his assimilation of all categories and fields of experience under the terms of his hypotheses through which mere mechanism, and causal determination, is overcome. Yet again the refunctioning of theology is essential, this time in building a bridge between processual fact and the values to be maximised in conduct:

> Prometheus comes into his own, especially when, after the disappearance of God and his objective world-value structure, mechanism does not remain the sole alternative . . . .The loss of objectivity of ready-made pre-ordered values is then more than compensated for by the end of the theological *hypostases* which had clogged and blocked up the whole open production - and projection - space before us. Value-atheism thus becomes the same as value-utopia, productive value-utopia, especially in alliance with objective useabilities, possibilities of transformation to value. (*PH* III, 1331)

Bloch regards the destruction of objective values as axiomatic, but not, however, on the basis of a Marxian critique of them as projections of class interests, but rather because of the extinction of their transcendent guarantor. In other words Bloch begins with Kant and not Marx: Kant conceded the merely practical and heuristic status of God and promulgated the continued reality of the moral law within us. Given his de-mythologisation of the God hypothesis then Bloch is bound to confront the transformation of God into Kingdom and the creativeness of humanity orientated to the future Front with the retention of a secularised moral law. His strategy is to retain the form of moral law inasmuch as it is assimilable into his new synthesis but to discard any pretence to defend a hierarchy of objective values; on the contrary: "the graduated structure is found only in objective utopia, in processive propensity" (*PH* III, 1332). The world exists as potential, not actual or organised value and the latter is only forthcoming as the consequence of the mediation of nature. In accordance with the spirit of the early Marx as seen, for example, in "Private Property and Communism" Bloch conceives the world as the capacity to perceive the potential, that is the capacity of man to humanize nature and nature to humanize man:

> What the world contains is and remains for the time being allied potential in value material; no more, but no less either. It contains the material, the time and the space to work on this material, to express and to naturalize man through it, to mediate nature with human history and to humanize nature through it. (*PH* III, 1332-3)

It is precisely here that Bloch, as the good left-wing Aristotelian he has become, is obliged to locate the driving force for his system in a source other than the God who extinguishes himself into the futurity of the Kingdom. The simple resuscitation of the pre-critical "real value statics" of medieval society is clearly undesirable and its reflection of a "mythological super-nature" (*PH* III, 1333) equally unacceptable. The alternative, a view of the world as "dead mechanism", is an affront to humanity. The "world material" has a "tendency-latency" (*Tendenz-Latenz*) to which human thought and labour can be allied. This then is the basis of Bloch's conception of value: "every formation of value is dependent on the tendency-latency in its material" (*PH* III, 1333). The maximum actualisation of future-orientated latency is the highest good; with this process and its fulfilment the many-layered synthesis is run together, its series of segments as it were impaled and thus unified by the metaphysical latency of matter itself. In consequence, hope,

the transposition of the God hypostasis into kingdom, material totality, the Absolute, Being-There (*Da-Sein*), liberation and de-alien-
ation, and finally the attainment of identity (the resolution of the subject-object distortion) are brought together in a way only comprehensible and remotely plausible when seen in the perspective created by examination of the whole text of *The Principle of Hope* in its relevant
context:

> The end of latency in the most positive-possible sense is the
> highest good, and it would not be the highest good if, in its
> highest subjectivity, it did not also contain highest object-
> basedness in spe within it, both as kingdomliness and as com-
> plete materiality. Only in this is it concrete; only in this can
> the desiderium find the Absolute of its intending and cease
> with it; only in this does subjectivity, which always has the
> unfulfilled That as ground and content, gain the tangibility of
> its content. The Being-There of the highest good is such an
> essential part of it that it can never be the highest good in mere
> inwardness but always also in uttered, objectively achieved ex-
> ternality. And as such of course then to disappear with its lib-
> erated subject, just as subjectivity disappears with the unalien-
> ated object: the subjective as well as the objective theory of
> value, like the entire still-separated subject-object relation,
> ceases in the *highest moment of the highest good.* (*PH* III,
> 1333)

This densely packed passage only renders its meaning on the basis
of informed appraisal. It is evident that the absence of the need to
communicate with a critical audience has allowed a degree of verbal
overcharge to impede the understanding (particularly in the Anglo-
Saxon world) of what is at a fundamental level a highly original synthesis, a confluence of intellectual streams that creates solid common
ground for the conjunction of largely disjoined interpretative traditions,
particularly as focussed in the consideration of the universal phenomenon of religion itself.

It is on the level of general appropriation of religion as a universal
human experience that Bloch turns, thirdly, to the further re-implan-
tation of his synthetic vision into the drive towards value. There is
once more a sudden change in style, a reversion to the informal phenomenology of the "pull" (*Zug*) that draws us into a "state of metaphysical hovering" (*Schwebung*), that is confrontation with the hard
material of the question of value, an existential state described aptly
by Kierkegaard as one in which we are half-aware of the enigmatic

"Something" that as it were haunts the evening. Against the lifeless internality of Stefan George and Schopenhauer, "the metaphysician of fundamental disappointment" (*PH* III, 1337) Bloch posits his restless future. The juxtaposition of the attained Egyptian Helen and the utopian, ideal Trojan Helen is curiously modified by the relation of "cipher" which Bloch tries to exploit as a means of retaining ideal distance without relapsing into idealism. There is a "plastic mode as well as a poetic one, a *figure of metaphysical hardness as well as a stage of metaphysical hovering*" (*PM* III, 1338). The former and the latter are obscurely differentiated as is likewise, Bloch's attempt to juxtapose Kierkegaard's "half-transparency of night mist" with George's "manifest sealedness" in the "situationless garden" (*PH* III, 1338). The following disquisition on the Buddha figure, "a figure of the most extreme repose-entrance to the highest good" (*PH* III, 1339), is truly extraordinary in the light of all what has gone before. The seated figure set in a triangle in timeless self-enclosedness (as opposed to the representation of the Buddha as teacher) attains a high point of symbolic representation in Bloch's scheme:

> This is the Buddha figure or the Indian seal of fulfilment of the final wish: to wish no more. It is not surprising that this most manifest cipher of salvation, though still abstract salvation, is located at the dialectical breaking point of exodus and entrance, of decay and significance: the truly metaphysical severity codifies ascent not Becomeness. Therefore every cipher contains the ultimatum of dawning, not only towards the side of coming up but also towards the side of passing what is habitual and fixed. (*PH* III, 1340)

Bloch's strange use of the image of the Buddha and through this his relativisation of the representations of Exodus and Kingdom in Judaism and Christianity, respectively, is defended thus: "But Buddha, despite subjectless-objectlessness nirvana, has an advantage ever other attempted final figures because - in the Nothing of his All - he does not posit a perfectissimum as already existent, as present in essence, though behind the appearance" (*PH* III, 1340). The mysterious biblical images of the divine chariot in Ezekiel[10] and of the heavenly Jerusalem provided the symbolic raw material for the cabbalistic interpretation and geometrical imagery that passes to Eckhart and Nicholas of Cusa;[11] these are parallel in function to the Buddha figure, the

---

[10]Ezekiel I, 5-28; 10, 19-22.

[11]Nicholas' statement "God is an intelligible sphere whose centre is everywhere, but whose circumference is nowhere" is cited without exact reference at PH III, p.1341.

"positive ultimum is intended as situationlessness, without storm and clouds" (*PH* III, 1341). There is then for Bloch a state, an unlocatable place beyond the imagery of any tradition which, by implication, arises out of nature mythology, that is the primal human act of the qualitative separation from the quantitative basis of life in physical processes. It is yet again in Goethe that Bloch locates the sensibility that holds together, yet in check, nature and the sense of the infinite without relapsing into dualism.[12] At the very end of the extraordinary intellectual adventure of *The Principle of Hope* the following perspective is clearly dominant: the conjunction of natural earth-boundedness with a ceaseless appetite for the infinite, quintessentially expressed in the highest and healthiest embodiment of the German Romantic temperament, that is in the person of Goethe.

It is the intense Germanic quality of Bloch's refunctioning of culture that strikes the reader as the real bedrock of *The Principle of Hope*. It is this that permits him to relocate religious striving in the "hugely bubbling world retort" (*PH* III, 1343). Christianity's adoption of the primal feasts associated with nature mythology and its aesthetic sensibility, as formulated initially by Augustine who taught "almost a formed premonition of salvation in the shapes of nature" (*PH* III, 1344), provided a notion eventually resurfacing in the aesthetics of Schopenhauer and Wagner. Thus Christianity (but not, notably, at this juncture Judaism) is related through its festivals to the pagan celebratory cycle, so that, for example, "although in the Christian Easter a different aurora was welcomed than that of the spring sun, it was equally one which could make user of the external signs of nature as if they were themselves symbolic" (*PH* III, 1344). The decipherment of nature in mythology and in Christianity prefigures the "function of a new, a material theory of signs" (*PH* III, 1345). Bloch asserts, in conformity with his principle of "not-yet-being" but at variance with the normal hermeneutics of mythology, that is "far from being present or complete in a hinter-world or supernatural world, has as its time only the future, as its form only the real cipher, as its degree of reality only latency" (*PH* III, 1345). Once Bloch begins to focus the actual quasi-empirical basis of his system in the mythology of nature, then a strain is apparent between this claim and the assertion that the products of the celebration of nature "converge in the direction forwards a *final figure*" (*PH* III, 1345). The conjunction of the massive exposure and recapitulation of the repressed and half-hidden of the utopian impulse and the ultimately slender natural basis for its existence outside the structure of hypostatic projection and future resolution becomes embar-

---

[12]Bloch cites Goethe's letter F. Stolberg of 2 Feb. 1789 on PH III, p.1343.

rassing. We have to ask ourselves whether Bloch's theory of the origin and meaning of religion can account for the extraordinary human flowering in religion and culture. Is there not, furthermore, something ludicrously inadequate about Bloch's conception of the discrepancy between natural man and the sublime products of his self-transcendence, once this uneasy relationship is placed in the paradigmatic anthropology of Goethe?

In the closing paragraphs of this, the penultimate section of *The Principle of Hope*, Bloch's argument peters out into a theory of "objective-utopian archetypes" (*PH* III, 1346) which provide the basis for the practice of decipherment. The theory of archetypes is related back to the "Foundation" (*PH* I, 164f.) where the archetypes are understood as "not at all formed merely out of human material, neither out of the archaic, nor out of later history; but rather they demonstrated a bit of the double inscription of nature itself, a kind of real cipher or real symbol" (*PH* III, 1346). The explanation of symbol Bloch offers comes dangerously close to the representation of his complete synthesis as the simple reduction of an unnecessary reduplication: "a real symbol is one where the thing signified is still disguised from itself, in the real object" and it is, therefore, "an expression for that which has not yet become manifest in the object itself, but rather is signified in the object and through the object; the human picture of the symbol is only a representative depiction of this" (*PH* III, 1346). It is the distinction of symbol from reality that is elided once the future-located identity of All and Nothing is attained. There is a real danger here that the circle of symbol and reality is closed with an implosive suddenness that radically subverts the grandiose projection that precedes it: all things might end not with a bang, but a whimper.

Allusions to Renaissance artists, Galileo, Paracelsus and Jakob Boehme lead to Bloch's restatement of the theory of signatures which comprises in its most economical and metaphysically least problematic form the metaphorical disjunction of sign and signification:

Returning to Paracelsus and Boehme, amid their theory of signatures stands the most critical-voluminous of all, with a direct neo-Pythagorean tradition, developed in the Jewish Middle Ages, and it came down to the Renaissance through Reuchlin. It is the theory of signatures of the Cabbala, expressed in Hebrew characters and the numerical values corresponding to them. (*PH* III, 1349).

On common ground with Walter Benjamin[13] Bloch extols the late
Baroque and Romantic use of metaphor, allegory and symbol which recalls the theory of signatures and transmits what he calls the
"qualitative and value-meaning of Pythagoreanism"(*PH* III, 1351).
Thus when the question of the "form problem of the highest good" is
raised in relation to the question of symbolic representation, the end result is an equivalence in Bloch's estimation between the ancient numerical and aesthetic theories and his conception of dialectical materialism in terms of the latency of matter:

> And so that there should be no misunderstanding at the end
> (caused for example by the reactionary use of 'marked form' for
> which neither Goethe nor Aristotle, nor even Paracelsus are to
> blame): all these problems together with that of a qualitative
> theory of the expression of natural qualities and natural forms
> do not stand of course contrary to analysable, causal-dialectical
> happening but are in the midst of it, they are solely *tension*-
> forms, dialectical-material *process*-figures and have around
> them, before them, the *uncompleteness* of latency. (*PH* III,
> 1351)

Having disposed of the tradition of radical transcendence through
a left-wing Hegelian critique informed by a future-based, atheistic
Messianic "kingdom", the sole means of sustaining the representation of
the *otherness* of things from their ultimate resolution in *identity* is in a
refunctioned "theory of signatures"; this itself, in turn, is commensurate,
even in the last analysis identified with, the *materialist* dialectics.
The qualitative therefore leaps out of the merely causal and quantitative. The most basic category for Bloch is, then, the "cipher of homecoming and of homeland, attempted signatures of the fundamental"
(*PH* III, 1352). Nature itself "surrounds us on all sides and arches over
us, with so much brooding, incompletedness, meaning and cipher in it, *is
not a bygone but rather incoming land*" (*PH* III, 1353). The ultimate goal
towards which the intentionalities of different traditions, including
that of Christianity, strive is subsumed into the fullest realisation of
matter:

> The Authentic is the highest good, it is the most qualified form
> of existence of What-Is according to possibility, hence of our
> matter. The Authentic dawns thus in the entire potential of
> matter - towards a final one, adequately qualified and figured.

[13]Bloch alludes here without exact citation to Benjamin's *Ursprung des deutschen
Trauerspiels* (1928), pp.155ff.

This, its kingdom-figure which does not yet exist, governs, throughout great dangers, hindrances and orbitings, all the other figures of the good path, and in it the Authentic according to the intention is formed like joy. *These are the frontier definitions of intention towards the highest good and the frontier concepts of every thought that moves towards the absolute of human wanting.* (PH III, 1353)

At this juncture, Bloch redescends from the heights of intellectual recapitulation of the tradition into a category, that of need, assimilable directly into the Marxist sphere of influence. *The Principle of Hope* therefore concludes with a passage entitled "Karl Marx and Humanity: the Stuff of Hope (PH III, 1354-76). With sudden, brutal, even misleading directness Bloch focusses upon the "unsurpassable Marx", whose teachings provide in unadulterated form "an all too certain model of the path of red intelligentsia: it is *humanity actively comprehending itself* (PH III, 1357). Like Münzer before him, Marx revolted against misery, comprehended the nullity of humbleness and recognised the proletariat as focal point of historical transformation. Whether Bloch's prevenient synthesis actually endorses this belated declaration of adherence to Marx is questionable:

The zero point of extremest alienation which the proletariat represents now at last becomes the dialectical point of change; Marx teaches us to find our All precisely in the Nothing of this zero point. Alienation, dehumanization, reification, this Becoming-Commodity of all people and things, which capitalism has to an increasing extent brought with it: this in Marx is the old enemy which is capitalism, as capitalism, finally triumphed as never before. Precisely humanity itself is the born enemy of dehumanization, indeed because Marxism in general is absolutely nothing but the struggle against the dehumanization which culminates in capitalism until it is completely cancelled out, it follows e contrario that genuine Marxism in its impetus, its class struggle and its goal-content is, can be, will be nothing but the promotion of humanity. (PH III, 1358)

Alienation, explicit in the young Marx but continuing, even if unnamed, in the later Marx of *Capital* is the negative against which the positive of the Humanum is set. How Bloch can justify Marx' location of world transformation in the proletariat in terms other than through the enactment of the dialectic of negation and affirmation, that is to say within the confines of the abstract, arbitrarily imposed polarities of the ancestral German-idealist dialectic, is not at all evident. "Creative Marxism" is to take up as a "theory-practice" the progressive secularization concomitant with a realization of humanity as conceived in an immanent Messianic eschatology. With urgency Bloch asserts: "Reason cannot blossom without hope, hope cannot speak without reason, both in Marxist unity - no other science has any other future, no other future any science" (PH III, 1367). In Bloch's fulfilled conception of Marxism, "cold" analysis and "warm" perspective are combined and the disclosure of material relations is complimented by the dream of the Golden Age. Bloch concludes by once more citing *Geist der Utopie*, thus illustrating in his own work a conjunction of both streams attributable in principle to Marx himself. In a final intellectual convulsion Bloch reverts to the conceptuality of the Novum now freed from merely contemplative status by the Marxian philosophy which bears within it the direction of history itself:

> Happiness, freedom, non-alienation, Golden Age, Land of Milk and Honey, the Eternally-Female, the trumpet signal in Fidelio and the Christ-likeness of the Day of Resurrection which follows it, but all are set up around that which speaks for itself by still remaining silent. (PH III, 1375)

The human wealth of which Marx speaks, and the wealth of nature as "tendency-latency" as Bloch conceives it, are mutual:

> *True genesis is not at the beginning but at the end*, and it starts to begin only when society and existence become radical, i.e. grasp their roots. But the root of history is the working, creating human being who reshapes and overhauls the given facts. Once he has grasped himself and established what is his, without expropriation and alienation, in real democracy, there arises in the world something which shines into the childhood of all and in which no-one has yet been, homeland. (PH III, 1375-6)

What the reader is to make of this eschatological genesis is the question to which now in our concluding chapter we turn our attention. Bloch's work, *The Principle of Hope*, is doubtless overblown and cumbersome, and suffers from excess, yet how should its powerful message be received? Our aim throughout has been to expound, to clarify and to contextualise. In the next chapter we offer a brief evaluation of Bloch's thought in the light of its reception. Here it will once more prove necessary to engage in "refunctioning", this time directing the problematic of post-modernity at Bloch's own complex, sometimes forced synthesis, so as to tease out the abiding value of an intellectual and asthetic creation, which when conceived as a totality, offers a comprehensive even if problematic rehabilitation of neglected and suppressed subcurrents in Western cultural and religious history. The florid splendours of *The Principle of Hope* are, however, but the pinnacle of an oeuvre that offers much that is distinctive. At the very least Bloch works out a grandiose strategy of very considerable consistency in a thought-experiment which may take its place amongst the few great post-Hegelian syntheses; this no-one can afford to neglect.

CHAPTER X

BLOCH AND THE POSTMODERN PROJECT

Wayne Hudson has described Ernst Bloch's early utopian philosophy as an "avant-garde philosophical modernism" in which he "attempted to refunction terminology drawn from philosophical, literary, mythological, mystical and religious sources in an activist philosophy, inspired by Nietzsche's summons to 'embark' and an imperative of incipient vita nova".[1] This characterisation emphasises the affinity of Bloch's work with that of his early contemporaries in an era of apocalyptic tension and nihilism. Thus the intellectual strategies of Bloch, together with those of Adorno, Heidegger, Lukács and their great theological contemporary, Karl Barth, have all to be understood in their historical and social context, that is under the impact of the First World War, the Russian Revolution and the German Third Reich. Each had his own way of recovering the past, a hermeneutic of the tradition which also implies a theoretical and practical relation with modernity. None of these thinkers can, however, be regarded as "modernist" to the degree that (say) the Da-Da or Surrealist writers and artists were; none of them carried into the fields of philosophy or theology (in the distinctive genres adopted or initiated by each) the extremes of the dissolution of form or minimalism characteristic of the avant-garde music (but not its theory) of the era. To a very considerable degree what is fundamental to their endeavours is that all retain an immense and continuing confidence in the power of the intellect, *regardless* and *despite* external circumstance and convoluted personal strategies. Each made a powerful bid to articulate the context of realisation, and then through highly diverse constructive strategies to articulate visions of the human condition; each, with greater or lesser degrees of success enacted the role of the heroic intellectual genius.

The consequent difficulty in all these major strategies that emerged out of the cultural ferment of the inter-war period is an astounding degree of intellectual isolation from the real forces of scientific, technological and, later, cybernetic modernity. For each of the thinkers to whom we have accorded representative status Marx and Nietzsche are taken in different ways as determinative figures; both the latter can,

---

[1]Hudson, op.cit., p.20.

however, be understood not only as prophets of forms of modernity but also its supreme *negative* critics. Thus Marx's attack upon capitalism and Nietzsche's passionate exaltation of the individual over against the political emergence of mass-humanity and the herd instinct foreran the sophisticated "lament over reification" (Adorno), the re-ontologisation of existence through the dialectics of nihilism (Heidegger), the critique of the novel as a means of decoding the rise of bourgeois civilisation (Lukács), and the explosive intrusion of the divine into the ever more banal yet terrifying world of *Technik* (Barth). The dilemmas of this stage in the evolution of modernity were tied to an underlying paradox: the positive identities offered to the contemporary era nevertheless bore the identifying marks of a decaying culture deeply compromised by its structural relationships with an economic and social order, most aspects of which appeared hostile to the human condition in terms of class structure and the distribution of wealth, and in the dehumanisation and degradation of industrial development and *Technik* that culminated in the hecatomb of the First World War. *Post*modernity in this regard ought perhaps rightly to be understood as the undeceived reappropriation of the pre-critical tradition out of which we have emerged.

Given the similarities in the intellectual formation of the thinkers we have set in parallel, that is a thorough grounding in the classical European cultural tradition, then their responses could not, without a quite astonishing (and largely unforthcoming) *volte-face*, have been other than what they were, that is a variety of strategies which all *negated* even as they sought to *recover* the only tradition with which they were thoroughly acquainted. Thus the oppressive encipherment of social, economic and political reality, the indirect embodiment of what lay outside an intrinsically elite, expertly propagated tradition, had to be exposed, but notably *not* by any direct confrontation with those forces that were taking control of the synthetic "second nature" which has, increasingly, been the power base of industrialised human life. There ensued a complex game of dialectical double-bluff in which the representation of reality had to be undertaken by that which was not and could not, without an extraordinary extension of sensibility, actually be such a representation, precisely because of the anachronistic status and concomitant disjunctions of these chosen fields of meaning and of their respective methodologies from modernity.

Out of such isolation of cultural discourse and its large failure to appropriate the as yet mostly inexpressed yet humanly relevant dimensions of the human and natural sciences there arises a pervasive problem: what is and ought to be the critical reception of the immanent dialectical representation of the disjunction of culture and context, superstructure and basis? If, and this will surely be increasingly the case, technology in all its glamorous splendour re-forms human life ever more extensively and yet generates further passive receptivity in a mass audience, then what alternative is there to an elite cultural atavism and regression? Does Ernst Bloch with his re-structuring of thought from the utopian, anticipatory Front in any way meet the questions we pose in terms of the strategy and the morality of cultural reappropriation? An adequate response to these questions must, of necessity, be fairly complex and the remainder of this concluding chapter is formulated accordingly.

Bloch, like the other writers to whom we have alluded, operated self-consciously in relation to the German idealist inheritance and in this he accorded particular weight to Kant and thereby presents certain similarities with the theologian Karl Barth. Both became "postmodern" thinkers in that whilst recognising the epistemological and ontological consequences of Kant's critiques, they sought for and asserted post-Kantian strategies of renewal which involved the re-appropriation of the theological and religious traditions of the West. In fact as regards their initial affinity, both produced "dialectical" texts in the context and aftermath of the First World War; and in their later divergence, both engaged in recoveries of tradition. These are parallels which illuminate the dilemmas of postmodernism. Bloch remained the more obviously consistent thinker as his concern with the Not-Yet-Being encountered in the Front of the future remained relatively unchanged throughout his intellectual career. Barth, by contrast, seemed to renege upon his dialectical phase and to revert to an ontological mode of thinking grounded in archaic categories brought back into use despite the risk of systematic regression. Bloch, by appealing to the *suppressed* utopian (and eschatological) aspects of the tradition was able to represent his own retreat into the past in the name of the future as a progressive, rather than regressive strategy. In reality *both* attempts retreat from *actual* modernity; yet both are "postmodern" in that each rebuilt a cultural identity through a reworked theology and a-theology, respectively. The disjunction in their assessments of the role and importance of theology and religion illustrates the complex parallel: Bloch refunctions religion at the expense of a theology which in its Western Judaeo-Christian form is in effect absorbed into the new religiously-informed apotheosis of the human; Barth refunctions theology on the basis of a calculated repudiation of religion as a human construct that impedes the revelatory uniqueness of God in Christ. Both, as Bloch himself pointed out, are in effect trying to defend the openness of human being against modes of pre-determination. Seen in this way both are defenders, through strangely alien yet parallel, strategies, of the autonomy of the human but both remain culture-bound, apparently ensnared in complex and fascinating strategies of anachronism.

In the later development of Bloch and Barth ontological assertion succeeds to some considerable degree the dialecticism of their earlier work, but the former less immediately so because of his exploration of the utopian genre with its complex "metaphorical logic" (Hudson) of futurity. Yet, in the final analysis both produced soteriologically-informed syntheses. Bloch's presentation of the massive Humanum of Goethe and Hegel's *Phenomenology* and the quasi-metaphysical extension of his humanity in the dimension of time and the *nunc stans*, and Barth's repristination of classical Christology are conceivable on similar grounds as postmodern recreations which both make the exploitation of temporal conceptuality and of ontological narrative the prime vehicles of their realisation.

It has been a consistent claim in this book that the threat of nihilism has been the predominant, even if concealed driving force behind the refunctioning activity of the figures to whom we have accorded paradigmatic status in relation to Bloch. Bloch and Barth, both thinkers who took up and re-interpreted the theological and religious inheritance were forced to re-engage, often obliquely, with metaphysical questions which re-appear within their chosen, parallel yet differing spheres and their concomitant intellectual strategies. The inverted character of the metaphysical re-appearance in quasi-metaphysics is a function of the constriction and self-enclosure of post-Kantian (or indeed post-Neo-Kantian) discourse. Ultimately neither Bloch nor Barth engaged wholly effectively with the problem of the *episteme*, that is of the field of knowledge which might, through common features *relate* different spheres of discourse rather than foster the sometimes ludicrous sphere-sovereignty of a chosen and excessively-developed single discourse. The triumphalist pursuit of hegemony in either Bloch's "Kingdom" or Barth's "God" risks an intellectual absurdity most apparent where the systematic and ontological self-consistency of both is most complete. Thus the concluding passages of Bloch's *The Principle of Hope* and the third volume of Barth's *Church Dogmatics* risk *reductio ad absurdum*, as on re-encountering contingency after their ontological adventures both writers face the charge that they represent merely the seamless rhetoric of transformation rather than an actual analysis of the possibility of translation of theory into social reality and practice. Their intellectual excursions into the grandiose inner logic of narratives extending, as it were into the future (Bloch) and the past (Barth), risk reduction to banal identity. Both have, in reality, reactivated quasi-idealist strategies that license massive literary self-advertisement but change little in any direct sense. The title of this concluding chapter hints at a moral dimension to the dilemmas of postmodernism. How ought we to engage with the disjunction of the "superstructure" of our cultural inheritance from its current "basis" in scientific, social and demographic reality? Perhaps the most ruthlessly honest of the figures we singled out at the outset of this chapter was Adorno who resisted all the temptations of system and did not attempt the questionable tactics of "open system" or "theory-practice" to be found in Bloch. However, history proved Adorno to be equally incapable of practical engagement and he paid the price of his own pessimism that did not even extend to a qualified endorsement of the events of 1968, as did Bloch's optimism. What is evident in the engagement of these leading twentieth-century artificers of culture with Hegel, Marx, and Nietzsche is a pervasive similarity of strategy, a move from dialectics to ontological assertion. This mode of operation (save perhaps in the case of Adorno) represented "reality" at the expense of a far more complex and perhaps as yet unattempted engagement with the series of disjunctions between cultural and intellectual traditions and socio-cultural *Sitz-im-Leben* which is inadequately and misleadingly represented through the instrumental use of Marxism as a subversive method. What therefore emerges is the indispensable, yet profoundly problematic role of Marxism itself when employed as a method of disclosure, that is as an incidental strategic tool.

On a superficial level, Bloch's *The Principle of Hope* presents the reader with the hopeless paradox of trying to enact a heroic culture enshrining the cult of the individual genius on the basis of Marxism, a belief-system and praxis dedicated to the collective triumph of the proletariat and the extinction of the bourgeois elite. History has moved on, Marxism outside Third World contexts (which exhibit the belated symptoms of early capitalist development) is in decay and retreat, not least in its socialist strongholds. What might there be to replace it as a means of recognising and interpreting the moral dimension of the restraints placed upon human growth and realisation by the distribution of all forms of resource? The morality of postmodernism includes the admission of this issue into the critique of the perverse self-enclosedness of spheres of discourse, which isolate even as they empower and grant hegemony to the creator of the meta-narrative. Above all, self-justificatory excursions into the past, however well-camouflaged in terms of their future-orientatedness, may well merely be complex forms of indulgence and power-play. Such strategies do little to regain the condition of critical holism absolutely essential if futurity as conceived by Ernst Bloch, that is in the grandiose secularised soteriology of the Prometheus-Christ reborn in the image of Goethe, is not to mock the *ac-*

tual present and the likely future degradation of the human condition and its ecological setting in the last decade of the twentieth century.

The judgment made above is hard, too hard, perhaps, because Bloch, unlike many of his contemporaries, did not indulge himself in the celebration of human despair and never abandoned his militant, often forced, optimism. If we were to recognise in Bloch the more modest paradox implicit in the aspirations of the best German thinkers to combine *both* the cultivation of a heroic culture *and* the desire for democracy, then we may as Anglo-Saxons find in Bloch significant stimulus to that beneficent militancy which resists the complacency and indifference of small-scale, "tick-tock" despair (or its simple hedonistic counterpart in consumer capitalism). We may therefore venture to dare a heroic realism and that lack of conformism which is to be found in the work of Ernst Bloch at its best.

It would not do, however, to end this book merely with such a rhetorical flourish. What might it be that gives Bloch's work its power to provoke fascination and, as we appreciate from Leszek Kolakowski's withering denigration, detestation and envy, even we may suspect, loathing?[2] The secondary literature, particularly that in German, is immense and ranges from numerous newspaper reviews of his work, and commentary upon his life in the many obituaries, through to learned articles, symposia and a not inconsiderable number of monographs. On the other side there are many, for example the distinguished Germanist J.P. Stern[3], besides Kolakowski, who clearly find Bloch and his work an extreme irritant. It is nevertheless evident that Bloch, like Ernst Jünger has had a representative intellectual career which spans the central and problematic role of Germany in the history of the twentieth century. Given the exalted status of the established *Schriftsteller* in German culture and society such individuals assume an importance far beyond that normally accorded to writers in contemporary Anglo-Saxon countries. Apart from a brief period of popularity amongst some English-speaking theologians in the 1970s Bloch remains a little-read near enigma in both Britain and North America. Distinguished enthusiasts like Fredric Jameson and George Steiner who write in English are relatively rare, both are, however, to a notable degree "outsiders" who practise an inter-disciplinary, ideologically-aware critique of culture into which many artifacts are drawn. It is only when

[2]Kolakowski describes Bloch as vastly learned but as having extremely poor powers of analysis and refers to him as a "preacher of intellectual irresponsibility" in *Main Currents of Marxism*, vol.III, p.445.

[3]Stern equals Kolakowski in dislike of Bloch but has a more pleasing literary touch when he alludes to the Principle of Hope as "Marxism on Stilts" in *The New Republic*, 9.3.1987, pp.38-42.

such multi-disciplinary width comes into some proximity with the immense learning of Bloch that critical, and not simply reductive, interaction may take place. Only those who bear within them a residual dissatisfaction, the sense that things should, and could be other than they are, and an inclusive, generous desire for an enlargement of soul and intellect will be sympathetically critical of Bloch.

Bloch's work embodies in an extreme way the tension between a heroic, individualised culture and the democratic intention of rendering its inheritance accessible. Bloch faces without flinching the cult of genius within his own tradition which is the very antitheses of the Marxist outlook he espoused in an extremely difficult, almost lifelong alliance. He is, in this regard, a writer of integrity who mocked ideological overdetermination by the crass representation, even caricature, of the demands of dogma. It is easy for those who have not lived under totalitarian regimes of the Left or Right to berate others who have with charges of compromise or collusion. No-one remotely aware of the dynamics of the social and political persecution of religion in communist lands could imagine that Bloch's consistent and obsessive concern with religion and its interpretation was the outlook of a time-server. What Bloch is prepared to address is the question of the nature of human identity in a culture which for a millenium and a half in the West lived with the sense of God. The integrative and synthetic power of Bloch's vision stems to a large degree from his honest realisation that the struggle between a static, past-occurrent awareness of transcendence and a dynamic, future-orientated and eschatological anticipatory consciousness is the backcloth against which the events of the Christian era have been worked out.

The inner tensions of Bloch's strange, often eclectic, yet unfailingly stimulating synthesis represent in a remythologised form that unresolved, inadequately recognised gulf between humanity as creator and bearer of culture and humanity as socio-biological agent ensnared in the dilemmas of social determination and the encoded patterns of phylogenetic inheritance. The huge burden of the cultural and literary past and its seemingly trivial and implausible basis in what amounts to a repristinated monistic vitalism re-opens the quest for human identity in terms which include the history of the God-hypothesis, that vision and sense of totality and teleology which once seemed adequate to both the grandeur and the squalid pathos of the human condition. In Bloch there is truly the awareness that an interpretation of this experience of God in his Messianic manifestations may constitute the only hypothesis adequate to deal with what otherwise seems some form of evolutionary excess, a superfluity in the history of humanity. In this

Bloch, like his fellow polymath Hans Blumenberg, takes up once more the challenge of Nietzsche as prescribed in the "death of God".[4] Thus how this God once "lived" and what form his "death" takes remain issues not only for Bloch and Blumenberg, but also for Adorno and, more recently for Derrida. This preoccupation may often seem strange to the Anglo-Saxon mind free from the immediacy of both Luther's Reformation and the pervasive presence of Judaism and of Jewish thinkers at the leading edge of cultural reflection.

Bloch confronts the alliance of power and knowledge exemplified in the mythology and ontological narratives of Enlightenment provided by Goethe and Hegel. Faust and the dialectic of lord and bondsman converge in the image of the one who grasps and breaks through limitation. Yet, at the same time as Bloch recognises that it is this drive to self-transcendence that spills over in cultural production, he is not fully prepared to concede, except peripherally and in passing, that mechanisms of self-limitation are equally, if not even more crucial if the paradoxes of human brutality and self-transcendence are to be contained within a benificent culture. Bloch's attempt to generate "value" and "quality" by a "leap" out of the quantitative dialectic of human and cosmic existence is grotesquely inadequate. It is here that his optimism founders on the rocks of individual and collective human depravity. The recognition of the religious dynamics of aggrandisement and the flawed splendour of humanity is doubtless unwelcome to those locked relatively unreflectingly, or even in a state of despair, in the iron cage of complex immanence. What might be yet more unwelcome would be that aspect of religion as limitation, as sacrifice- even prostration, that is the concomitant of both the vertical and the future transcendence which features in Bloch's work. There is an as yet unwritten and now perhaps unrecordable history of the relationship of Bloch with his first wife, Else von Stritzky, who apparently impressed upon him an indelible sense of the unexpectedness of grace. This is a grace that Bloch, following Feuerbach saw as an indispensable adjunct of the image of a humanity conceived in an immanence, into which "God" exhausted himself in a continual transition from "vertical" transcendence into "future anticipatory consciousness".

Bloch as a Marxist was inevitably aware of the historical compact between Christianity and the "religion of the Lord" and thus with temporal power and the consequent exploitation of ideologies of dependence and submission, that is seen in the consistent infantilisation of

---

[4]Hans Blumenberg's *The Legitimacy of the Modern Age* is one of the most important yet not well-known socio-theoretical works to emerge in the post-war period see p.88 u.22 above.

believers.[5] In this setting, ultimately that summed up in the representation of Christianity as "slave morality" by Nietzsche and thus of "sacrifice" as a perversion, Bloch remains caught in the dialectic of aggrandisement yet, strangely and simultaneously aware that it is "love" that, somehow, ought to lie at the base of human life. Bloch appeared, unlike Marx, to have respected the rights and integrity of the individual, besides this he considered humanity in universal terms rather than as corrupted by a Messianic partisanship on behalf of a single class. His is a socialism which, despite all its faults, has a human face, albeit on occasion a physiognomy over which pass the traits of Lenin, Goethe and Hegel. What Bloch fails to undertake, even as Marx failed, is to engage with the inevitability of alienation, and the sacrifice that in Hegelian terminology risks the seeming impossibility and risk of the miracle of grace itself, the transition from being in itself and for itself to being *for another*. Some of the pervasively problematic tensions and fissures in Bloch's philosophy of hope represent, but do not overcome, the problems we have alluded to. What we do find is a grandiose articulation that at the very least brings religion out of its alienated, peripheral status, and puts it once more into a relation with the Marxist tradition in all its diversity, and, above all, restores it to the centre of life.

The fact that we now live in what is frequently described as a "post-Marxist" and "post-Christian" era does not detract from Bloch's achievement, inasmuch as he has been as it were *through* both traditions and rebuilt a relationship of what amounts, on his terms, to a mutual dependence. We do not need to identify ourselves with this particular formulation in order to learn from this original if often problematic thinker. Bloch has broken down some of the barriers that obstruct the path to an integrated, Humanum built on the basis of complementarity rather than subverted through an annihilative struggle between alternatives. In the truest sense ground has been opened up for dialogue, a postmodern dialogue in which the activity of "re-functioning" suggests a mode of thought and action which may permit the explicit re-appearance of motifs apparently displaced and banished from the living agenda of human discourse. Of these that of "sacrifice" and its cognates is in this writer's view the most pressing and yet problematic. Seriously to engage with the work of Ernst Bloch is to show evidence of intellectual vitality; to understand him is to know with Bakhtin that

---

[5]See R.H. Roberts, "Lord, Bondsman and Churchman: Integrity, Identity and Power in Anglicanism" in C.E. Gunton and D.W. Handy (eds.), *On Being the Church: Essays on the Christian Community* (Edinburgh: T. and T. Clark, 1989).

Nothing is absolutely dead;
everything will have its homecoming festival[6].

---

[6]M.M. Bakhtin, op.cit., p.170. J.-F. Lyotard's characterization of the "postmodern" is especially apt: "*Post-modern* would have to be understood according to the paradox of the future (*post*) anterior (*mode*)", *The Postmodern Condition: A Report on Knowledge*, tr. G. Bennington and B. Massumi (Manchester: Manchester University Press, 1980) p.81. A more succinct summary of the primal structure of Bloch's enterprise could scarcely be imagined.

BIOGRAPHICAL OUTLINE

1885   Born on the 8th July, son of Max Bloch and Bertha Bloch (née Feitel).

1898   School essay: *"Das Weltall im Lichte des Atheismus"*.

1902   Essay accepted for publication: *"Über Kraft und ihr Wesen"*.

1902-1903   Correspondence with Ernst Mach, Theodor Lipps, Eduard von Hartmann and Wilhelm Windelband. (Surviving letters in the Mach exchange appear in *Ernst Bloch Briefe*).

1905   *Abitur* taken in the Ludwigshafen Gymnasium.

1905-1906   Matriculation and study of philosophy with Theodor Lipps at the University of Munich.

1907-1908   Continuation of study of philosophy (together with music and physics) at the University of Würzberg under the direction of Oswald Külpe.

1908   Graduation (*Promotion*) with a dissertation entitled *"Kritische Erörterungen über Rickert und das Problem der modernen Erkenntnis Theorie"* published in 1909.

1908-1911   Move to Berlin, participation in Georg Simmel's private solloquium. Beginning of friendship with Georg Lukács and Margarete Susman.

1911   Residence in Garmisch. Acquaintance with Else von Stritzky. Work begun on the anticipatory consciousness.

1912   Italian journey with Lukács. Residence in Heidelberg and entry into the Max Weber circle. Return to Garmisch.

1913   Marriage in Garmisch to Else von Stritzky, sculptor and heiress from Riga. Return and residence in Heidelberg.

1914-1917   Emigration to Grünwald in Isartal. Composition of *Geist der Utopie*.

1917   Work on Swiss political and utopian programmes for Weber's *Archiv für Sozialwissenschaft*. Journalistic activity.

1918   Publication of *Geist der Utopie* in Munich.

1919   Return to Germany, Berlin and then Munich.

1920-1921   *Thomas Münzer als Theologe der Revolution* written and then published in Munich in 1921.

1921   Death of Else von Stritzky-Bloch. Move to Berlin.

1922   Unsuccessful marriage in July to Linda Oppenheimer, an artist from Frankfurt.

1923   Publication of new, heavily revised edition of *Geist der Utopie*.

1924   Journeys to Italy, France and North Africa.

1925-1926   Visits to France and Tunisia.

1926   Residence in Berlin and association with Siegfried Kracauer, T.W. Adorno and Walter Benjamin.

1928   Journalism for the *Frankfurter Zeitung*. Friendship with Bertold Brecht, Kurt Weill, Otto Klemperer. Separation from Linda Oppenheimer. Birth of daughter Miriam.

1929   Residence in Vienna with Karola Piotrowska.

1930-1933   Residence in Berlin. Publication of *Spuren*. Preparation of *Erbschaft dieser Zeit*.

1933   Emigration to Zurich in early March.

1934   Residence in Vienna. Marriage to the Polish architect Karola Piotrowska in November.

1935   Residence in Paris. Publication of *Erbschaft dieser Zeit* in Zurich.

1936-1938   Residence in Prague. Birth of son Jan Robert. Work for the Prague *Weltbühne*.

1938-1939   Emigration to the U.S.A. Preparation of *Das Prinzip Hoffnung, Naturrecht und menschliche Würde* und *Subjekt-Objekt-Erläuterungen zu Hegel*.

1948   Called to the chair of philosophy in the reconstituted University of Leipzig.

1949   Return to Europe with wife and son, residence in Leipzig. Publication of *Subjekt-Objekt* (East Berlin).

1952   Publication *Avicenna und die Aristotelische Linke* (East Berlin).

1953   Publication of *Christian Thomasius. Ein deutscher Gelehrter ohne Misere* (East Berlin).

1954-1959   Publication of *Das Prinzip Hoffnung* (East Berlin) in three volumes (1954, 1955, 1959).

1955   Award of National Prize of the German Democratic Republic. Election to German Academy of Sciences in the GDR.

1956   Twentieth Conference of the Communist Party of the Soviet Union. Hungarian Revolution and deportation of Lukács to Romania.

1957   Bloch involved in political conflict. Enforced retirement and progressive isolation. Preparation of the *Leipziger Vorlesungen*.

1959   Visit to the Hegel conference in Frankfurt am Main. Contract with Suhrkamp Verlag for *Spuren* and *Das Prinzip Hoffnung* and their publication.

1960   Lectures in Tübingen, Heidelberg and Stuttgart. Invitation
            to guest professorship from the University of Tübingen.

1961   During a summer visit to Bayreuth the construction of the
            Berlin Wall precipitated Bloch's decision to remain in the
            West. Thus begins his much contended tenure of the guest
            professorship in Tübingen with the lecture *"Kann Hoffnung
            entauscht werden?"* Active in lectures until 1966 and in
            seminars and conferences during retirement.

1968   Publication of *Atheismus im Christentum* 1968. Rapid
            appearance of major texts 1968-1977.

1977   Death from heart attack on 4th August followed by a
            controversial funeral ceremony attended by 2,500 people.

SELECT BIBLIOGRAPHY

The bibliographical material associated with Ernst Bloch is extensive and the following selection is intended to afford initial guidance relating primarily to issues raised in this book.

a) *Primary Sources*

Bloch's works are readily accessible in the complete collected edition published by Suhrkamp Verlag in 1977:

1. *Spuren*
2. *Thomas Münzer als Theologe der Revolution*
3. *Geist der Utopie (1923)*
4. *Erbshaft dieser Zeit*
5. *Das Prinzip Hoffnung* (in three volumes)
6. *Naturrecht und menschliche Würde*
7. *Das Materialismusproblem - seine Geschichte und Substanz*
8. *Subjekt-Objekt - Erläuterungen zu Hegel*
9. *Literarische Aufsätze*
10. *Philosophische Aufsatze zur objektiven Phantasie*
11. *Politische Messungen - Pestzeit Vörmarz*
12. *Zwischenwelten in der Philosophiegeschichte (Aus Leipziger Vorlesungen)*
13. *Tübinger Einleitung in die Philosophie*
14. *Atheismus im Christentum*
15. *Experimentum Mundi - Frage, Kategorien des Herausbringens, Praxis*
16. *Geist der Utopie* (facsimile of 1918 edition)
    To this edition have been added: *Tendenz - Latenz - Utopie* (1978) Beat Dietschy and Hanna Gekte (eds.) *Ernst Bloch - Leipziger Vorlesurgen zur Geschichte der Philosophie* (Frankfurt am Main: Suhrkamp, 1985). Karola Bloch (et al), *Ernst Bloch Briefe 1903-1975* (Frankfurt am Main: Suhrkamp, 1985), vols I and II.

Major English translations

Peter Palmer (tr.), David Drew (introd.) *Essays on the Philosophy of Music* (Cambridge: Cambridge University Press, 1985). Extracts from *Geist der Utopie* and *Das Prinzip Hoffnung*).

Neville Plaice, Stephen Plaice and Paul Knight (trs.), *The Principle of Hope* (Oxford: Basil Blackwell, 1986).

E.B. Ashton (tr.), *Man on his Own* Essays in the Philosophy of Religion, (New York: Herder, 1970). (This is a short selection of texts in translation.)

Neville Plaice and Stephen Plaice (trs.), *Heritage of Our Times* (Cambridge: Polity Press, 1989).

D.J.Schmidt (tr.), *Natural Law and Human Dignity* (Cambridge, Mass.: MIT Press, 1986).

J. Zipes (tr.), *The Utopian Function of Art and Literature* (Cambridge, Mass.: MIT Press, 1987).

b) *Biographical studies*

Ehrhard Bahr, *Ernst Bloch* (Berlin, 1974).

Silvia Markun, *Ernst Bloch in Selbstzeugnissen und Bilddokumenten* (Hamburg: Rowolt, 1977).

Peter Zudeieck, *Der Hintern des Teufels. Ernst Bloch, Leben und Werk* (Moos: Elster Verlag, 1987).

c) *Comprehensive presentations*

Helmut Fahrenbach, *Die Philosophie Ernst Blochs im Zeitgenössischen Kontext* (Frankfurt am Main: Suhrkamp, 1987).

Wayne Hudson, *The Marxist Philosophy of Ernst Bloch* (London: Macmillan, 1982). (A distinguished work - the only full-scale presentation of Bloch's thought in English).

d) *Collections*

Arnold, Heinz Ludwig, *Ernst Bloch Sonderband* (Munich: Text und Kritik GmbH, 1985).

Bloch, Karola and Reif, Adelbert, *Denken heisst Überschreiten. In memoriam Ernst Bloch 1885-1977* (Frankfurt am Main: Europäische Verlagsanstalt, 1978).

Ernst Blochs Wirkung. Ein Arbeitsbuch zum 90 Geburtstag (Frankfurt am Main: Suhrkamp, 1975).

Flego, Gvozden and Schmied-Kowarzik, Wolfdietrich (eds.), *Ernst Bloch - Utopische Ontologie BdII des Bloch - Lukács Symposiums 1985 in Dubrovnik* (Bochum: Germinal, 1987).

Gropp, Rugard Otto, *Ernst Bloch Festschrift zum siebzigsten Geburtstag* (East Berlin: Deutscher Verlag der Wissenschaften, 1955).

Gropp, Rugard Otto, (et al), *Ernst Blochs Revision des Marxismus. Kritische Auseinandersetzung marxistischen Wissenschaften mit der Blochschen Philosophie* (East Berlin, 1957).

Löwy, Michael, Münster, Arno, and Tertulian, Nicolaus, (eds.) *Verdinglichung und Utopie Ernst Bloch und Georg Lukács zum 100. Geburtstag, Beiträge des internationalen Kolloqiums in Paris, März, 1985* (Frankfurt am Main: Sendler Verlag, 1985).

Münster, Arno (ed.), *Tagträume von aufrechten Gang* (Frankfurt am Main: Suhrkamp 1970).

Schmidt, Burghardt (ed.), *Materialen zu Ernst Blochs "Prinzip Hoffnung"* (Frankfurt am Main: Suhrkamp, 1978). (Extensive bibliography).

Schmidt, Burghart (ed.), *Seminar Zur Philosophie Ernst Blochs* (Frankfurt am Main: Suhrkamp Verlag, 1983).

Traub, R. and Weiser, H. (eds.), *Gespräche mit Ernst Bloch*, (Frankfurt am Main: Suhrkamp Verlag, 1975).

Über Ernst Bloch (Frankfurt am Main: Suhrkamp, 1968) (Survey of newspaper reviews in extensive bibliography).

Ueding, Gert, *Glanzvolles Elend-Versuch über Kitsch und Kolportage* (Frankfurt: Suhrkamp, 1973).

Unseld, Siegfried, *Ernst Bloch zu ehren*, (Frankfurt am Main: Suhrkamp, 1965.

e) *Secondary Literature*

Adorno, Theodor W., *"Grosse Blochmusik"* in *Neue Deutsche Hefte*, April 1960.

Adorno, Theodor W., *"Henkel, Krug und Frühe Erfahrung"* in Unseld, S., op.cit., pp.

Buhr, Manfred, *"Kritische Bemerkungen zu Ernst Blochs Hauptwerk Das Prinzip Hoffnung, Deutsche Zeitschrift für Philosophie*, 8, 1960, pp.365 ff.

Buhr, Manfred, *"Der religiöse Ursprung und Charakter der Hoffnungsphilosophie Ernst Blochs"*, *Deutsche Zeitschrift für Philosophie*, 6, 1958, pp.576 ff.

Deuser, Hermann and Steinacker, Peter (eds.), *Ernst Blochs Vermittlung zur Theologie* (Munich: Chr. Kaiser Verlag, 1983) Eckert, Michael, *Transzendieren und immanente Transzendenz Die Transformation der traditionellen Zweiweltentheorie von Transzendenz und Immanenz in Ernst Blochs Zweiseitentheorie* (Vienna: Herder, 1981).

Fetscher, Iring, *"Ernst Bloch auf Hegels Spuren"* in Unseld, S., op.cit., pp.83-98.

Frenzel, Ivo, *"Philosophie zwischen Traum und Apokalypse"*, *Frankfurter Hefte*, 15, 1960, pp.457 ff. and pp.545 ff.

Gollwitzer, H., *Krummes Holz, aufrechten Gang Zur Frage nach dem Sinn des Lebens* (Münich: Chr. Kaiser Verlag, 1973).

Green, Ronald M., "Ernst Bloch's Revision of Atheism", *Journal of Religion*, 49, 1969, pp.128-135.

Gropp, R.O., *"Die marxistische dialektische Methode und ihr Gegensatz zur idealistisch Dialektik Hegels"*, Deutsche Zeitschrift für Philosophie, 2, 1954, pp.69-112.

Gropp, R.O., *"Ernst Blochs Hoffnungsphilosophie-eine antimarxistische Welterlösungslehre"* in Gropp, R.O. (ed.) op.cit.

Habermas, Jürgen, *"Ein marxistischer Schelling. Zu Ernst Blochs spekulativem Materialismus"* in Philosophisch- politische Profile (Frankfurt am Main: Suhrkamp, 1981) pp.141-159.

Holz, Hans Heinz, *"Kategorie Möglichkeit und Moduslehre"*, Unseld, S., op.cit., pp.99-120.

Hurbon, Laennec, *"Der Thomas - Münzer - Ton im 'Prinzip Hoffnung'"*, in Schmidt, B., (ed.), op.cit., pp.533-547.

Jäger, A., *Reich ohne Gott Zur Eschatologie Ernst Blochs* (Zurich: EVZ - Verlag, 1969).

Jameson, Fredric, *Marxism and Form, Twentieth-Century Dialectical Theories of Literature* (New Jersey: Princeton University Press, 1971).

Kneif, Tibor, *"Ernst Bloch und der musikalische Expressionismus"*, in Unseld, S., op.cit., pp.277-326.

Kolakowski, Leszek, *Main Currents of Marxism* (Oxford: Clarendon Press, 1978) vol. III, ch. XII.

Koschel, Ansgar, *Dialog um Jesus mit Ernst Bloch und Milan Machovec* (Frankfurt am Main: Peter Lang, 1982).

Kracauer, Siegfried, *"Thomas Münzer als Theologe der Revolution,* Frankfurter Zeitung, 27.8.1922.

Lochman, Jan Milic, *Christus oder Prometheus? Die Kernfrage des christlich-marxistischen Dialogs und die Christologie* (Hamburg: Furche, 1982) .

Ludz, Peter, *"Religionskritik und utopische Revolution"*, in Probleme der Religionssoziologie (Kölner Zeitschrift für Soziologie, Sonderheft 6), 1962, pp.313-335.

Marsch, Wolf-Dieter, *"Nach-idealistische Erneuerung von Teleologie. Bloch: Der homo absconditus auf der Suche nach Identität"*, in Schmidt, B., (ed.), op.cit., pp.493-501.

Metz, Johann Baptiz, *"Gott vor uns Statt eines theologischen Arguments"* in Unseld, S., op.cit., pp.227-242.

Moltmann, Jürgen, *"Ernst Bloch: Messianismus und Marxismus. Einführende Bemerkungen zum Prinzip Hoffnung"*, Kirche in der Zeit, 15, 1960, pp.291 ff.

Moltmann, Jürgen, Theology of Hope (London: SCM Press, 1967).

Moltmann, Jürgen, *"Die Zukunft als neues Paradigma der Transzendenz"*, Internationale Dialog - Zeitschrift, 2, 1969, pp.2-13.

Moltmann, Jürgen, *Im Gespräch mit Ernst Bloch Eine theologische Wegbegleitung* (Munich: Chr. Kaiser Verlag, 1976) (Contains Moltmann's main contributions).

O'Collins, Gerald, "The Principle and Theology of Hope", Scottish Journal of Theology, 21, 1968, pp.129-144.

Pannenberg, Wolfhart, *"Der Gott der Hoffnung"* in Unseld, S., op.cit., pp.209-225.

Ratschow, C.H., "Ernst Bloch, *Theologische Realenzyklopädie*, 6, pp.715-719.

Roberts, Richard H., "Review article: An Introductory Reading of Ernst Bloch's *The Principle of Hope* in *Journal of Literature and Theology*, 1, 1987, pp.89-112.

Rühle, Jürgen, "The Philosopher of Hope: Ernst Bloch" in Labedz, L. (ed.), Revisionism (London: Allen and Unwin, 1962).

Rühle, Jürgen, *"Über Ernst Bloch"*, Literatur und Revolution. Die Schriftsteller und der Kommunismus (Cologne, 1960), pp.321 ff.

Sauter, G., *Zukunft und Verheissung. Das Problem der Zukunft in der gegenwartigen theologischen und philosophischen Diskussion* (Zurich / Stuttgart: Zwingli Verlag, 1965).

Schaeffler, Richard, *Was dürfen wir hoffen? Die Katholische Theologie der Hoffnung zwischen Blochs utopischem Denken und der reformatorischen Rechtfertigungslehre* (Darmstadt: WBG, 1979).

Schmidt, Burghart, *"Ein Bericht: Zu Entstehung und Wirkungsgeschichte des Prinzips Hoffnung"* in Schmidt, B. (ed.), op.cit., pp.15-40.

Schreiter, Robert, "Ernst Bloch: the man and his work", *Philosophy Today*, 4, 1970.

Simons, Eberhard, *Das expressive Denken Ernst Blochs Kategorien und Logik kunstlerischer Produktion und Imagination* (Freiburg: Verlag Karl Alber, 1984).

Splett, J., *"Docta Spes. Zu Ernst Blochs Ontologie des Noch- Nicht-Sein"*, *Theologie und Philosophie*, 3, 1969, pp.383-394.

Steinacker, Peter, *"Der verkleinerte Held-Gott im höchster Menschennähe. Überlegungen zur Wirkung Blochs auf die Christologie"*, in Deuser, H., Steinacker, P. (eds.), op.cit., pp.186-210.

Steinacker - Berghauser, Peter, *"Mystischer Marxismus? Das Verhältnis der Philosophie Ernst Blochs zur Mystik"*, *Neue Zeitschrift für systematische Theologie und Religionsphilosophie*, 17, 1975, pp.39-60.

Susman, Margarete, *"Geist der Utopie"*, *Frankfurter Zeitung* 12.1.1919, Unself, S., op.cit., pp.383-394.

Taylor, Ronald (ed.), *Aesthetics and Politics* (London: NLB, 1977).

Steiner, George, "The Pythagorean Genre", Unseld, S. op.cit., pp.327-344.

Vilmar, Fritz, *"Welt als Laboratorium Salutis"*, in *Ernst Bloch zu ehren*.

Walser, Martin, *"Prophet mit Marx und Engelszungen, zum Erscheinen des Hauptwerkes Ernst Blochs in Westdeutschland"*, *Süddeutsche Zeitung*, 26/27 Sept. 1959.

INDEX OF SUBJECTS

INDEX OF PROPER NAMES

The names of persons, real, mythological and fictional are included together with an indication of substantial discussions of topics or texts related to them.